Possibilities and Paradox

An Introduction to Modal and Many-Valued Logic

Possibilities and Paradox

An Introduction to Modal and Many-Valued Logic

J.C. Beall and Bas C. van Fraassen

OXFORD
UNIVERSITY PRESS

OXFORD
UNIVERSITY PRESS

Great Clarendon Street, Oxford OX2 6DP

Oxford University Press is a department of the University of Oxford.
It furthers the University's objective of excellence in research, scholarship,
and education by publishing worldwide in

Oxford New York

Auckland Bangkok Buenos Aires Cape Town Chennai
Dar es Salaam Delhi Hong Kong Istanbul Karachi Kolkata
Kuala Lumpur Madrid Melbourne Mexico City Mumbai Nairobi
São Paulo Shanghai Taipei Tokyo Toronto

Oxford is a registered trade mark of Oxford University Press
in the UK and in certain other countries

Published in the United States
by Oxford University Press Inc., New York

First published 2003

A catalogue record for this title is available from the British Library

Library of Congress Cataloging in Publication Data
(Data available)

ISBN 0 19 925987 9
10 9 8 7 6 5 4 3 2 1

Typeset by the authors using LaTeX
Printed in Great Britain
on acid-free paper by
Biddles Ltd, *www.biddles.co.uk*

To our logic teachers

Richard Trammell and Gary Hardegree

Karel Lambert and Nuel Belnap

Acknowledgements

For their comments we thank Sandy Boucher, Caitlin Brady, Lillian Carrasquillo, Donovan Cox, Sean Doherty, Aaron Exum, Daniel Gordon, Wendeline Hardenberg, Daniel Kelly, Sarah-Jane Leslie, Elizabeth Liedel, Fallon Mattis, Michael McGlone, Doug Osborne, Neal Robinson, Helen Rosner, Efrat Seiberg, Shyvonne Shaw, Dahlia Terhesieu, Jonathan Weinberg, and Lindsay Wishnick.

Jay Garfield, Michael Glanzberg, Scott Lehmann, David Ripley, Joshua Schechter, and Brad Skow provided very extensive comments, for which we are grateful.

For discussion we thank Brad Armour Garb, Jonathan Beere, Otávio Bueno, Mark Colyvan, Daniel Nolan, Richard Otte, Graham Priest, and Greg Restall.

For Style: We are indebted to Greg Restall for his general help with the style-files underwriting this book. Greg's generosity continues a stream of generosity and creative brilliance in the LaTeX community. To all those people in the LaTeX community—including the makers of TeXShop and teTeX (especially Gerben Wierda and Thomas Esser)—we express thanks.

For their guidance we thank Ruth Anderson and Katy Plowright of Oxford University Press.

From BvF: Thanks to Nicholas Rescher, Frederick Fitch, Richmond Thomason, and David Kaplan for further logic lessons along the way.

From JCB: Thanks to Tim Elder for his unfailing support as department head. Thanks to Charles and Bev Beall for their long-standing support over many years. Thanks especially to Katrina Higgins for her ongoing encouragement, understanding, patience, coffee, and curry.

JC Beall
Storrs

Bas van Fraassen
Princeton

January, 2003

Preface

Our aim in this book, as in courses we have taught at various universities over several decades, is to give philosophy students a basic grounding in philosophical logic, in a way that connects with the motivations they derive from elsewhere in philosophy. Competence in modal and many-valued logic and semantics is a sort of literacy requirement in many contemporary philosophical debates—in metaphysics and philosophy of language especially, but more recently also in epistemology and philosophy of mind.

The point of view we emphasize throughout is that logic derives from the structure of language, and that therefore a plurality of logics will derive systematically from a plurality of differently structured forms of discourse. The syntax and semantics presented must accordingly amount to a (albeit very simple and limited) theory of language in general. With an eye on logic the aspects of language on which we focus pertain to patterns of valid inference: the concept of premises validly implying a certain conclusion is general, not language specific. A unified point of view, with special application to the fundamental parallels between modal and many-valued logic, is presented in Chapters One and Three and the first section of Chapter Twelve; together with the tools of Chapters Two, Four, and Ten the unified view allows us to develop a large variety of logical systems, all of them to be found in philosophical literature as well as in more purely logical studies. The canvassed systems comprise normal modal logics (Chapter Four), some of the non-normal ones that early authors such as C. I. Lewis favored, logic of conditionals and intuitionistic logic (Chapter Six), variously motivated introductions of values beyond the traditional True and False, as well as a few elementary "paraconsistent" logics (Chapters Seven through Nine). All of these are revisited from a more advanced point of view in Chapters Eleven and Twelve, with proofs of the most important meta-theorems. At the end of each chapter we have listed suggestions for further reading, with special emphasis on philosophical applications.

The variety in our subject matter comes of course at the price of other limitations. All the logics presented remain at the propositional level and ignore the complications of context-dependence. We would very much have liked to include, on one hand, quantifiers, names, and definite descriptions, and on the other hand the two-dimensional modal logic that has recently begun to play an important part in philosophy of mind. Fortunately, the techniques used in those areas involve simple extensions of the ones the students will learn in this book, so the text should prepare them well for encounters with those topics. That said, we do include such topics in courses of our own, and will make resources available on our websites:

`http://vm.uconn.edu/~wwwphil/beall.html`

`http://web.princeton.edu/vanfraas/`

We also plan to maintain a list of new information for this book there, with corrections (if needed), additions, hints for exercises, and supplementary material. Critical comments and suggestions will be welcome!

NOTE ON CONVENTIONS

» *Chapters, Sections*: We follow a simple system: Chapters, sections, and subsections are referred to by the given number preceded by '§'. So, for example, Chapter 5 is §5; Section 2 of Chapter 5 is §5.2; and so on. Note that an unnumbered "section" (like the current *Note on conventions*) within some §n is none the less cross-referenced as §n.

» *Abbreviations*: We sometimes use 'st' or 's.t.' for 'such that', and 'wrt' for 'with respect to'.

» We generally shorten 'if and only if' to 'iff' (pronounced either 'if and only if', 'if-if' or, following David Lewis, 'iffffffff'). Similarly, when too many 'if's would otherwise pile up in a definition or the like, we use 'just in case', 'exactly if', or 'precisely if' as synonyms of 'if and only if'.

» With respect to the two "directions" of a given biconditional we sometimes use 'lrd' and 'rld' for 'left-right direction' and 'right-left direction', respectively.

» *Sentence/Statement names*: We frequently name a sentence (or statement) by displaying it to the right of a numeral or some such symbol. For example, the sentence 'Snow is white' is dubbed (1) by displaying it thus:

1. Snow is white

What is important to note is that '(1)' may be used to name different sentences in different sections; however, no confusion will arise if the reader treats each such sentence-name as implicitly indexed to the section in which it was introduced (for a given sentence). So, e.g., if 'snow is green' is displayed in §4.3 with the name '(2)', then '(2)' (in that context) is short for '§4.3 (2)', which may be read 'sentence (2) in Section 4.3'.

» *Citations*: We use brackets to refer to bibliographic material; for example, '[1]' denotes the corresponding entry in the Bibliography (at the back of the book). One may read 'Anderson and Belnap [1]' as 'Anderson and Belnap (in their work corresponding to item 1 in the Bibliography)'. Similarly, 'some philosophers [1, 2] have argued' may be read 'some philosophers (in the work corresponding to items 1 and 2 in the Bibliography) have argued'. And so on. Similarly, 'See [1]' may be read 'see the entry corresponding to item 1 in the bibliography', and 'Anderson and Belnap's [1]' may be read 'Anderson and Belnap's work corresponding to item 1 in the Bibliography'.

» *Index of Names*: We do not list cited authors in the Index; they are in the Bibliography with a reference like '<see n>', where page n is the page on which the given author is cited.

» *Use–Mention*: With Robert K. Meyer [72] we follow the conventions of *Principia Mathematica*. In other words: Let context be your guide!

List of Systems

Classical logic	CPL	§4.1	§9.2	§11.3
	CPL(Der)	§11.2		
	CPL(NAT)	§11.2	§11.5	
Normal modal logic	K	§5.5	§12.2	
	T	§5.5	§12.2	
	D	§5.5	§12.2	
	B	§5.4.2	§12.2	§12.2.1
	S4	§5.5	§12.2	
	S5	§5.5	§12.2	
Non-normal modal logic	NN	§6.1		
	S2	§6.1		
Logic of conditionals	CK	§12.3		
Intuitionistic logic	I	§6.4	§12.4	
Many-valued logics	FDE	§7.5	§12.5	
	K3	§8.2	§9.2	
	Ł3	§8.2	§11.4	
	LP	§8.3		
	RM3	§8.3		
	B3	§8.4		
	Ł$_{\aleph}$	§9.3		
	B2	§11.3		
	B4	§11.3		
Paraconsistent logics	FDE	§7.5	§12.5	
	LP	§8.3		
	RM3	§8.3		

LIST OF SYMBOLS

Set theory	$\in$	§2.1					
	$\notin$	§2.1					
	$\{x : \ldots\}$	§2.1					
	$\subseteq$	§2.1					
	$\subset$	§2.1					
	$\cap$	§2.1					
	$\cup$	§2.1					
	$\emptyset$	§2.1					
	$\wp$	§2.1					
	$\bigcap$	§2.1					
	$\bigcup$	§2.1					
	$\langle\,\rangle$	§2.2					
	$\times$	§2.2					
Connectives	&	§3.2	§6.3	§12.3			
	$\veebar$	§3.2					
	$\leftrightarrow$	§3.2	§11.4				
	$\neg$	§3.2					
	$\Rightarrow$	§3.2	§6.3	§12.3			
	$\rightarrow$	§2.3	§3.2	§8.2	§9.3	§11.4	§12.4
	$\wedge$	§3.2	§4.1				
	$\vee$	§3.2	§4.1				
	$\sim$	§3.2	§4.1				
	$\supset$	§3.2	§4.1				
	$\equiv$	§3.2	§4.1				
	$\Box$	§5.2					
	$\Diamond$	§5.2					
	⥽	§5.6.1	§6.2				
	$\bot$	§6.2	§6.4	§12.4			
	π	§11.4					
Inference and validity	$\Vdash$	§3.4					
	$\vdash$	§3.6	§11.1				
	Cn	§3.6.1	§6.4.1	§10.1			
Other symbols	$\odot$	§3.3	§7.2				
	$\oplus$	§6.4	§7.5				
	$\ominus$	§6.4.7	§7.5				
	$\top$	§8.4.1					
	∇	§12.6					

Contents

Part I

Preliminaries

Chapter 1
Philosophical Motives

Are there many logics or is there just one Logic—its principles eternal, immutable, and absolute? In the history of philosophy there was for many centuries one standard logic, deriving from Aristotle's Syllogistic. Today we once again teach one standard logic, deriving from Frege and his contemporaries about a century ago. But throughout this history there were also other logics, sometimes extending and sometimes rivaling the standard logic. Modal logic, intuitionistic logic, many-valued logic, and relevance logic are today's main contenders, though there are many more.[1] How shall we view this embarrassment of riches?

1.1 Many Languages, Many Logics

We may think here of a parallel in moral philosophy. On the face of it there are many ethical systems, exemplified in different cultures and different strata of society. One possible view is that just one of these is right (our own of course!) and that what counts as moral in other ethics, if different, is really morally indifferent or even immoral. Another view is that, since what is "right" is a value judgment, it makes no sense to try and stand outside of all ethical systems and ask which of them is right.

Against the first two views is a third, to the effect that there is really one underlying moral consciousness, which is differently exemplified simply because people exist under very different conditions and in very different circumstances.

We shall explore philosophical logic with an analogue of this third point of view. Logic pertains to language. In a logical system we attempt to catalogue the valid arguments and distinguish them from the ones that are invalid. Arguments are products of reasoning expressed in language. But there are many languages and different languages may have a different structure, which is then reflected in the appropriate logical principles.

[1] We shall take up examples of each of these listed, but even there we have to content ourselves with a small sample, for there is a great diversity of modal, many-valued, and relevance logics. Apart from these families there are also the quantum logics, probability logics, higher-order logics, fuzzy logic, dynamic logics,... and more still, some as yet unborn.

By *languages* we do not mean here the natural languages English, French, German, Russian, Latin, Greek, and so on; to the extent that these are translatable into each other they amount to a single language. But these natural languages offer the resources to frame special small languages that are circumscribed in various ways. An article in a mathematics or physics journal is quite rigidly confined to a certain vocabulary and style of discourse; so is an article in a journal of art criticism. Logic as studied by philosophers focuses on very simple languages, though there are good arguments for the conclusion that at least some of these are adequate to the needs of at least mathematics and the empirical sciences.[2]

If different languages can be studied from a single point of view, it will be possible to see different logics as exemplifying a single logical point of view applying itself in those different circumstances.

1.2 ARISTOTLE'S SEA BATTLE

To introduce both modal and many-valued logic we can begin with a single tantalizing passage from Aristotle's *On Interpretation* [3, 19a, 29–36] which has itself been interpreted in two very different ways:

> [A] sea-fight must either take place on the morrow or not. No necessity is there, however, that it should come to pass or should not. What is necessary is that it either should happen tomorrow or not. And so, as truth of propositions consists in corresponding with facts, it is clear in the case of events where contingency or potentiality in opposite directions is found that the two contradictory statements about them will have the same character.

The two contradictory statements are 'There will be a sea-fight tomorrow' and 'There will not be a sea-fight tomorrow'. There are no facts as yet that determine which is true, so (Aristotle maintains) these two statements "must have the same character". What character is that?

One answer is that they would have a different character if one of them were true and the other were false. On that view, Aristotle is denying that really one of them is true and the other false, already today, though we do not know which is which. In that case the example shows a violation of the Law of Bivalence (viz., that every statement is either true or false), which has generally been thought of as at the very foundation of logic.

A different answer is that these two statements may well be unlike with respect to actual truth and falsity (whether we know it or not), but have the same character with respect to necessity and possibility. On this reading the crucial part of Aristotle's text is "No necessity is there, however, that

[2]There are also arguments against this. Intuitionistic logic, which we will take up, pertains to mathematical discourse of a different form from that to which standard logic pertains, and was developed originally in the conviction that standard logic is not adequate to mathematical discourse in general.

[the sea-fight] should come to pass or should not." Neither is necessary, both are possible. To explore this idea one needs no third option between *True* and *False*, but one does have to inquire into the logical role of such words as 'Necessarily' and 'Possibly'. And this still implies that a mere division into the true and the false is inadequate: both the true and the false statements are further subdivided into the necessary and the non-necessary, the possible and the impossible.

These two different responses to Aristotle's example are amply represented in philosophical commentaries. They are of interest to us here because they introduce two major ways of departing from the narrow confines of standard logic, and even point to still further departures. We'll conclude this initial discussion of our subject with a brief introduction to each.

1.3 Manifold Paths to Truth

In the first two decades of the 1900s Polish logicans and philosophers developed views on this subject which led to formulation of systems of many-valued logic: logic which pertains to the sort of language for which the Law of Bivalence does not hold. The following passage from Łukasiewicz (pronounced 'woo-kah-zay-vitz') reflects the tenor of these views:

> [T]here are possible propositions, besides true and false ones. And corresponding to them are possible events, something which is a third matter besides existence and non-existence.

The term 'many-valued' was introduced by adjusting the logical terminology to allow for truth-values other than *True* and *False*—values that correspond to a different "character" which statements may have.

It would seem that Łukasiewicz is pointing here to different *ways of not being true*: among those which are not true, some are false and some have a third status. (There is at this point no call for values that correspond to different *ways of being true*, though introducing those would seem to be a natural next step.) What difference would one expect this to make to logic? The most obvious question to ask is: "What happens to the word 'not'?" If with Aristotle we maintain that 'There will be a sea-fight tomorrow' and 'There will not be a sea-fight tomorrow' have the same character, and if we take this to mean that they have the same truth-value, we arrive at the schema for any statement A:

» A is true if and only if its negation ~A is false.

» A is false if and only if its negation ~A is true.

» A is neither true nor false (has third value) if and only if its negation ~A is neither true nor false (but has third value).

Some familiar logical laws will clearly remain in force: if statement A is true then ~A is false and so ~~A is true; hence, the classically valid argument 'A, therefore ~~A' is still valid.

On the other hand, we should also expect some classically valid arguments to be no longer valid. For example, in classical logic, if A implies B and ~A also implies B, then B must be true no matter what (a tautology); however, this principle derives from the assumption that in all possible cases, either A is true or ~A is true. If that assumption does not hold for our language, this classical form of reasoning is no longer valid.

But we can also imagine some discontent with this. The word 'not' could be read differently, more broadly so to speak, with the negation ~A taken to be true in all cases in which A does not have the truth-value *True*. In that case, the above schema would not apply: negations would always have one of the two values *True* or *False*. The drawback is that Aristotle's contention about the sea-battle (as Łukasiewicz construes it) cannot be represented in this language. Why not then have two sorts of 'not' in this language? You can see how various options open up for constructing many-valued languages and determining their appropriate logics.

1.4 Modal Character, Modal Logic

However many ways there are of being true and of not being true, we recall that we can distinguish in Aristotle's example also another characteristic that statements may or may not have: necessity. The traditional modalities are necessity, possibility, non-necessity, and impossibility, and they were already a subject of study throughout the history of logic. In the twentieth century, under the impetus mainly of C. I. Lewis [62, 64] in America (though also of those same Polish logicians that we mentioned before) this study took a new form. One outcome was the recognition of many more than four modal characters, in view of such questions as: Is a necessary statement necessarily necessary, or is it possibly non-necessary, or even possibly impossible?[3]

Modal logic is then logic as applied to a language in which there are statements of form 'Necessarily, there will be a sea-battle tomorrow', 'There will necessarily be a sea-battle tomorrow', 'There may not be a sea-battle tomorrow', 'Possibly, no sea-battle will take place tomorrow'. Will this simply be an extension of the standard logic to more complex forms of discourse?

Yes and no. It is possible to construct a modal logic by first stipulating that all classically valid arguments are valid, and then adding that some other arguments are valid due to the logical connections between these

[3]These were not questions introduced initially by C. I. Lewis but, rather, by the German philosopher Oskar Becker in an early response, which was then taken up at length in the seminal Lewis and Langford textbook [64].

modal qualifiers. In that sense modal logic will indeed be just an extension of standard logic. But there is a subtler sense in which standard logic was too confining to accommodate these new ideas. Consider any three sentences A, B, and C. In classical propositional logic we can prove that:

1. $(A \equiv B) \vee (A \equiv C) \vee (B \equiv C)$

is valid.[4] So if $A \equiv B$ is not true, then every statement C is materially equivalent to either A or B. Moreover, material equivalence seems to blot out any other distinction, for

2. $(A \equiv B)$, therefore $[(\ldots A \ldots) \equiv (\ldots B \ldots)]$

is also valid in classical logic, where $(\ldots A \ldots)$ is any sentence with A as component that can be framed in classical propositional logic, and $(\ldots B \ldots)$ is the same sentence with A replaced by B. As long as we have these two results and regard them as general logical principles, there is no way to express something like the assertion that A, B, and C have three different modal characters.

Principle (2) is generally called a *principle of extensionality* and its failure in modal logic makes modal logic *non-extensional* or (to use a common antonym) *intensional*. This failure of a classical principle shows that at some level at least we cannot think of modal logic as simply adding to or extending standard logic.

1.5 Possible Worlds

The development of modal logic reached a new level some decades after Lewis' pioneering work, with the revival of yet another tradition in modern logic. Leibniz first explicated notions of necessity and possibility in terms of possible worlds. The world we live in is the actual world; it is but one of infinitely many possible worlds that God could have created. A statement is logically true, or valid, exactly if it is true in all possible worlds—for logical laws are the only constraints on what God could create. In its new dress this idea is of course divested of theological connotations: the idea of alternative possible worlds is simply taken as understood, without such explication.[5]

This view offers us a way to represent the varieties of modal character that statements can have, and also a new and useful handle on logical relations between statements.

---

[4]Here we use $\equiv$ for material equivalence ('if and only if') and $\vee$ ('or') for inclusive disjunction.

[5]To express his view that alternative possible worlds are real David Lewis [66] famously wrote: "I believe, and so do you, that there are many ways the world could have been." That view need not be held in order to do or understand logic; it suffices to use it as an aid to the imagination.

Truth and falsity *in* (or *at*) possible worlds gives us a classificatory scheme for statements. If A is a statement and $\mathcal{X}$ a set of possible worlds, then there is a case, call it *Case* $\mathcal{X}$, namely:

» the worlds in which A is true are exactly the worlds in $\mathcal{X}$.

If $\mathcal{X}$ includes all worlds then A is necessary. If $\mathcal{X}$ is at least not empty then A is possible. If the actual world is a member of $\mathcal{X}$ then A is true; if not, then A is false. This is a cross-classification: some true sentences are necessary and some are not, some false ones are impossible and some possible. That is the beginning of a schema which assigns not different truth-values but certainly values that represent subdivisions among the true and among the false (hence, different ways of being true and of being false).[6]

Logical relationships among statements derive from the relations (such as inclusion, overlap, and disjointness) among the sets of worlds in which they are true. During the nineteen-fifties and sixties a number of logicians, notably Saul Kripke [58, 59], worked out this account systematically and found that it could be used to explain C. I. Lewis' modal logics, as well as various other logics.

1.6 A UNIFIED VIEW?

Some of our ideas concerning the unification of our treatment of the different logics will already be quite clear now. We see the study of logic as grounded in a very general characterization of languages to which they pertain. Such basic notions as validity are the same for all: an argument is valid if its conclusion must be true if its premises are true. But in different languages, sentences can have many distinct characters that cut across the classification into *True* and *False*.

These characters that sentences can have may be represented by assigning different values to those sentences—sometimes but not always appropriately called truth-values—and logical relations will derive from relations among these values. Certainly other ideas will come into play as well, as we look farther afield to, for example, intuitionistic logic, the logic of conditionals, and relevance logics. But this uniform approach will extend to all, and we shall make a point of exploiting the advantages that this unity will provide.

EXERCISES 1.6.1

1 Evaluate Łukasiewicz's following argument. Is it a plausible argument? If it is a sound argument, what is its logical structure?

[6] What we are not yet indicating here is how this sort of representation can accommodate the more recondite modal characters such as being possibly but not necessarily necessary. We save that for the chapters on modal logic.

> I can assume without contradiction that my presence in Warsaw at a certain moment of next year, e.g., at noon on 21 December, is at the present time determined neither positively nor negatively. Hence it is *possible*, but not *necessary*, that I shall be present in Warsaw at the given time. On this assumption the proposition 'I shall be in Warsaw at noon on 21 December of next year', can at the present time be neither true nor false. For if it were true now, my future presence in Warsaw would have to be necessary, which is contradictory to the assumption. If it were false now, on the other hand, my future presence in Warsaw would have to be impossible, which is also contradictory to the assumption. Therefore, the proposition considered is at the moment *neither true nor false* and must possess a third value, different from '0' or falsity and '1' or truth. This value we can designate by '$\frac{1}{2}$'. It represents 'the possible', and joins 'the true' and 'the false' as a third value. [67]

2 Discuss: To what extent, if any, is *logic* a theory? Are there universally true "logical laws", not open to "revision"? How, if at all, do logical laws differ from, say, laws of physics?

FURTHER READING

A potentially useful supplement to the philosophical discussion in this book is Stephen Read's [83]. Another recent book is Susan Haack's [42].

With respect to Aristotle's sea-battle and responses thereto, see especially Jaakko Hintikka's [48].

Histories of logic include Joseph Bocheński's [12], William and Martha Kneale's [57], and Heinrich Scholz's [88], among others. For the history of the possible worlds scheme in modal logic see Jack Copeland's [22].

For a different approach to logical pluralism than that presented in §1.1, see Beall and Restall's [8, 9].

> [I]t is a wholesome plan,
> in thinking about logic,
> to stock the mind with as many puzzles as possible,
> since these serve much the same purpose
> as is served by experiments in physical science.
> – Bertrand Russell [87]

Chapter 2
Set-Theoretic Tools

This book utilizes contemporary set-theoretic jargon. Accordingly, the aim of this chapter is to introduce the basic terminology and corresponding notions. We do not give a full set theory; we give just the amount required for understanding the rest of the book.

2.1 Sets

For present purposes we rely on an intuitive notion of set or collection. With such entities the reader is familiar: the set comprising all and only Tasmanian devils, the set of all (and only) even integers, and so on. We call the specified devils and the integers *elements* or *members* of the given sets.

A set is exactly specified if its members are given. This identity condition for sets is codified in the principle:

Definition 2.1 (Extensionality) If sets $\mathcal{X}$ and $\mathcal{Y}$ have the same members then they are the *same set*.

Symbolizing 'x is a member of $\mathcal{Z}$' as '$x \in \mathcal{Z}$' (and, correspondingly, 'x is not a member of $\mathcal{Z}$' as '$x \notin \mathcal{Z}$'), this amounts to:

» If $\mathcal{X}$ and $\mathcal{Y}$ are sets such that $x \in \mathcal{X}$ iff $x \in \mathcal{Y}$, then $\mathcal{X} = \mathcal{Y}$.[1]

The Principle or Axiom of Extensionality justifies the designation of the set of positive odd numbers below 10 as $\{9, 7, 5, 3, 1\}$. We also want to designate sets by descriptions less definite than lists—for example, the set of all odd numbers above 10, a set we may designate as $\{x : x > 10 \text{ and } x \text{ is odd}\}$. That there is at most one set so designated follows from Extensionality. The special use of this designation is given by:

Definition 2.2 (Abstraction) $y \in \{x : Px\}$ iff Py.

[1]For the sake of readability we drop explicit universal quantifiers from definitions, so that 'x' in the above definition is (implicitly) universally quantified.

In words: Anything that has the property P is a member of $\{x : Px\}$ and vice versa, for any (well-formed) predicate P. As most people know, careless combination of this principle with other principles leads to contradictions.[2] For present purposes we content ourselves with living dangerously; we rely only on "naive set theory" alone.

Relations among sets (beyond identity) are given by the following definitions:

DEFINITION 2.3 (PART, SUBSET) $\mathcal{X} \subseteq \mathcal{Y}$ ($\mathcal{X}$ is a *part*, or *subset*, of $\mathcal{Y}$) iff every member of $\mathcal{X}$ is a member of $\mathcal{Y}$.

DEFINITION 2.4 (PROPER PART) $\mathcal{X} \subset \mathcal{Y}$ ($\mathcal{X}$ is a *proper part*, or *proper subset*, of $\mathcal{Y}$) iff $\mathcal{X}$ is a part of $\mathcal{Y}$ and there is some member of $\mathcal{Y}$ which is not a member of $\mathcal{X}$.

DEFINITION 2.5 (UNION) $\mathcal{X} \cup \mathcal{Y}$ (the *union* of $\mathcal{X}$ and $\mathcal{Y}$) is the set comprising anything that is a member of $\mathcal{X}$ or $\mathcal{Y}$ or both.

DEFINITION 2.6 (INTERSECTION) $\mathcal{X} \cap \mathcal{Y}$ (the *intersection* of $\mathcal{X}$ and $\mathcal{Y}$) is the set comprising anything that is a member of $\mathcal{X}$ *and* a member of $\mathcal{Y}$.

DEFINITION 2.7 (COMPLEMENT) $\overline{\mathcal{X}}$ (the *complement* of $\mathcal{X}$) comprises everything that is not a member of $\mathcal{X}$.

DEFINITION 2.8 (RELATIVE COMPLEMENT) $\mathcal{Y} - \mathcal{X}$ (the *complement of $\mathcal{X}$ relative to $\mathcal{Y}$*) is the set comprising all members of $\mathcal{Y}$ that are not members of $\mathcal{X}$.

So go relations among sets. But what are relations? Before turning to this question we tidy up conventions and summarise some of what we have thus far.

When x is a member of set $\mathcal{X}$ we also say 'x is in $\mathcal{X}$'. Accordingly, $\mathcal{X}$ is a subset of $\mathcal{Y}$ exactly if everything that is in $\mathcal{X}$ is also in $\mathcal{Y}$; and the members of $\mathcal{Y} - \mathcal{X}$ are in $\mathcal{Y}$ but not in $\mathcal{X}$. We use capital (scripted) letters to denote sets; a lower case letter such as 'x' may, of course, also denote a set because it may denote anything. When both sentences and sets are discussed we try to keep A, B, C,... for sentences and $\mathcal{X}$, $\mathcal{Y}$, $\mathcal{Z}$ for sets; but convenience will dictate when context covers us.

One way to calculate intuitively with sets is to think of classical propositional logic, which will be reviewed in a subsequent chapter. Whatever

[2]Consider the property: $x \notin x$! (This is the Zermelo-Russell paradox.)

you can prove about sentences with $\sim$, $\wedge$, $\vee$ and $\vdash$ (under their standard classical interpretations) you can also prove about sets with $-$, $\cap$, $\cup$, and $\subseteq$. Accordingly, principles such as De Morgan, Double Negation, Disjunctive Syllogism, Distribution, Associativity, etc., all carry over *mutatis mutandis*.[3]

Before moving on to *relations* we should discuss two more items. First, the *empty set*, which is *the* set containing no elements:

DEFINITION 2.9 (EMPTY SET) $\emptyset = \{x : x \neq x\}$.

Second, given a set $\mathcal{K}$ we have a special set, the *power set* of $\mathcal{K}$, which is the set of all its parts or subsets:

DEFINITION 2.10 (POWER SET) $\wp(\mathcal{K}) = \{\mathcal{X} : \mathcal{X} \subseteq \mathcal{K}\}$.

Both $\mathcal{K}$ and $\emptyset$ are in $\wp(\mathcal{K})$. When $\mathcal{K} = \{b, c\}$, then $\wp(\mathcal{K})$ has four members:

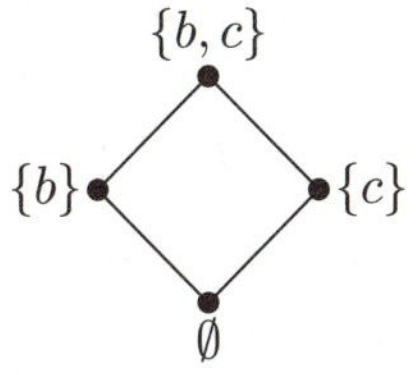

The lines, read from bottom ($\emptyset$) to top ($\mathcal{K}$), indicate the *part of* or *subset* relation:

$$\emptyset \subseteq \{b\} \subseteq \mathcal{K}$$

$$\emptyset \subseteq \{c\} \subseteq \mathcal{K}$$

and $\{b\}$ and $\{c\}$ are each other's relative completement in $\wp(\mathcal{K})$; that is, $\{b\} = \mathcal{K} - \{c\}$ and $\{c\} = \mathcal{K} - \{b\}$.

More generally, if $\mathcal{Q}$ is any set of sets—or, as we shall say interchangeably, to avoid monotony, *family of sets* or *class of sets*—then the following are also sets:

$$\bigcap \mathcal{Q} = \{x : \text{ if } \mathcal{Y} \in \mathcal{Q} \text{ then } x \in \mathcal{Y}\}$$

$$\bigcup \mathcal{Q} = \{x : \text{ for some } \mathcal{Y},\ \mathcal{Y} \in \mathcal{Q} \text{ and } x \in \mathcal{Y}\}$$

These are the generalised operations of intersection and union. If $\mathcal{Q} = \{\mathcal{X}, \mathcal{Y}, \mathcal{Z}\}$ then $\bigcap \mathcal{Q} = \mathcal{X} \cap \mathcal{Y} \cap \mathcal{Z}$ and $\bigcup \mathcal{Q} = \mathcal{X} \cup \mathcal{Y} \cup \mathcal{Z}$, and so on.

For now, we should turn to the "nature" of relations and various related matters.

[3]The reader should not panic if she has forgotten what these principles amount to. The important task, for now, is simply to get a handle on the basic set-theoretic jargon.

2.2 RELATIONS

Relations, for present purposes, are sets of ordered pairs (or, more generally, ordered n-tuples). When we have two entities, b and c, we may form the ordered pair comprising exactly b and c in a particular order: either $\langle b, c\rangle$ or $\langle c, b\rangle$. Consider the x *loves* y relation. Suppose that b loves c but not vice versa. (Tragic love.) Then the relation of *love* contains the element $\langle b, c\rangle$ but not $\langle c, b\rangle$. b is called the ***first component*** (sometimes 'first coordinate') of $\langle b, c\rangle$, and c the ***second component***.

We say that ordered pairs are identical just in case their respective first components are identical and their respective second components are identical:

DEFINITION 2.11 (ORDERED PAIRS) $\langle b, c\rangle = \langle d, e\rangle$ if and only if $b = d$ and $c = e$.

A common way of avoiding "ontological buildup" is to define ordered pairs thus:

$$\langle b, c\rangle = \{\{b\}, \{b, c\}\}$$

For our purposes, however, we shall not worry about the exact "nature" of ordered pairs (or n-tuples, generally); what is important is that (Def 2.11) be satisfied.

Since the *order* of elements matters to the identity of $\langle b, c\rangle$ but not to the identity of $\{b, c\}$, these two sets are not identical. This is a key point to keep in mind.

Beyond ordered pairs are ordered triples, ordered quadruples and, in general, ordered n-tuples: $\langle b_1, \ldots, b_n\rangle$, for $n \geq 2$. With respect to such ordered n-tuples we need only know that

$$\langle b_1, \ldots, b_n\rangle = \langle c_1, \ldots, c_n\rangle \text{ iff } b_1 = c_1 \text{ and} \ldots \text{and } b_n = c_n$$

CARTESIAN PRODUCTS

Given two sets, $\mathcal{X}$ and $\mathcal{Y}$, the *Cartesian Product* of $\mathcal{X}$ and $\mathcal{Y}$, namely $\mathcal{X} \times \mathcal{Y}$, is the set of all ordered pairs, $\langle x, y\rangle$, where $x \in \mathcal{X}$ and $y \in \mathcal{Y}$.

Generalising, we define the *Cartesian Product of* $\mathcal{X}_1, \ldots, \mathcal{X}_n$ to be the set comprising all ordered n-tuples, $\langle x_1, \ldots, x_n\rangle$, where $x_1 \in \mathcal{X}_1, \ldots, x_n \in \mathcal{X}_n$.[4]

BINARY RELATIONS

Binary relations will play a big role in the following chapters. What are they? For present purposes:

[4] In the case where the "various" $\mathcal{X}_i$ are identical to $\mathcal{X}$, the product $\mathcal{X}_1 \times \ldots \times \mathcal{X}_n$ is frequently written as $\mathcal{X}^n$, and is called *the* n^{th} *Cartesian power of* $\mathcal{X}$.

DEFINITION 2.12 A *binary relation*, $\mathcal{R}$, is a set of ordered pairs; and a *binary relation from $\mathcal{X}$ to $\mathcal{Y}$* is a subset of $\mathcal{X} \times \mathcal{Y}$.

Where $\mathcal{R}$ is any binary relation we sometimes use '$x\mathcal{R}y$' to mean that $\langle x, y\rangle \in \mathcal{R}$. We say that the *domain of* $\mathcal{R}$ is the minimal set $\mathcal{X}$ such that $\mathcal{R}$ is a relation from $\mathcal{X}$ to some set $\mathcal{Y}$. Likewise, the *codomain of* $\mathcal{R}$ is the minimal set $\mathcal{Y}$ such that $\mathcal{R}$ is a relation to $\mathcal{Y}$ from some set $\mathcal{X}$.

Given this terminology, a binary relation with domain $\mathcal{X}$ and codomain $\mathcal{Y}$ is a subset of $\mathcal{X} \times \mathcal{Y}$, but it is also a relation from any set $\mathcal{U}$ to to any set $\mathcal{Z}$ such that $\mathcal{X}$ is a subset of $\mathcal{U}$ and $\mathcal{Y}$ a subset of $\mathcal{Z}$.

EQUIVALENCE RELATIONS

The notion of *equivalence* is very important in logic, and philosophy (and mathematics) generally. For present purposes we need the idea of an *equivalence relation* (relative to some set, $\mathcal{X}$).

Before giving the definition of *equivalence relation* we first need its essential ingredients, which are various properties of relations.

DEFINITION 2.13 $\mathcal{R}$ is *reflexive* iff $x\mathcal{R}x$, for all x in the (co-) domain of $\mathcal{R}$.

DEFINITION 2.14 $\mathcal{R}$ is *symmetric* just in case $x\mathcal{R}y$ iff $y\mathcal{R}x$, for all x and y in the (co-) domain of $\mathcal{R}$.

DEFINITION 2.15 $\mathcal{R}$ is *anti-symmetric* just in case if $x\mathcal{R}y$ and $y\mathcal{R}x$, then $x = y$, for all x and y in the (co-) domain of $\mathcal{R}$.

DEFINITION 2.16 $\mathcal{R}$ is *transitive* just in case if $x\mathcal{R}y$ and $y\mathcal{R}z$, then $x\mathcal{R}z$, for all x, y, and z in the (co-) domain of $\mathcal{R}$.

DEFINITION 2.17 $\mathcal{R}$ is *total* iff either $x\mathcal{R}y$ or $y\mathcal{R}x$ (or both), for all x and y in the (co-) domain of $\mathcal{R}$.

We say that $\mathcal{R}$ is a *relation on* $\mathcal{X}$ if $\mathcal{X}$ is the domain and codomain of $\mathcal{R}$. With this and the foregoing ingredients in hand the notion of an *equivalence relation* may be understood thus:

DEFINITION 2.18 $\mathcal{R}$ is an *equivalence relation* on $\mathcal{X}$ if and only if $\mathcal{R}$ is a reflexive, symmetric, and transitive relation on $\mathcal{X}$.

An obvious example of an equivalence relation is *identity*, which comprises all ordered pairs of the "form" $\langle x, x\rangle$. Likewise, *having the same latitude* is an equivalence relation between earthly locations. (*Having the same longitude* is not an equivalence relation. Why not?)

2.3 FUNCTIONS

Functions will play a prominent role in subsequent chapters and the reader should make sure that she understands the basic notion. For present purposes, a *function from set $\mathcal{X}$ to set $\mathcal{Y}$* is simply a relation from $\mathcal{X}$ to $\mathcal{Y}$. But not all relations from $\mathcal{X}$ to $\mathcal{Y}$ are functions. We devote this section to discussing various important features of functions. We leave the general *definition* as an exercise.

There are many familiar functions, encountered in elementary mathematics. One is the positive square-root function and another the squaring function:

a) $\sqrt{x}$ is the positive number y such that $y^2 = x$

b) x^2 is the number $x \cdot x$

In (a) it has to be understood that x itself is positive, at least as long as we do not move outside the subject of real numbers. So a function may have restrictions on what it can be applied to. Here is another example.

c) f is the function such that $f(x) = \frac{0}{x}$

Division by zero, we say, is *not defined*; so, $f(0)$ is not defined.

In general we shall use lower case letters like f, g, and h to stand for functions. Their definitions will typically have the form of (c). This may be shortened to

c′) $f : f(x) = \frac{0}{x}$

and the examples, (a) and (b), could be put in like form:

a′) $g : g(x) = \sqrt{x}$

b′) $h : h(x) = x^2$

These are all numerical functions. But all that is necessary for a *function*—all that is "essential to its nature"—is that it assign exactly one object to anything over which it is defined. Here are two non-numerical examples:

» The function q is defined on the alphabetical letters before z; if x is a letter then $q(x)$ is the next letter.

» The function β (beta, pronounced 'bay-ta') is defined on the members of the human race; if x is a person then $\beta(x)$ is the father of x.

When f is a function, and $f(x) = y$, then we say that y is *the value of* f *at argument* x. The set of all arguments on which f is defined is its *domain*, and the set of all values f takes is its *range*.

We also say that f *maps* set $\mathcal{W}$ *into* set $\mathcal{Z}$ to mean that $\mathcal{W}$ is part of the domain of f, and the values of f at arguments in $\mathcal{W}$ are all in $\mathcal{Z}$. In that case, we may sometimes write $f : \mathcal{W} \longrightarrow \mathcal{Z}$.

Degrees and Operators

Functions have *degrees*. All the examples so far have been functions of degree 1 and are called 'one-place' or 'unary' functions. Examples of functions of degree 2 and 3 are respectively

» $f'(x, y) = x + y$

» $g'(x, y, z) = \frac{x^2}{(y+z)}$

Functions of degree 2 are also called *binary*. Some special properties of binary functions are these:

DEFINITION 2.19 f is *commutative* iff $f(x, y) = f(y, x)$.

DEFINITION 2.20 f is *associative* iff $f(x, f(y, z)) = f(f(x, y), z)$.

The arithmetical function +, for example, is both commutative and associative, because

$$x + y = y + x \text{ and } x + (y + z) = (x + y) + z$$

A function is called an *operator* if all its values are also arguments on which it is defined. As the reader may recall from her first logic course many sentential operators are binary; some such operators are unary. (Which ones?)

2.4 INDUCTIVELY DEFINED SETS

Some sets, as we have seen, can be defined quite simply by abstraction or, as a special case, by listing their members. Thus the set of odd numbers below 10 can be defined either as

$$\{x : x < 10 \text{ and } x \text{ is an odd natural number}\}$$

or as $\{1, 3, 5, 7, 9\}$. But there is another procedure for defining sets that are built up systematically in a certain way, called *definition by induction* or, more usually, *inductive definition*. An informal example from a familiar mythology would be the following definition of the set of human beings:

» Adam and Eve are human;

» if x and y are human and z is a child of x and y, then z is human;

» nothing is human except in virtue of the above.

The first clause is called the *basis clause* and the elements it introduces the *basis elements*. The second clause is called the *generating clause* and the relationship it relies on (the relation *being a child of*, in our example) the *generating relation* or *mode of generation*. Very important, of course, is the third clause, called the *closure clause*. While the first two clauses introduce elements, the closure clause excludes membership for anything not so introduced.

There can be more than one mode of generation, in which case the second clause has several parts. Thus in our example, the generating clause could have been two-fold:

» if x and y are human and z is a son of x and y, then z is human;

» if x and y are human and z is a daughter of x and y, then z is human.

If the generating relationship is not known or given, then of course there is no telling what is in the thus defined set. But when it is known we can start listing members. So in our example, we could begin:

» Adam is human

» Eve is human

» Abel is a child of Adam and Eve

» Abel is human

» Cain is a child of Adam and Eve

» Cain is human

and so on, through the documented genealogy. In fact, in this case (even if we accept the documentation!) the relationship is at best known only to a small extent, for we do not know who are the children of our great-great-grand children (which are not born yet).

In elementary logic you will already have encountered an inductively defined set that will be one of our main topics of concern: the set of sentences of classical propositional logic. While we shall present its precise definition in the next chapter, you already know that the basis elements are the atomic sentences. The modes of generation will consist in combining sentences by means of the connectives, such as 'and' and 'or'. Nothing will count as a sentence unless it is made up from atomic sentences by means of the specified connectives.

A more artificial but illustrative example is the set of powers of the numbers 3 and 5—call this set $\mathcal{P}$ for brevity and define it as follows;

» Basis Clauses:

  » 1 is in $\mathcal{P}$

  » 3 is in $\mathcal{P}$

  » 5 is in $\mathcal{P}$

- Generative Clauses:
  - if $x \cdot 3$ is in $\mathcal{P}$ then so is $x \cdot 3 \cdot 3$
  - if $x \cdot 5$ is in $\mathcal{P}$ then so is $x \cdot 5 \cdot 5$
- Closure Clause: nothing is in $\mathcal{P}$ except by virtue of the above.

Here 1 is the zero-th power of 3 and of 5, but 3 and 5 have no other powers in common.

While we will frequently use this method of definition by induction throughout what follows, we will also eventually find it to give us the wherewithal for a powerful proof method, *proof by (mathematical) induction*. You may already have some inkling of how that would work. For example, in a quite informal way at least, would you not be able to show that each member of the set $\mathcal{P}$ is a multiple of an odd number? But we will return to this when needed.

Exercises 2.4.1

1 There is exactly one empty set. Why?

2 Give a definition of *functions*, based on what has been said in this chapter. Be sure to make the definition general enough, so as to capture functions of any finite degree.

3 Compare the notions of domain and co-domain of a relation with those of the domain and range of a function. What is the connection?

4 Give a proof of each of the following claims:

1. If $\mathcal{X} \subset \mathcal{Y}$ and $\mathcal{Y} \subset \mathcal{Z}$, then $\mathcal{X} \subset \mathcal{Z}$
2. $\mathcal{X} \cup \mathcal{X} = \mathcal{X} \cap \mathcal{X} = \mathcal{X}$
3. $\mathcal{X} \cap \emptyset = \emptyset$
4. $\mathcal{X} \cup \emptyset = \mathcal{X}$
5. $\mathcal{X} \cap \mathcal{Y} \subseteq \mathcal{X}$
6. $\mathcal{X} \subseteq \mathcal{X} \cup \mathcal{Y}$
7. $\mathcal{X} \subseteq \mathcal{Y}$ iff $\mathcal{X} \cap \mathcal{Y} = \mathcal{X}$
8. $\mathcal{X} \subseteq \mathcal{Y}$ *and* $\mathcal{X} \subseteq \mathcal{Z}$. iff $\mathcal{X} \subseteq \mathcal{Y} \cap \mathcal{Z}$
9. $(\mathcal{X} \cup \mathcal{Y}) \cap \mathcal{Z} = (\mathcal{X} \cap \mathcal{Z}) \cup (\mathcal{Y} \cap \mathcal{Z})$
10. $(\mathcal{X} \cap \mathcal{Y}) \cup \mathcal{Z} = (\mathcal{X} \cup \mathcal{Z}) \cap (\mathcal{Y} \cup \mathcal{Z})$
11. $\mathcal{X} - (\mathcal{Y} \cup \mathcal{Z}) = (\mathcal{X} - \mathcal{Y}) \cap (\mathcal{X} - \mathcal{Z})$

12. $\mathcal{X} \subseteq \mathcal{Y}$ iff $\wp(\mathcal{X}) \subseteq \wp(\mathcal{Y})$
13. $\wp(\mathcal{X} \cap \mathcal{Y}) = \wp(\mathcal{X}) \cap \wp(\mathcal{Y})$
14. $\bigcup \emptyset = \emptyset$
15. $\bigcup(\mathcal{K} \cup \mathcal{K}') = (\bigcup \mathcal{K}) \cup (\bigcup \mathcal{K}')$, for families $\mathcal{K}$ and $\mathcal{K}'$ of sets
16. $\bigcup\{\mathcal{X}\} = \mathcal{X}$
17. $\bigcap\{\mathcal{X}\} = \mathcal{X}$
18. $\bigcup \wp(\mathcal{X}) = \mathcal{X}$
19. $\mathcal{X} \times \mathcal{Y} = \emptyset$ iff $\mathcal{X} = \emptyset$ or $\mathcal{Y} = \emptyset$
20. $\mathcal{X} \times (\mathcal{Y} \cap \mathcal{Z}) = (\mathcal{X} \times \mathcal{Y}) \cap (\mathcal{X} \times \mathcal{Z})$
21. $(\mathcal{X} \times \mathcal{Y}) \cup (\mathcal{Z} \times \mathcal{Q}) \subseteq (\mathcal{X} \cup \mathcal{Z}) \times (\mathcal{Y} \cup \mathcal{Q})$

5 In plane geometry the points are labeled with ordered pairs of numbers $\langle x, y \rangle$, the co-ordinates. Relations among the points and sets of points can be defined through relations on these co-ordinates. For example, the X-axis is the set $\{\langle x, y \rangle : y = 0\}$. Define the 3-place relation of lying on the same line (*collinearity*).

6 For simplicity let us say that each person is a descendant of him- or herself, and, of course, children of descendants are descendants. Formalize this explanation by means of a properly formulated inductive definition of the *descendant* relation.

7 Is the following binary relation $\mathcal{R}$ an equivalence relation on the set of ordered pairs of positive integers?

$$\langle x, y \rangle \mathcal{R} \langle u, v \rangle \text{ iff } x \cdot v = y \cdot u$$

8 Let $\mathcal{R}$ be an equivalence relation on $\mathcal{X}$ and let $\mathcal{Y}$ be a set. Show that $\mathcal{R} \cap (\mathcal{Y} \times \mathcal{Y})$ is also an equivalence relation on $\mathcal{X}$.

9 Let $\mathcal{R}$ and $\mathcal{S}$ be equivalence relations on $\mathcal{X}$. Show that $\mathcal{R} \cap \mathcal{S}$ is also an equivalence relation on $\mathcal{X}$.

10 The set of all functions with domain $\mathcal{X}$ and range $\mathcal{Y}$ is denoted $\mathcal{Y}^{\mathcal{X}}$. What set is $\mathcal{Y}^{\mathcal{X}}$ if $\mathcal{X}$ is empty? How many members does $\mathcal{Y}^{\mathcal{X}}$ have if $\mathcal{X}$ has two members and $\mathcal{Y}$ has three members?

11 If f is a function with domain $\mathcal{X}$ and range $\mathcal{Y}$, it is *one-to-one* iff its values are distinct for distinct arguments. With f so understood, show that the *inverse of* f, defined by

$$f^{-1}(y) = x \text{ iff } f(x) = y$$

is well-defined and is a function (with what domain and range?). Is the function $f(x) = 2x + 1$ defined on the natural numbers a one-to-one function? If so, what is its inverse?

12 When f is a function and $\mathcal{X}$ a set we define

$$f[\mathcal{X}] = \{f(x) : x \in \mathcal{X} \text{ and } x \text{ is in the domain of } f\}.$$

Are the following correct in general? If not, is there something similar that is correct?

1. $f[\mathcal{X}] \cap f[\mathcal{Y}] = f[\mathcal{X} \cap \mathcal{Y}]$
2. $f[\mathcal{X}] \cup f[\mathcal{Y}] = f[\mathcal{X} \cup \mathcal{Y}]$
3. If $\mathcal{X} \subseteq \mathcal{Y}$ then $f[\mathcal{X}] \subseteq f[\mathcal{Y}]$

13 The notions of intersection and union were also defined for collections of sets in general. Consider the following definition:

» The set of humans is the intersection of all the sets $\mathcal{X}$ such that:
  » Adam and Eve are members of $\mathcal{X}$.
  » If anything is a child of two members of $\mathcal{X}$ then it is a member of $\mathcal{X}$.

Does this pick out the same set as the previously defined set of humans?

FURTHER READING

Two useful introductions to contemporary set theory are Enderton's [32] and Potter's [75]. Both texts focus on the so-called iterative conception of sets, which is dominant in contemporary philosophy and mathematics, and both texts briefly discuss the set-theoretic paradoxes that largely motivated the iterative conception. Stoll [94] and Quine [80] likewise provide useful texts, though with different philosophical motivations.

Every mathematician agrees
that every mathematician must know some set theory;
the disagreement begins
in trying to decide how much is some.
– Paul Halmos [44]

Chapter 3
Languages and Logics

The point of view we shall develop is that logic studies certain relations in language. These relations themselves must first be described in general. To do this we construct models of language—called 'languages'—of a simple sort to begin, and slightly more complex as we go on.

3.1 What is a Language?

An English speaker has a finite vocabulary but, from her finite vocabulary, she knows how to generate infinitely many expressions that will be understood by other English speakers. The rules that govern (implicitly or explicitly) the way complex but grammatical expressions are formed are said to form the *grammar* or *syntax* of English.

In venturing to formulate a rule of grammar we are stating a theoretical hypothesis. To test this hypothesis we can make complex expressions following a suggested rule, checking to see whether people accept the results as good English. Most rules in the old grammar texts fare rather badly in such tests; they have to be qualified with lists of exceptions.

In logical syntax we study languages with simple rules of grammar given, and also possible new forms for grammatical rules. The subject of syntax is the relations among expressions which are grammatical expressions of the same language.

Expressions do not just have relations to each other; they also "stand for" things in the world. In *semantics* we consider the relations of expressions to other things, while taking syntax for granted. For example, suppose that 'Cicero' refers to Tully; then 'the father of Cicero' refers to the father of Tully. (We take it for granted in this example that if 'Cicero' is a name, then 'the father of Cicero' is also a grammatically acceptable expression.) Similarly, if 'Cicero' refers to Tully and Tully is a man, then 'Cicero is the same man as Tully' is *true*. The terms 'refer' and 'true' will be basic terms of semantics.

What exactly is the ground of semantic facts? We say confidently that 'Cicero' refers to Tully. The reasons for this lie not in nature but, rather, in the things done and said by and around Cicero at an early age. In some cases we can trace conscious decisions: 'Marilyn Monroe' was a stage name consciously adopted and agreed to by others. In other cases the relevant linguistic behaviour just grows like Topsy: there may have been no conscious decisions to enrich the language involved at all in the process by which 'dope' and 'rotter' became English words.

The questions we have just raised do not belong to semantics, at least not logical semantics. In logical semantics we take the *standing for* relations for granted, in the way that we assume grammatical rules given. But the relations between expressions and their users—which determine grammaticality and reference in some way—can also be taken into account; their study is called *pragmatics*.[1]

The progression—syntax, semantics, pragmatics—is one of diminishing idealisation. Terms which seem absolute, or are treated without analysis, on one level, may be relativised or analysed on the next. In semantics we assume that each expression stands for something definite; but in pragmatics we say that what 'I' stands for depends on who says it, and what 'he' stands for depends on still further factors in the context of usage.

In the same way we could relativise syntactic concepts when we turn to semantics. This is not fashionable today but there are certainly historical examples of grammatical rules which were formulated in partly semantic terms. Aristotle, for example, characterised 'noun' and 'sentence' in terms of 'independent meaning' and 'expressing a complete thought' or 'capable of being true or false' (*On Interpretation*). The procedure in logical *semiotics*—the combination of syntax, semantics and pragmatics—is to idealise to the extent of assuming that there is a separate syntactic category for each semantic category, and that each syntactic category can be defined purely syntactically. We will accept that idealization here.

3.2 Syntax

Syntax is like bookkeeping, easy to get impatient with. Concepts easy to handle on an intuitive level need enormous precision and complication when we try to characterise them in purely syntactic terms—even when they are concepts relating only to relations among grammatical expressions.

That said, syntax studies little structures of an especially simple sort *in principle*, which help later to study structures that are more complex even in principle.

In this book we shall deal almost entirely with languages whose only important syntactic category is that of *sentences*. Complex sentences are built up from simpler ones by means of connectives. The following are typical rules of grammar, for use in connection with the classical propositional (or

---

[1]This three-fold terminology of 'syntax', 'semantics' and 'pragmatics' is due to Charles Morris, who introduced it in a seminal article in the *Encyclopedia of Unified Science*.

sentential) logic:

i) if A is a sentence, so is ~A

ii) if A and B are sentences, so is $(A \wedge B)$.

The simplest sentences of a language are called *atomic*.

Because we shall construct languages richer than that of classical logic we need further connectives as well. For example, negation has several analogues if there are three "truth values", depending on whether the extra value is thought of as a special way of being false, a special way of being true, or as being its own "opposite". Each connective typically has a name; for example, & is called 'ampersand' and ~ 'tilde'. But usually it is convenient to use putative English equivalents, such as 'and' for & or $\wedge$. Here is a short list of connective symbols with their English readings:

'and'	'or'	'not'	'if...then'	'if and only if'
$\wedge$	$\vee$	~	$\supset$	$\equiv$
&	$\veebar$	$-$	$\rightarrow$	$\leftrightarrow$
.	$\Cup$	$\neg$	$\Rightarrow$	$\Leftrightarrow$

$\supset$ is called 'hook', $\equiv$ 'tribar', $\vee$ 'wedge', $\wedge$ 'carrot', and, as above, ~ 'tilde'. For CPL it is possible to take just two of the connectives as basic and define the others in terms of them. When we refer to the *usual* way of defining connectives we shall mean that '$A \vee B$' is short for '$\sim(\sim A \wedge \sim B)$', '$A \supset B$' for '$\sim(A \wedge \sim B)$', and '$A \equiv B$' for '$(A \supset B) \wedge (B \supset A)$'. When it comes to other logics (or other languages that share the syntax of CPL), there is no guarantee that some of the connectives are definable in terms of the others.

The syntax for classical propositional (or sentential) logic—what we dub 'S_{cpl}'—may be given as follows.

S_{cpl} has a vocabulary and a set of sentences.

Vocabulary:

a) infinitely many atomic sentences

b) connectives ~ (unary) and $\wedge$, $\vee$, $\supset$, $\equiv$ (all binary);

c) punctuation marks:) and (

Sentences:

1) All atomic sentences are sentences;

2) If A is a sentence, then ~A is a sentence; and if A and B are sentences, so are $(A \wedge B)$, $(A \vee B)$, $(A \supset B)$, and $(A \equiv B)$;

3) Nothing is a sentence except by virtue of clauses (1) and (2).

As in Chapter 2, clause (3) is called the *closure clause*; and clauses (1)–(3) together form an *inductive definition* of the set of S_{cpl}-sentences.

Two remarks. We pretended to define a specific syntax, called 'S_{cpl}'. But really we didn't; for we did not say which entities are the atomic sentences. So really we might as well have said that we were defining *an* S_{cpl}, which is a *sort of* syntax. The pretense, however, gives the discussion a more concrete flavour. Second, the definition of S_{cpl} gives an indication of how to define a large class of syntaxes, which differ from S_{cpl} by having different connectives.

To give the general definition we agree to write '$\varphi(A_1, \ldots, A_n)$' for the result of constructing a complex sentence from sentences $A_1, \ldots, A_n$ by means of connective φ. Note well: the order matters. For example, the result of doing this for A and B, by means of $\wedge$ in S_{cpl}, is really $(A \wedge B)$, but we agree that '$\wedge(A, B)$' will stand for that same result.

DEFINITION 3.1 A *sentential syntax*, Synt, is a syntax which has a vocabulary and a set of sentences of the following sort.

Vocabularly:

a) a set $\mathcal{A}$ of atomic sentences
b) a set $\mathcal{C}$ of connectives, of various degrees
c) punctuation marks:) and (
d) there is no overlap of any sort between signs which are atomic sentences, connectives, or punctuation marks.

Sentences: the set $\mathcal{S}$ of sentences is defined:

1) All atomic sentences are in $\mathcal{S}$;
2) If φ is a connective of degree n, and $A_1, \ldots, A_n$ are in $\mathcal{S}$, then so is $\varphi(A_1, \ldots, A_n)$;
3) Nothing is in $\mathcal{S}$ except by virtue of clauses (1) and (2).

We summarise this definition by saying that $\mathtt{Synt} = \langle \mathcal{A}, \mathcal{C}, \mathcal{S} \rangle$.

3.3 SEMANTICS AND VALUATIONS

In a sentential syntax we may not see any structure in the atomic sentences, so in general we cannot place any restriction on how they are assigned values. For complex sentences, on the other hand, we may be able to give conditions of truth or falsity. When we do lay down such conditions it is of course important to avoid vicious circularity. The way we shall guard against that, in all the cases taken up in this book, is to place no restrictions at all on how atomic sentences can be true or false together, and to describe the assignment of values to complex sentences in terms of the values of their parts (though other factors may be involved as well). The main concept we shall keep very general:

» a *valuation of a syntax* is an assignment of values (of some sort or other) to the sentences of that syntax.

One example of a valuation is the assignment of T or F to each sentence when we construct truth-tables in elementary logic. (In this book we will use '1' and '0' rather than 'T' and 'F' for *True* and *False*.) But as we saw in §1, many other sorts of values can be assigned.

SENTENCES AND BASES

Sometimes there are operations on these assigned values that we can use to explain how the values of complex sentences are related to the values of their parts. In that case we say that the valuation has a *base*.

DEFINITION 3.2 Let v be a valuation of sentential syntax S. A *base* $\mathcal{B}$ for v is a triple $\langle \mathcal{V}, \mathbb{C}, \odot \rangle$, where $\mathcal{V}$ is a set of elements, $\mathbb{C}$ a set of operators on $\mathcal{V}$, and $\odot$ is a rule associating one operation $\odot_\varphi$ in $\mathbb{C}$ with each connective φ of the syntax, in such a way that

» $\mathsf{v}(\mathsf{A}) \in \mathcal{V}$, for each sentence A of S

» for all sentences $\mathsf{A}_1, \ldots, \mathsf{A}_n$ and each n-ary connective φ of S:

$$\mathsf{v}(\varphi(\mathsf{A}_1, \ldots, \mathsf{A}_n)) = \odot_\varphi(\mathsf{v}(\mathsf{A}_1), \ldots, \mathsf{v}(\mathsf{A}_n)).$$

For example, we might assign numbers to sentences in such a way that $(\mathsf{A} \wedge \mathsf{B})$ receives the *product* of the numbers received by A and by B. Suppose that v is a valuation of S_{cpl} that obeys the usual rules of truth-table construction. Then we shall have

$$\mathsf{v}(\sim\mathsf{A}) = \begin{cases} 1 & \text{if } \mathsf{v}(\mathsf{A}) = 0 \\ 0 & \text{if } \mathsf{v}(\mathsf{A}) = 1 \end{cases}$$

$$\mathsf{v}(\mathsf{A} \wedge \mathsf{B}) = \begin{cases} 1 & \text{if } \mathsf{v}(\mathsf{A}) = \mathsf{v}(\mathsf{B}) = 1 \\ 0 & \text{otherwise} \end{cases}$$

We need not especially look at $\vee$, $\supset$, or $\equiv$ since in classical propositional logic these can be characterized in terms of $\wedge$ and $\sim$. Can we find a base for v? Clearly the set of elements can be very small: $\mathcal{V} = \{1, 0\}$. These elements are numbers, and we are familiar with various operations on them, such as subtraction, multiplication, and addition. A bit of reflection shows that we can express the above equivalently by:

$$\begin{aligned} \mathsf{v}(\sim\mathsf{A}) &= 1 - \mathsf{v}(\mathsf{A}) \\ \mathsf{v}(\mathsf{A} \wedge \mathsf{B}) &= \mathsf{v}(\mathsf{A}) \cdot \mathsf{v}(\mathsf{B}) \end{aligned}$$

where the operations are *one minus* and *product*, respectively. So the set of operators includes these two. The rule that associates connectives and operators is, for ~ and ∧, the following:

$$\odot: \quad \begin{aligned} \odot_{\sim}(n) &= 1 - n \\ \odot_{\wedge}(m, n) &= m \cdot n \end{aligned}$$

Each of the connectives has such an associated operator. All valuations that agree with the usual rules of truth-table construction have this base.

A language has both a syntax and semantics. Both may be very rich but the syntax must at least specify *the set of sentences* of the language. And the semantics must at least specify a set of valuations of sentences, *the admissible valuations* of the language. The notion of *base* will be useful both in many-valued and in modal logic. A main difference between these two subjects is that in a many-valued language any two admissible valuations are explicitly made up with a common base. In modal logic this is not so. The relation between modal and many-valued logic will be taken up in Part IV.

EXERCISES 3.3.1

1 Let v be a valuation of S_{cpl} that obeys the rules of truth-table construction. We discussed a base for v where $\mathcal{V} = \{1, 0\}$ and the operators corresponding to ~ and ∧ are *one minus* and *product*, respectively. What are the operators corresponding to ∨, ⊃, and ≡?

2 Let S be a sentential syntax with only one atomic sentence p, and ~ as only connective. Consider the valuations:

» $v_1(p) = 1$; and if $v_1(A) = 1$ then $v_1({\sim}A) = 0$; also, if $v_1(A) = 0$ then $v_1({\sim}A) = 0$.

» $v_2(p) = 1 = v_2({\sim}p)$; and if A is not p or ~p, then $v_2(A) = 0$.

Does v_1 have a base? Does v_2? If either has a base, make up a third valuation with the same base.

3 Can you give an informal example of a valuation of S_{cpl} which does not have a base?

3.4 SEMANTIC PROPERTIES AND RELATIONS

Some values represent ways of being true; others not. When describing a language, we typically mention for each valuation which of the values it assigns to sentences are true ones—these are called the 'designated values'. This is the *typical* way to do it, not the only possible way. But if a valuation assigns one of the designated values to a sentence, we say that the valuation *satisfies* that sentence—or that the sentence *is true on* that valuation.

Generalizing upon this: it is part of the specification of a language to say which valuations satisfy which sentences. Accordingly, we shall say

DEFINITION 3.3 A *language* comprises

a) a syntax, which includes a set of *sentences*

b) a semantics, which includes

» a set of valuations of the sentences (the *admissible valuations*)

» a relation between admissible valuations and sentences (*satisfaction*)

For example, in classical propositional logic the syntax is S_{cpl}, the valuations, v, are assignments of 1 and 0 that follow the rules for truth-table construction, and v satisfies A if and only if v assigns 1 to A.

Once the basic components of any language are in hand, various "universal concepts", applicable to any language, are easily explained.

DEFINITION 3.4 A is a *valid sentence* (*tautology*, *logical truth*) of language $\mathcal{L}$ if all admissible valuations of $\mathcal{L}$ satisfy A. (Briefly: $\Vdash$ A in $\mathcal{L}$.)

DEFINITION 3.5 A is a *satisfiable sentence* of language $\mathcal{L}$ exactly if some admissible valuation of $\mathcal{L}$ satisfies A.

DEFINITION 3.6 A *implies* B in language $\mathcal{L}$ exactly if every admissible valuation of $\mathcal{L}$ which satisfies A also satisfies B. (Briefly: A $\Vdash$ B in $\mathcal{L}$.)

The relation of *implication* between sentences clearly corresponds to the notion of valid argument: the conclusion must be true if the premise is. Since arguments often have more than one premise, we generalise these notions to sets of sentences, as follows.

DEFINITION 3.7 A set $\mathcal{X}$ of $\mathcal{L}$-sentences is *satisfiable* in $\mathcal{L}$ exactly if some admissible valuation of $\mathcal{L}$ satisfies every A $\in \mathcal{X}$. (Briefly: 'satisfies $\mathcal{X}$'.)

DEFINITION 3.8 A set $\mathcal{X}$ of $\mathcal{L}$-sentences *implies* A in $\mathcal{L}$ exactly if every admissible valuation of $\mathcal{L}$ that satisfies $\mathcal{X}$ also satisfies A. (Briefly: $\mathcal{X} \Vdash$ A in $\mathcal{L}$.)

When $\mathcal{X}$ implies A in $\mathcal{L}$, we will also frequently say that A is a (semantic) *consequence* of $\mathcal{X}$ (in $\mathcal{L}$), and similarly that $\Vdash$ is the semantic consequence relation.

3.5 WHAT IS A LOGIC?

How shall we find out which sentences are logically true in a given language, and which arguments are valid? It is, and always has been, precisely the task of logic, as a discipline, to answer these questions. Aristotle first broached the task by means of his system of syllogisms, which catalogued the valid argument forms for a select family of sentences in natural language. The first two such forms had the names *Barbara* and *Celarent*:

BARBARA	CELARENT
All A are B. All B are C. Therefore: All A are C.	Some A are B. All B are C. Therefore: Some A are C.

and the entire system of such syllogistic forms was avidly memorized by students in the Middle Ages and for some centuries thereafter. The principles of "syllogistic" provided the first systematic catalogue of valid arguments. Since there are many different languages and sorts of languages (counting also such fragments of bigger languages as e.g. the family of sentences that can occur in syllogisms), there must accordingly be many different logics. There must in principle be one such systematic catalogue for each language (though different languages could agree in their sets of valid sentences and/or valid arguments, so their logics could be the same).

THE FIRST CONSTRAINT

The sets of valid sentences and of valid arguments of a language are defined, as we have seen, in terms of the admissible valuations, that is, with recourse to the semantics of the language. The *first constraint* logic accepts is that logic is to describe these sets purely syntactically, that is, purely in terms of the syntactic form of the expressions. Aristotle's syllogistic provides a good example: it tells us whether a syllogism is valid purely on the basis of the forms of the sentences involved. A sentence of type 'All ... is ...' has form A and one of type 'Some ... is ...' has form E. The first syllogism displayed has form A-A-A, with mnemonic 'BARBARA' and the second has form E-A-E, with mnemonic 'CELARENT'.

Will it always be possible to satisfy the first constraint—to specify the sets of valid sentences and of valid arguments of a language purely syntactically? That is not guaranteed at all! The language may lack the needed expressive power; its syntax may be poor in relation to the complex structures that appear in its semantics. But then of course the logician will have the task of showing whether it is possible or not, and of doing so if it is.

THE SECOND CONSTRAINT

The second constraint logic accepts is that it should be user-friendly; it should provide mechanical or effective, humanly usable, procedures to answer the central questions (validity and so on). At the very least, procedures for determining (in-) validity ought to be easily checkable as to whether they have been properly applied. Is that always possible for the questions of interest? That is again not guaranteed at all. Here too the logician's task is to show whether it is possible or not, and to do so if it is.

Of course, there are mechanical procedures that are more feasible for computers than for humans. Inductive definitions give us in effect good illustrations of this. After writing down the basis elements of the defined class, the generating clauses provide a procedure for producing all the other elements. In general this will take forever. But each element that belongs to the class will definitely appear in finitely many steps—we just may not know how many steps! Thus it may be possible for a given language to give an inductive definition of the set of valid sentences, in purely syntactic terms, and that is typical of a logical system. But having such a definition doesn't automatically afford a practically useful way to spot theorems. If you just start generating theorems via the inductive definition and hope that the one you are interested in will appear, you could be in for a very long day—to say the least.

A *decision procedure* is one that will give a definite yes or no answer in finitely many steps. Again there are decision procedures that are not exactly a great boon to the unaided pencil-and-paper operation. Suppose for example that you could give an inductive definition of the set of valid sentences, and also an inductive definition of the set of sentences that are not valid sentences. Then you and your sister could each take one; you could start generating the valid sentences and she could start generating the others. In finitely many steps the sentence of interest would appear either in your list or in hers—but who is to say how long it would take?

In subsequent chapters we will provide genuinely user-friendly logical systems, by means of the *tableaux method*, originally devised by the Dutch logician Evert W. Beth but amended, simplified, and adapted in many ways since. When available, the tableaux method provides a decision procedure for validity.

3.6 Appraisal of Logical Systems

Consider a given language $\mathcal{L}$ and the semantic consequence relation $\Vdash$ in $\mathcal{L}$ (implication in $\mathcal{L}$). A logical system LS for $\mathcal{L}$ will specify a syntactically defined consequence relation $\vdash$ (a *logical consequence* relation of LS).[2] For both we have a limiting case:

» A is a *valid* sentence of $\mathcal{L}$ iff the empty set implies A in $\mathcal{L}$.

[2] We will refer to '$\vdash$' and '$\Vdash$' as the single turnstile and double turnstile, respectively. To the left of either the single or double turnstile we will write '$\mathcal{X}$, A' for the union of premise-set $\mathcal{X}$ and {A}, and we will also write '$\mathcal{X}, \mathcal{Y}$' for the union of premise-sets $\mathcal{X}$ and $\mathcal{Y}$.

» A is a *theorem* of LS iff A is a logical consequence of the empty set in LS.

If everything goes well these relations will really be the same: the semantics and the logic will in effect provide us with two different descriptions of the same relation among sentences in $\mathcal{L}$. Not everything may go so well; so we will here define some terms that pertain to the various sorts of match and mismatch between a given language and a given logic.

DEFINITION 3.9 LS is *statement sound* for $\mathcal{L}$ iff all theorems of LS are valid sentences of $\mathcal{L}$.

DEFINITION 3.10 LS is *statement complete* for $\mathcal{L}$ iff all valid sentences of $\mathcal{L}$ are theorems of LS.

DEFINITION 3.11 LS is *argument sound* for $\mathcal{L}$ iff $\mathcal{X} \Vdash$ A in $\mathcal{L}$ whenever $\mathcal{X} \vdash$ A in LS, for all finite sets $\mathcal{X}$ of sentences of $\mathcal{L}$ and all sentences A of $\mathcal{L}$.

DEFINITION 3.12 LS is *argument complete* for $\mathcal{L}$ iff $\mathcal{X} \vdash$ A in LS whenever $\mathcal{X} \Vdash$ A in $\mathcal{L}$, for all finite sets $\mathcal{X}$ of sentences of $\mathcal{L}$ and all sentences A of $\mathcal{L}$.

DEFINITION 3.13 LS is *strongly sound* for $\mathcal{L}$ iff $\mathcal{X} \Vdash$ A in $\mathcal{L}$ whenever $\mathcal{X} \vdash$ A in LS, for all sets $\mathcal{X}$ of sentences of $\mathcal{L}$ and all sentences A of $\mathcal{L}$.

DEFINITION 3.14 LS is *strongly complete* for $\mathcal{L}$ iff $\mathcal{X} \vdash$ A in LS whenever $\mathcal{X} \Vdash$ A in $\mathcal{L}$, for all sets $\mathcal{X}$ of sentences of $\mathcal{L}$ and all sentences A of $\mathcal{L}$.

Strong soundness and completeness are the ideal but sometimes it is useful enough to have a logic with a weaker property. By way of illustrating how it might not be so easy to enjoy the ideal, consider an example.[3] The following is an argument with conclusion 'There are infinitely many cats'. The set $\mathcal{X}$ of premises of the argument is infinite; it has the members

1. There is at least one cat
2. There are at least two cats
3. There are at least three cats

$$\vdots$$

[3]This is a variant of an example Alfred Tarski gave in his seminal paper on consequence relations [96].

and so forth. If we take only the first n members of $\mathcal{X}$, then the conclusion does not follow—the argument is not valid. But the conclusion does follow from $\mathcal{X}$ as a whole. Therefore there can be a sort of quantum leap—from the finite cases to the infinite cases—in the consequence relation, and a given logic may not be able to keep up with it. (As we shall take up in a later chapter, classical propositional logic is strongly complete, as is standard quantificational logic. In both these logics it is also the case that an argument is valid only if some finite sub-argument is valid, so the above example can definitely not be handled there.)

EXERCISES 3.6.1

1 Prove that if $\mathcal{X}$ is not satisfiable (in language $\mathcal{L}$) then $\mathcal{X}$ implies every sentence (in $\mathcal{L}$).

2 The relation of implication will always have some very general structural properties, regardless of what language $\mathcal{L}$ is like. Prove each of the following for all languages, as they are defined in this chapter.

1. If A is a member of $\mathcal{X}$ then $\mathcal{X} \Vdash A$.
2. If $\mathcal{X} \Vdash A$ then $\mathcal{X}, \mathcal{Y} \Vdash A$.
3. If $\mathcal{X} \Vdash A$ for every $A \in \mathcal{Y}$ and $\mathcal{Y} \Vdash B$, then $\mathcal{X} \Vdash B$. [This is called the principle of *transitivity* for $\Vdash$.]
4. $\emptyset \Vdash A$ iff for every set $\mathcal{X}$ of sentences, $\mathcal{X} \Vdash A$.

3 Show informally that in classical propositional logic the argument from A, B to C is valid iff the argument from A to $B \supset C$ is valid or the set $\{A, \sim(B \supset C)\}$ is unsatisfiable.

4 CALCULUS OF DEDUCTIVE SYSTEMS: We define the following function on sets of sentences of a given language $\mathcal{L}$:

$$Cn(\mathcal{X}) \quad = \quad \{A : \mathcal{X} \Vdash A\}$$

(suppressing the reference to $\mathcal{L}$ in our notation here). A *deductive system* is a set that is "closed under" the operation of function *Cn*:

» $\mathcal{X}$ is a *deductive system* (of $\mathcal{L}$) iff $\mathcal{X} = Cn(\mathcal{X})$.

Complete the following:

1. Prove the following for the function *Cn* (properties which make it a *closure operator* on sets):
   (a) $\mathcal{X} \subseteq Cn(\mathcal{X})$.

(b) $Cn(Cn(\mathcal{X})) \subseteq Cn(\mathcal{X})$.

(c) $Cn(\mathcal{X} \cup \mathcal{Y}) = Cn(Cn(\mathcal{X}) \cup Cn(\mathcal{Y}))$.

2. For deductive systems $\mathcal{X}$, $\mathcal{Y}$ prove the following:

   (a) $\mathcal{X} \cap \mathcal{Y}$ is a deductive system, and is the largest such system contained in both $\mathcal{X}$ and $\mathcal{Y}$.

   (b) $Cn(\mathcal{X} \cup \mathcal{Y})$ is a deductive system and is the smallest such system that contains both $\mathcal{X}$ and $\mathcal{Y}$.

FURTHER READING

Forbes [35] and Bach [4] provide related introductory discussion of languages. A useful but advanced discussion of languages is Cresswell's [23].

In logic there are no morals.
Everyone is at liberty to build up his own logic,
i.e. his own form of language, as he wishes.
– Rudolph Carnap [19]

Chapter 4 Tableaux

In this chapter we briefly introduce *analytic tableaux* (singular: tableau) or *trees* (singular: tree); such trees will serve as our primary proof procedure in Parts II and III. Aiming at familiarity we begin with tree rules for classical propositional logic (CPL). We first review the syntax and semantics of CPL, and then introduce trees.

4.1 Syntax of CPL

We have already discussed the syntax of CPL, which is a structure, $\mathrm{S}_{\mathrm{cpl}} = \langle \mathcal{A}, \mathcal{C}, \mathcal{S} \rangle$, where, for present purposes, $\mathcal{A}$ comprises the following letters with or without positive integer subscripts:

$$\mathrm{p}, \mathrm{q}, \mathrm{r}$$

$\mathcal{C}$ comprises the unary connective $\sim$ and binary connectives $\wedge$, $\vee$, $\supset$ and $\equiv$. $\mathcal{S}$, the set of CPL-sentences, is specified thus:

» All elements of $\mathcal{A}$ are elements of $\mathcal{S}$;

» If A is in $\mathcal{S}$, then $\sim$A is in $\mathcal{S}$; and if A and B are in $\mathcal{S}$, so are $(A \wedge B)$, $(A \vee B)$, $(A \supset B)$, and $(A \equiv B)$;

» Nothing is in $\mathcal{S}$ except by virtue of the above two clauses.

4.2 Semantics

The *admissible valuations* are those functions $\mathrm{v} : \mathcal{S} \longrightarrow \{1, 0\}$ such that

$$\mathrm{v}(\sim A) = 1 \text{ iff } \mathrm{v}(A) = 0$$

$$\mathrm{v}((A \wedge B)) = 1 \text{ iff } \mathrm{v}(A) = 1 \text{ and } \mathrm{v}(B) = 1$$

$$\mathrm{v}((A \vee B)) = 1 \text{ iff } \mathrm{v}(A) = 1 \text{ or } \mathrm{v}(B) = 1$$

$$\mathrm{v}((A \supset B)) = 1 \text{ iff } \mathrm{v}(A) = 0 \text{ or } \mathrm{v}(B) = 1$$

$$\mathrm{v}((A \equiv B)) = 1 \text{ iff } \mathrm{v}(A) = \mathrm{v}(B)$$

An admissible valuation ν *satisfies* A iff $\nu(A) = 1$. The important semantic properties and relations, of course, are defined as in §3.4.[1]

We will use '$\mathcal{L}_{cp1}$' to denote the language specified by the syntax and semantics above—the language of classical propositional (or sentential) logic. We will leave it tacitly understood in this chapter that $\mathcal{L}_{cp1}$ is the language under discussion; when we speak of an admissible valuation, ν, we leave it as understood that this is an admissible valuation of S_{cpl}.

4.3 Analytic Tableaux: Trees

Recall from (Def 3.7) that a set $\mathcal{X}$ of $\mathcal{L}_{cp1}$-sentences is *satisfiable* exactly if there is some admissible valuation that satisfies every A in $\mathcal{X}$, where A is an $\mathcal{L}_{cp1}$-sentence. Trees provide a mechanical (syntactic) procedure for checking such satisfiability—and eventually semantic validity of arguments. Once the tree construction procedure has been outlined we will discuss the question of how the semantic concept of satisfiability (and, eventually, semantic validity) and the mechanical procedure align with each other.

The Basic Idea

Is the set $\mathcal{H} = \{p, (p \supset q), {\sim}q\}$ satisfiable $\mathcal{L}_{cp1}$? One way of checking is via "truth tables", with which the reader is familiar. Another way, however, is by a version of *reductio*: Suppose that $\mathcal{H}$ is satisfiable. Then some admissible valuation, ν, satisfies each element of $\mathcal{H}$, in which case we have

$$\nu(p) = \nu((p \supset q)) = \nu({\sim}q) = 1$$

But any admissible valuation assigns 1 to ${\sim}q$ iff it assigns 0 to q. So, $\nu(q) = 0$. Likewise, since ν is an admissible valuation, $\nu((p \supset q)) = 1$ iff $\nu(p) = 0$ or $\nu(q) = 1$. As $\nu(q) \neq 1$ (i.e., $\nu(q)$ is not 1), $\nu(p) = 0$. But, as above, $\nu(p) = 1$. Since ν is a *function* it cannot assign *both* 1 and 0 to p. Hence, $\mathcal{H}$ is not satisfiable.

Tree procedures are closely related to the foregoing idea; they are systematic, mechanical searches for an admissible valuation that satisfies a given set of sentences. For now, we turn to a quick glance at what trees look like.

[1] Note that one may—and we often will—take only two elements of C to be primitive, defining all others in terms of the primitive pair. For example, by taking the primitive connectives to be only $\sim$ and $\wedge$ one may specify the admissible valuations by giving only the first two clauses above; in turn, one may define $\vee$, $\supset$, $\equiv$ in terms of the clauses governing $\sim$ and $\wedge$. We leave this as an exercise in §4.3.1.

The Basic Picture

Trees look something like this:

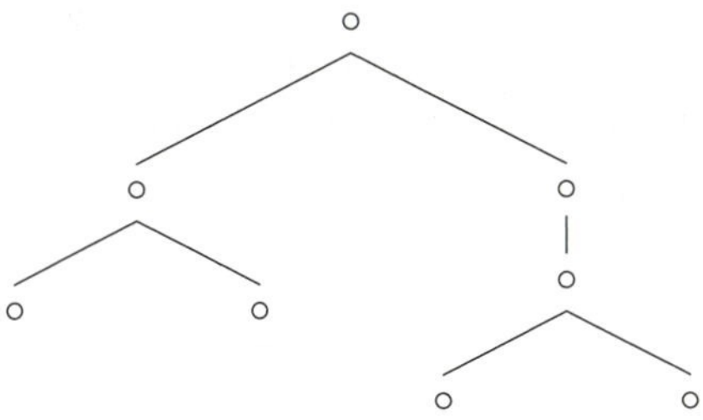

They grow upside-down, as it were. The circles are called *nodes*, the top node *the root*.[2] The bottom nodes are called *tips* (sometimes *leaves*), and any path from the root to a tip—or, strictly speaking, from the root to as far as the path goes—is called a *branch*. (As far as the path goes? We will deal mostly with *finite* branches, and certainly only finite branches in this chapter; however, we will consider infinite branches in subsequent chapters.)

For our purposes trees come equipped with *rules* which, intuitively, tell you how to "grow branches" from given nodes. Since our concern is with satisfiability (and eventually validity) our trees will be grown from sentences and our rules, accordingly, will apply to such sentences.

As example consider, once again, the set $\mathcal{H} = \{(p \supset q), p, \sim q\}$. In using trees to test the satisfiability of $\mathcal{H}$ we begin by constructing the following initial branch.

$$(p \supset q)$$
$$p$$
$$\sim q$$

This list is called *the initial list* (or *trunk*) and the sentences in this list are the first three nodes of the tree. At this stage of the tree construction we would simply begin to apply *resolution rules*—tree rules—to the initial list; this is how our tree grows. Such rules will be given below. For now, we reason as follows.

The initial list is satisfiable iff there is some admissible valuation that satisfies each element in the initial list—an admissible valuation according to which every sentence in the initial list is true. In our tree construction

[2] Trees always have a unique root, though we won't pause to discuss a general definition in this chapter. (We do provide a definition in Part IV, and also an important result on which our tree procedure relies (viz., König's Lemma).)

we hypothesize, in effect, that there is some such admissible valuation satisfying each element in the initial list. Let us take each element of the list in turn, starting from the top.

If (p ⊃ q) is satisfied, then either ~p is true (assigned 1 by the given admissible valuation) or q is true. We can indicate this disjunction by branching. (Ignore, for now, the so-called closed off sign—viz., ⊗.)

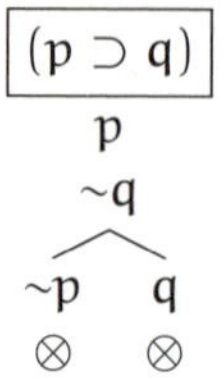

So, if some admissible valuation satisfies (p ⊃ q) then either it satisfies ~p or it satisfies q. This is the upshot of the branching. Notice, too, that the first element of the list is now *boxed-up* (or boxed), as we will say. Boxing (in this context) is a device to remind us that we have *fully processed* the given element—we have done all that is required to ensure that (p ⊃ q) is satisfied (viz., by indicating that either ~p is satisfied or q is satisfied). The *closed off* sign ⊗ indicates a *closed branch*. We say

» A branch is *closed* iff there are two nodes on the branch such that A occurs by itself at one node and ~A by itself at the other, for some sentence A in $\mathcal{S}$.

» A branch is *open* iff it is not closed.

This should explain why the *closed off* sign occurs where it does on the tree above; in each case there are sentences of the form A and ~A on two of the nodes of the given branch.

Just as a branch may be open or closed so too can a tree be open or closed. Likewise, trees may be *finished*—in which case no further rules can be applied.

» A tree is *closed* iff every branch of the tree is closed.

» A tree is *open* iff the tree is not closed.

» A tree is *finished* iff the tree is closed or at every node of the tree is (only) an atomic sentence, the negation of an atomic, or a *boxed* sentence.[3]

[3]'finished' is not a standard term; usually, the term 'complete' is used in this context, but we reserve 'complete' for other uses.

What does a *closed tree* indicate? If the tree procedure is doing its job, a closed tree indicates that the initial list is not satisfiable. A branch closes exactly when sentences of the form A and ~A occur (by themselves) at nodes on the branch. Intuitively, one can think of branches as searching for admissible valuations that make each element (sentence) on the branch true; since no admissible valuation assigns 1 to both A and ~A, any branch on which both A and ~A occur (by themselves) is a branch that closes—the search for satisfying all elements of that branch comes to an end, as there is no such satisfaction to be found.

Consider another example. Is $\mathcal{H}' = \{(p \supset q), (r \vee {\sim}q), {\sim}r, {\sim}p\}$ satisfiable? Our tree for $\mathcal{H}'$ begins, as above, with the following initial branch:

$$\begin{array}{c} (p \supset q) \\ (r \vee {\sim}q) \\ {\sim}r \\ {\sim}p \end{array}$$

Once again, we assume that some admissible valuation satisfies this initial list. We build our tree in search of such a valuation.

If $(p \supset q)$ is satisfied, then either ~p is true or q is true. As above, we indicate this disjunction by branching:

$$\begin{array}{c} \boxed{(p \supset q)} \\ (r \vee {\sim}q) \\ {\sim}r \\ {\sim}p \\ \diagup \quad \diagdown \\ {\sim}p \qquad q \end{array}$$

As per the convention discussed above, the boxing indicates that we have fully processed $(p \supset q)$.

Turning to the second element of the initial list, we have a disjunction, $(r \vee {\sim}q)$, which is satisfied iff at least one of its disjuncts, r or ~q, is satisfied. Using the same branching technique we indicate the relevant possibilities thus:

$$\begin{array}{c} \vdots \\ \diagup \qquad \diagdown \\ r \qquad\qquad {\sim}q \end{array}$$

But where does this new branching go? Prior to the new branching the tree has exactly two branches, one ending with ~p, the other with q. On which branch does the further branching grow? The answer is: *on both branches.*

Why both branches? Recall where we are. We are assuming that some admissible valuation, v, satisfies the initial list, in which case v satisfies

$(p \supset q)$, in which case $\nu(\sim p) = 1$ or $\nu(q) = 1$. This 'either...or' gave rise to the first branching. This branching, in turn, represents 'possible paths' that ν might take; but *which* path ν follows is not known. Accordingly, our second branching step, arising from the second line of the initial list (viz., $(r \vee \sim q)$), produces branches at both $\sim p$ and q, yielding:

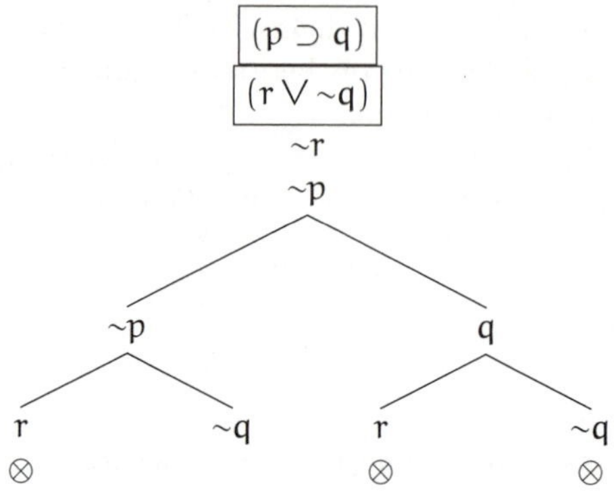

Notice that this example is a finished, open tree. That it is *open* is telling; its open branch gives an easy clue to whether the initial list is satisfiable. In particular, consider the following valuation, ν, which we construct by "climbing" the open branch:[4]

$$\nu(q) = \nu(p) = \nu(r) = 0$$

Our method of constructing such a valuation is straightforward:[5]

» Start at the tip of any open branch, b.

» Ignore all boxed-up sentences in b.

» If A is an atomic sentence occurring by itself on some node of b, let $\nu(A) = 1$;

» If A is an atomic sentence and $\sim A$ occurs by itself on some node of b, let $\nu(A) = 0$.

» If A is an atomic sentence and neither it nor $\sim A$ occurs by itself at some node of b, let $\nu(A)$ be 1 or 0.

[4]The following doesn't specify a unique valuation; rather, it specifies a relevant collection of valuations—all the ones assigning 0 to q, p and r. That said, we shall continue to speak of *the* valuation, ν, corresponding to an open branch, trusting that no confusion will arise.

[5]Though we're not giving a precise definition of trees, we need to mention that there is exactly one sentence per node of any given tree.

By following these instructions on the finished, open tree above, we come up with ν's assignments described above. What is important to notice is that ν is an admissible valuation that satisfies the initial list of the tree—it satisfies our specified set $\mathcal{H}'$.

FROM SATISFACTION TO SEMANTIC VALIDITY

Before outlining the tree construction procedure for $\mathcal{L}$ we should point out an important relation between satisfaction and semantic validity. The point is this: that with a test of satisfiability we automatically have a test for argument (semantic) validity and tautology-hood. That this is so follows from the following result: If $\mathcal{X}$ implies A ($\mathcal{X} \Vdash A$)—that is, if the argument from $\mathcal{X}$ to A is (semantically) valid—then $\mathcal{X} \cup \{\sim A\}$ is *not satisfiable*. (Again, all of this is implicitly referenced to $\mathcal{L}_{\text{cpl}}$.) The converse holds as well: If $\mathcal{X} \cup \{\sim A\}$ is not satisfiable, then $\mathcal{X} \Vdash A$. This result is important enough to warrant a rigorous proof but, for present purposes, we shall just sketch the proof.

» Suppose that $\mathcal{X} \Vdash A$. Then any admissible valuation that satisfies $\mathcal{X}$ satisfies A. Suppose, for reductio, that $\mathcal{X} \cup \{\sim A\}$ *is* satisfiable. Then some admissible valuation satisfies every element of $\mathcal{X} \cup \{\sim A\}$ and, hence, satisfies every element of $\mathcal{X}$ and every element of $\{\sim A\}$. Let ν be such an admissible valuation. Then ν satisfies $\mathcal{X}$ and $\nu(\sim A) = 1$. But as ν satisfies $\mathcal{X}$, ν also satisfies A, that is, $\nu(A) = 1$. But no admissible valuation assigns 1 to both ~A and A.

» Suppose that $\mathcal{X} \cup \{\sim A\}$ is not satisfiable. Then no admissible valuation satisfies every element of $\mathcal{X} \cup \{\sim A\}$ and, so, no admissible valuation satisfies every element of $\mathcal{X}$ and every element of $\{\sim A\}$. Suppose, now, that $\mathcal{X} \nVdash A$ (that is, that $\mathcal{X}$ does not imply A). Then some admissible valuation—call it 'ν'—satisfies $\mathcal{X}$ but does not satisfy A, in which case $\nu(A) = 0$. Since ν is an admissible valuation $\nu(A) = 0$ iff $\nu(\sim A) = 1$. But, then, ν satisfies $\mathcal{X}$ *and* $\{\sim A\}$, contrary to the initial supposition.

With this result in mind we can use trees to test for argument (semantic) validity and tautology-hood. In the case of an argument from premise set $\mathcal{X}$ to conclusion A, we grow a tree having as its initial list the elements of $\mathcal{X}$ and the *negation* of A. Our initial list, then, comprises all elements of $\mathcal{X} \cup \{\sim A\}$. The order in the list does not matter but it is customary to put the negated conclusion last—a custom we will follow.

Similarly, we can test whether a sentence is a tautology by growing a tree from its negation—a tree with its negation as root. Example: Suppose we want to test whether $(p \supset (q \supset p))$ is a tautology. In constructing our tree the initial list is simply: $\sim(p \supset (q \supset p))$. If some admissible valuation satisfies the initial list, then it assigns 0 to the *negatum*, namely,

$(p \supset (q \supset p))$, our original sentence. Now, if $(p \supset (q \supset p))$ is false (i.e., is assigned 0 by our given admissible valuation) then the antecedent is true *and* the consequent is false. Thus, no new "branching possibilities" emerge; we simply stay on the initial path. We represent this stage of the tree as follows.

$$\boxed{\sim(p \supset (q \supset p))}$$
$$|$$
$$p$$
$$\sim(q \supset p)$$

We box-up, as above, to indicate that we are finished resolving $\sim(p \supset (q \supset p))$. At this stage the bottom node is "filled" with another negated conditional, and so the same reasoning applies—the antecedent is true and the consequent false. As before, this yields a *continued* path along the initial branch; no new branching possibilities emerge:

$$\boxed{\sim(p \supset (q \supset p))}$$
$$|$$
$$p$$
$$\boxed{\sim(q \supset p)}$$
$$|$$
$$q$$
$$\sim p$$
$$\otimes$$

We have a closed tree. Provided the tree procedure is doing its intended job, a closed tree indicates that the initial list is not satisfiable; in this case, this means that the original sentence is a tautology: every admissible valuation satisfies it. Whether a given tree procedure does its intended job is an issue concerning the soundness and completeness of the tree procedure, an issue to which we briefly turn below.

TREES FOR $\mathcal{L}_{cpl}$

As a heuristic guide, one can think of the following rules thus: If A is true on some admissible valuation, then applying a resolution rule to A will yield all true sentences (relative to the given valuation) on at least one branch generated by the rule. But note: this is *only* a heuristic guide, since tree rules are purely formal rules and, so, devoid of such "meaning". (Still, a useful guide is a useful guide.)

Rules for $\mathcal{L}_{cpl}$ Trees

For each binary S_{cpl}-connective there are two rules, a positive and negative rule. We name the rules by using the following names for connectives: $\supset$

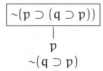

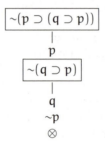

called 'hook', $\equiv$ called 'tribar', $\vee$ called 'wedge', $\wedge$ called 'carrot', and $\sim$ called 'tilde'. The rules for the binary connectives run as follows.

(H1) Hook (Pos): A sentence of the form $(A \supset B)$ is resolved by extending the tip of any open branch in which $(A \supset B)$ occurs into two new *branches*, with $\sim A$ at the tip of one new branch and B at the other. (Convention: When $(A \supset B)$ is so resolved, it is *boxed-up*.) We write this thus:

$$\boxed{(A \supset B)}$$

$$\sim A \qquad B$$

(H2) Hook (Neg): A sentence of the form $\sim(A \supset B)$ is resolved by extending the tip of any open branch in which $\sim(A \supset B)$ occurs into two new *nodes* (not branches), with A at one new node and $\sim B$ at the other. (Convention: When $\sim(A \supset B)$ is so resolved, it is *boxed-up*.) We write this thus:

$$\boxed{\sim(A \supset B)}$$

$$A$$
$$\sim B$$

(W1) Wedge (Pos): A sentence of the form $(A \vee B)$ is resolved by extending the tip of any open branch in which $(A \vee B)$ occurs into two new *branches*, with A at the tip of one new branch and B at the other. (Convention: When $(A \vee B)$ is so resolved, it is *boxed-up*.) We write this thus:

$$\boxed{(A \vee B)}$$

$$A \qquad B$$

(W2) Wedge (Neg): A sentence of the form $\sim(A \vee B)$ is resolved by extending the tip of any open branch in which $\sim(A \vee B)$ occurs into two new *nodes* (not branches), with $\sim A$ at one new node and $\sim B$ at the other. (Convention: When $\sim(A \vee B)$ is so resolved, it is *boxed-up*.) We write this thus:

$$\boxed{\sim(A \vee B)}$$

$$\sim A$$
$$\sim B$$

(C1) CARROT (POS): A sentence of the form $(A \wedge B)$ is resolved by extending the tip of any open branch in which $(A \wedge B)$ occurs into two new *nodes* (not branches), with A at one new node and B at the other. (Convention: When $(A \wedge B)$ is so resolved, it is *boxed-up*.) We write this thus:

$$\boxed{(A \wedge B)}$$

$$\begin{array}{c} | \\ A \\ B \end{array}$$

(C2) CARROT (NEG): A sentence of the form $\sim(A \wedge B)$ is resolved by extending the tip of any open branch in which $\sim(A \wedge B)$ occurs into two new *branches*, with $\sim A$ at the tip of one new branch and $\sim B$ at the other. (Convention: When $\sim(A \wedge B)$ is so resolved, it is *boxed-up*.) We write this thus:

$$\boxed{\sim(A \wedge B)}$$

$$\begin{array}{cc} / & \backslash \\ \sim A & \sim B \end{array}$$

(T1) TRIBAR (POS): A sentence of the form $(A \equiv B)$ is resolved by extending the tip of any open branch in which $(A \equiv B)$ occurs into two new *branches*, with A and B at nodes of one new branch and $\sim A$ and $\sim B$ at nodes of the other. (Convention: When $(A \equiv B)$ is so resolved, it is *boxed-up*.) We write this thus:

$$\boxed{(A \equiv B)}$$

$$\begin{array}{cc} / & \backslash \\ A & \sim A \\ B & \sim B \end{array}$$

(T2) TRIBAR (NEG): A sentence of the form $\sim(A \equiv B)$ is resolved by extending the tip of any open branch in which $\sim(A \equiv B)$ occurs into two new *branches*, with A and $\sim B$ at nodes of one new branch and $\sim A$ and B at nodes of the other. (Convention: When $\sim(A \equiv B)$ is so resolved, it is *boxed-up*.) We write this thus:

$$\boxed{\sim(A \equiv B)}$$

$$\begin{array}{cc} / & \backslash \\ A & \sim A \\ \sim B & B \end{array}$$

So go the rules for binary connectives. There is exactly one rule for the unary connective of $\mathcal{L}_{cpl}$. The rule is as follows.

(TT) TILDE TILDE: A sentence of the form ~~A is resolved by extending the tip of any open branch in which ~~A occurs into one new *node* (not branch), with A at the new node. (Convention: When ~~A is so resolved, it is *boxed-up*.) We write this thus:

$$\begin{array}{c} \boxed{\sim\sim A} \\ | \\ A \end{array}$$

With the $\mathcal{L}_{cpl}$-rules in hand we define *initial list*, *closed branch*, *open branch*, *finished tree*, *closed tree* and *open tree* as in §4.3. The *closed off* symbol, ⊗, is likewise used as above. Similarly, the basic recipe for constructing *counterexamples* to an argument remains as before—the instructions for "climbing" an open branch of a (finished) tree and constructing an admissible valuation that satisfies the initial list.

What needs to be defined is a notion of *proof-theoretic validity* or *proof-theoretic consequence*, with respect to $\mathcal{L}_{cpl}$. The tableau system is a logical system in the sense of §3. Our syntactic (logical) consequence relation, also called *proof-theoretic consequence*, is represented by the single turnstile:

DEFINITION 4.1 ($\vdash_{CPL}$) An $\mathcal{L}_{cpl}$-sentence, A, is a *proof-theoretic consequence* of a (possibly empty) set $\mathcal{X}$ of $\mathcal{L}$-sentences exactly if there is a finished, closed tree the initial list of which comprises the elements of $\mathcal{X}$ and the negation of A.[6]

Given Definition 4.1 the reader can see that, for example, arguments such as the following are proof-theoretically valid: the argument from premise set $\{(p \supset q), \sim q, p\}$ to conclusion r. That is, one can see that

$$\{(p \supset q), \sim q, p\} \vdash_{CPL} r.$$

A finished, closed tree for the given argument looks like this:[7]

$$\begin{array}{c} \boxed{(p \supset q)} \\ \sim q \\ p \\ \sim r \\ \swarrow \quad \searrow \\ \begin{array}{cc} \sim p & q \\ \otimes & \otimes \end{array} \end{array}$$

[6]There may be many different finished, closed trees for a given CPL-argument; fortunately, they all give the same result, though we won't prove this.

[7]Of course, *your* tree might look different, depending on the order of steps you take. This makes no difference to the tree test.

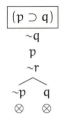

METATHEORY

Of course, as in §3, once we have a notion of proof-theoretic consequence, one immediately wonders about the fit between it and our prior semantic notion—implication, semantic consequence. The good news is that our tableaux system for classical logic is sound and complete with respect to $\mathcal{L}_{\mathtt{cpl}}$. We will provide the resources for a proof in Part IV.

EXERCISES 4.3.1

1 Give definitions of $\vee$, $\supset$, and $\equiv$ in terms of the semantic clauses governing $\sim$ and $\wedge$ (see §4.2). Can $\sim$ and $\vee$ similarly be taken to be primitive? What about other pairs?

2 Using the CPL tree rules determine which of the following claims are true. If the claim is not true, provide a counterexample which shows that the corresponding claim about semantic validity is not true—that is, construct an admissible CPL valuation that satisfies the premise set but fails to satisfy the conclusion.

1. $\emptyset \vdash_{\mathsf{CPL}} (((p \equiv q) \vee (p \equiv r)) \vee (q \equiv r))$
2. $(p \wedge {\sim}q), ({\sim}q \supset {\sim}p) \vdash_{\mathsf{CPL}} r$
3. $(p \supset q), (q \supset r) \vdash_{\mathsf{CPL}} (p \supset r)$
4. $({\sim}p \vee q), p \vdash_{\mathsf{CPL}} q$
5. $((p \supset q) \supset r) \vdash_{\mathsf{CPL}} (p \supset (q \supset r))$
6. $((p \vee q) \vee r) \vdash_{\mathsf{CPL}} (p \vee (q \vee r))$
7. $p, {\sim}p \vdash_{\mathsf{CPL}} q$
8. $q \vdash_{\mathsf{CPL}} (q \vee (p \supset (r_1 \wedge r_2)))$
9. $\emptyset \vdash_{\mathsf{CPL}} ({\sim}p \vee q) \equiv (p \supset q)$
10. $(p \supset q) \vdash_{\mathsf{CPL}} ({\sim}q \supset {\sim}p)$
11. $(p \supset r) \vdash_{\mathsf{CPL}} ((p \wedge q) \supset r)$
12. ${\sim}p \vdash_{\mathsf{CPL}} (p \supset q)$
13. ${\sim}(p \supset q) \vdash_{\mathsf{CPL}} p$
14. $p, ({\sim}q \supset {\sim}p), r \vdash_{\mathsf{CPL}} q$
15. $q \vdash_{\mathsf{CPL}} (p \supset q)$
16. $((p \wedge q) \supset r) \vdash_{\mathsf{CPL}} ((p \supset r) \vee (q \supset r))$

3 Show that if $\emptyset \Vdash_{\mathcal{L}} (p \supset q)$ then $p \Vdash_{\mathcal{L}} q$, and vice versa. (Tools for a more rigorous proof of such results will be available in Part IV. For now, be as precise as you can with the tools available.)

4 $\vee$ in $\mathcal{L}$ is so-called *inclusive disjunction*. Let $\veebar$ be *exclusive disjunction*, so that an admissible CPL valuation ν assigns 1 to $(A \veebar B)$ exactly if $\nu(A) \neq \nu(B)$. Exercise: Give tree rules appropriate for $\veebar$.

Further Reading

Further introductory discussion of trees can be found in Howson's [50], Jeffrey's [54], Restall's [86] and Bostok's [15].

Priest [79] covers many of the tableaux systems that we cover; he also gives proofs of the soundness and completeness results for the various systems. Bell, DeVidi, and Solomon [10] provide a similar approach to the one we take here, and they also cover some of the topics that we omit.

A mathematically precise account of trees is in Smullyan's [90], which is a classic on the technique.

The wonder is
that we can see these trees
and not wonder more.
– Ralph Waldo Emerson

Part II

Possibilities

Chapter 5
Normal Modal Logics

Modal operators are ubiquitous in natural language. Consider the following three claims:

a) If it is necessarily the case that 2 is the smallest prime number, then 2 is the smallest prime number.

b) If it is known that Max is bigger than Agnes, then Max is bigger than Agnes.

c) If it is morally obligatory that you love your neighbor, then you love your neighbor.

The first two appear to be true while the third appears to be false.[1] In each case the sentence has an antecedent beginning with what appears to be a unary connective of the form 'it is... that'. Classical logic has no non-trivial connectives of that sort except for 'it is not the case that'. Not only does it not have them but there is an ostensible reason why classical logic cannot have them. The language $\mathcal{L}_{cpl}$ is *truth-functional*: if two sentences A and B have the same truth-value then so do any two complex sentences (...A...) and (...B...) that differ only in that the second has B where the first has A. The operators in (a)–(c), on the other hand, appear to be non-truth-functional. To see this, notice that each of the following is true:[2]

d) The US flag has 50 stars on it.

e) 2 is the smallest prime number.

f) It is necessarily the case that 2 is the smallest prime number.

If 'it is necessarily the case that...' is truth-functional, then

g) It is necessarily the case that the US flag has fifty stars on it

[1] Some might be of the view that ethical claims are neither true nor false. We'll ignore this here, although the issue is relevant to Part III.

[2] We assume that all theorems of standard number theory are necessarily true, but the example can be changed if this turns out to be false (in which case, necessarily false?).

must be true, given that (e) and (f) are true.[3] The trouble is that (g) seems to be false; the US flag could have had fewer than fifty stars on it (if, e.g., Russia hadn't sold Alaska to the US). Accordingly, 'it is necessarily the case that' is not truth-functional. Similar examples will show that the operators in (b) and (c) are not truth-functional.

Operators such as 'it is necessarily the case that', 'it is known that' and 'it is morally obligatory that' are frequently called *modal operators*.[4] 'It is necessarily the case that' and 'it is possible that' are called *alethic modal operators* (pronounced 'ah-lee-thic', from the Greek 'althetheia' meaning *truth*), as such operators have something to do with the mode in which statements may be true. 'It is morally obligatory that' and 'it is morally permissible that' are called *deontic (modal) operators* (from the Greek 'deon', meaning *duty*). Modal operators having to do with belief or knowledge are often called *epistemic operators*, from *episteme* (knowledge);[5] modal operators having to do with *provability* are called *apodeictic*, from the Greek *apodeiknunai* (demonstrate); and operators having to do with *time* are often called *tense operators*, from the English *tense*.

Needless to say, modal operators play a fairly active role in philosophical discourse. Philosophers continue to pursue questions in ethics, epistemology, time, proof and the like; and frequently such questions concern whether such and so is *possible*, *impossible* and so on. The point of modal logic is (in part) to provide clear, formal models of such notions, models that reflect the logic of such operators.

In this chapter we set out a few so-called *normal modal logics*. (The tag 'normal' will be explained in due course; it is a technical term, although perhaps its technical usage coincides with some views about the corresponding modal logics.) Before moving to the logics, we will briefly sketch the basic philosophical picture behind the various logics (and, in particular, behind their semantics).

5.1 ON WAYS THINGS COULD BE

For purposes of illustration we concentrate on the alethic modal operators, *it is possible that* and *it is necessary that*. The other modalities are treated in the same basic fashion.

You could have been rock-climbing right now; instead, you are reading. Accordingly, it is not a necessary truth that you are reading right now. What

[3] Recall that, in virtue of being a function, no truth function can assign different values to the same argument.

[4] Such terminology is now standard, although a useful alternative and not entirely non-standard terminology calls such operators *intensional*. At the very least, intensional operators are not truth-functional; they are not, as it is sometimes put, *extensional*. See Carnap [18].

[5] When *belief* is treated as a modal operator (e.g., 'it is believed that') the operator is called a *doxastic* operator, from the Greek 'doxa', meaning *opinion*.

is a necessary truth is that you are identical to yourself, as you couldn't but be identical to yourself.

What is it to say that some statement is necessary, that it is necessarily true? To say that A is necessarily true is to say that it is impossible for A to be untrue. But what is it to say *that*?

Following the lead of Leibniz (and more recently Kripke [58, 59]), alethic modal operators are taken to be quantifiers over "possible worlds".[6] As David Lewis [66] put it, possible worlds are *ways things could be*. There are lots of ways things could be. One way things could be is precisely the way things actually are; this is the actual (possible) world. But, as above, things could've been different: you could've been rock-climbing right now instead of reading. On this approach, to say that A is necessarily true is to say that A is true at/in *every* possible world; to say that A is possibly true is to say that A is true at some (possible) world or other.

Some of this may appear to be fanciful thinking. Maybe so. Yet there is a sense in which this way of thinking is already very familiar from CPL, namely through the use of truth-tables. Think of a truth table for the sentences p, q, $p \wedge q$. The first row has entries $1, 1, 1$, and the second has $1, 0, 0$. These surely represent ways in which the various sentences could be true together. If p and q are 'Snow is white' and 'Some paper is white', respectively, then they represent the actual way things are and also a way things could have been. Now, truth-table rows correspond to (partially depicted) admissible CPL valuations. So, we can think of (admissible) CPL-valuations as representing possible worlds, representing *ways things could be*, at least in so far as the connectives go.[7] If v is such a valuation we can suppose that there is a world w corresponding to v in the sense that any sentence A is true in w exactly if $v(A) = 1$.

This provides us with a good grasp on at least one sort of (alethic) "logical" necessity. The metaphysically loaded talk of alternative possible worlds has a simple cash value here: it amounts to talk of all the different admissible valuations of the language. While this is clearly not the only meaning alethic (or other sorts of) modal discourse can have, it is one easily grasped meaning. With this in mind, one can say that a sentence A is necessary (or necessarily true) iff it is true at/in all valuations (all worlds); A is possible iff it is true at/in some valuation (some world); A is contingent iff it is true at/in some valuation (some world) and false at/in some valuation (some world); and A is impossible iff A is unsatisfiable. The point is that "quantification over worlds" is not nearly as unfamiliar as it may at first appear.

---

[6]Note well that we are not endorsing any ontology or philosophical account of modality here. Our concern is only with the formal structure of modal discourse.

[7]We are not suggesting that CPL valuations exhaust the range of what possible worlds are like—whatever, in the end, they are like—or that every CPL valuation represents a real possibility (whatever that may be). For now, we are using them merely as examples.

ACCESSIBILITY AND RELATIVE POSSIBILITY

As useful as the preceding illustration may be it would be a mistake to regard it as fixing the meaning of our modal terms. 'Necessarily' and 'possibly' are not univocal in our language. If, for example, you suggest that Max could have been rock climbing instead of working today he might retort "No, for I have injured my ankle." To be sure, your suggestion poses a logical possibility but, given the state of Max's body, not a physical possibility. Other examples would similarly suggest distinctions between what is physically possible in principle and what is technically possible. (Travel faster than light is not physically possible; travel at half the speed of light is physically but not technically possible. And so on.)

To allow for such different modalities, and for various standards of argument validity in modal discourse, we introduce into the semantics the idea of accessibility. In our models we place, in addition to the worlds, a binary relation $\mathcal{R}$ on worlds, with '$w_1 \mathcal{R} w_2$' read as *there is access from* w_1 *to* w_2 or as w_2 *is accessible from* w_1. (We will sometimes use 'w-accessible world' to mean *a world accessible from* w, so that w' is a w-accessible world iff $w\mathcal{R}w'$.) The accessibility relation is also sometimes called *relative possibility*, with '$w_1 \mathcal{R} w_2$' read as 'w_2 is possible relative to w_1'. We equate something being necessary in a world w with its being true in all w-accessible worlds. Similarly, we say that something is possible in w just in case it is true in some w-accessible world. The example of physical possibility is then sometimes explained by saying that *it is physically possible that* A iff A is true in some world subject to the same laws of nature as our world; and in this case, the accessibility relation is that of *being subject to the same laws of nature*.

We can think of our preceding illustration, in which worlds correspond simply to CPL-valuations, as a limiting case in which every world is accessible to every other world. Then we think of each valuation v as representing a world in the sense that it assigns 1 precisely to the sentences true in that world. Of course, we can then introduce a "universal" relation $\mathcal{R}$ that holds between any two valuations. As we shall see below (page 66) the logic of modal discourse will be the same if we do that (or not mention $\mathcal{R}$ at all) or if we require of $\mathcal{R}$ only that it be an equivalence relation (reflexive, symmetric, and transitive); for what the logic must be like will depend precisely on the properties we require of this access relation.

EXERCISES 5.1.1

1 The following argument was inspired by Aristotle's famous sea-battle passage:

> If I give the order to attack, then there will necessarily be a sea-battle tomorrow. If I do not give that order, then there will necessarily not be a sea-battle tomorrow. But I either give the order or do not give the order. Therefore,

> either there will necessarily be a sea-battle tomorrow or there will necessarily not be one.

It has been argued that this argument has two readings: on one reading it is valid but its premises are false; on the other its premises could be true but it is invalid. Display two such readings and discuss. (Hint: Pay special attention to the scope of the word 'necessarily'. Does 'necessarily' govern the entire sentence or only part of it?)

2 Inspired by Willard Van Ormen Quine's critique of modal discourse:

> Mathematicians are necessarily rational but not necessarily bipeds. Cyclists are necessarily bipeds but not necessarily rational. P. K. Z. is a mathematician and a cyclist. Therefore, P. K. Z. does not exist.

Display at least two possible readings and discuss the validity of the argument as thus read.

5.2 MODAL PROPOSITIONAL SYNTAX

Our modal propositional syntax augments $\mathtt{S}_{\mathtt{cpl}}$ by adding two new elements to $\mathcal{C}$. The new elements are $\Box$ (the box) and $\Diamond$ (the diamond), which are unary connectives.[8] Accordingly, our modal propositional syntax is a structure $\mathtt{S}_{\mathtt{mpl}} = \langle \mathcal{A}, \mathcal{C}, \mathcal{S} \rangle$ where $\mathcal{A}$ comprises the following letters with or without positive integer subscripts:

$$\mathtt{p}, \mathtt{q}, \mathtt{r}$$

$\mathcal{C}$ comprises the unary connectives $\sim$, $\Box$ and $\Diamond$ and binary connectives $\wedge$, $\vee$, $\supset$ and $\equiv$. $\mathcal{S}$, the set of $\mathtt{S}_{\mathtt{mpl}}$-sentences, is specified thus:

- All elements of $\mathcal{A}$ are elements of $\mathcal{S}$;
- If A is in $\mathcal{S}$, then each of $\sim$A, $\Box$A and $\Diamond$A is in $\mathcal{S}$; and if A and B are in $\mathcal{S}$, so are $(A \wedge B)$, $(A \vee B)$, $(A \supset B)$, and $(A \equiv B)$;
- Nothing is in $\mathcal{S}$ except by virtue of the two clauses above.

We use these new connectives to symbolize our examples. Thus if A is the sentence '2 is the smallest prime number' then $\Box$A symbolizes 'It is necessarily the case that 2 is the smallest prime number' and, among other variants, '2 is necessarily the smallest prime number'. Similarly, $\Diamond$A symbolizes 'It is possible that 2 is the smallest prime number' or '2 is possibly the smallest prime number'.

[8] The box and diamond are sometimes written *L* and *M*, respectively, but we shall not use this notation.

Each of the (modal) languages discussed in this chapter is generated from S_{mpl}. We distinguish the languages in terms of their respective semantics. We begin with the language, $\mathcal{L}_K$.[9]

5.3 BASIC NORMAL SEMANTICS

To display the semantics of $\mathcal{L}_K$ we must specify the admissible valuations and define satisfaction. As will be clear from the foregoing, we will have to do this in a slightly roundabout way.

$\mathcal{L}_K$ interprets S_{mpl} by way of a structure $\langle \mathcal{W}, \mathcal{R}, \nu \rangle$ where $\mathcal{W}$ is a non-empty set comprising "worlds" (or, more neutrally, "points"), $\mathcal{R}$ is a binary relation on $\mathcal{W}$ (i.e., $\mathcal{R} \subseteq \mathcal{W} \times \mathcal{W}$), the "access" relation, and ν is a function from $\mathcal{W} \times \mathcal{S}$ into $\{1, 0\}$. In effect, ν assigns a truth value to each sentence at each world (but we will return to ν below).

$\mathcal{L}_K$-*models* are structures of the sort above: $\langle \mathcal{W}, \mathcal{R}, \nu \rangle$. Specifically, where $\nu(w, A)$ is the value of ν for the argument $\langle w, A \rangle$ (and may be read 'the value of A at w under ν') we say that an $\mathcal{L}_K$-*model* is any $\mathcal{L}_K$-structure such that:

$$
\begin{array}{rcl}
\nu(w, {\sim}A) = 1 & \text{iff} & \nu(w, A) = 0 \\
\nu(w, (A \wedge B)) = 1 & \text{iff} & \nu(w, A) = 1 \text{ and } \nu(w, B) = 1 \\
\nu(w, (A \vee B)) = 1 & \text{iff} & \nu(w, A) = 1 \text{ or } \nu(w, B) = 1 \\
\nu(w, (A \supset B)) = 1 & \text{iff} & \nu(w, A) = 0 \text{ or } \nu(w, B) = 1 \\
\nu(w, (A \equiv B)) = 1 & \text{iff} & \nu(w, A) = \nu(w, B) \\
\nu(w, \Diamond A) = 1 & \text{iff} & \text{for some } w' \in \mathcal{W}, \\
 & & \langle w, w' \rangle \in \mathcal{R} \text{ and } \nu(w'A) = 1 \\
\nu(w, \Box A) = 1 & \text{iff} & \text{for all } w' \in \mathcal{W}, \\
 & & \text{if } \langle w, w' \rangle \in \mathcal{R} \text{ then } \nu(w', A) = 1
\end{array}
$$

Neither $\mathcal{R}$ nor the "worlds" (elements of $\mathcal{W}$) play a major role in the clauses for extensional connectives ($\sim$, $\wedge$, $\vee$, $\supset$, $\equiv$); they play a major role in the clauses for the modal connectives ($\Diamond$ and $\Box$). Let A be any S_{cpl}-sentence. Determing the value of A at w never involves going beyond w itself—its value depends only on what is happening at home (as it were). Modal (intensional) sentences are different; the value of $\Box$A at w depends on what is happening at *all* worlds (or, more accurately, at all w-accessible worlds).

VALUATIONS

What will be the admissible valuations for this language, associated with this model? The function ν is clearly not a valuation, since its domain does not have sentences as members, but ordered pairs consisting of sentences

[9] The corresponding logic is standardly called 'K'.

and worlds; however, we can think of v as specifying for each sentence A the *set of worlds* at which A is true.[10] Therefore, we can define one valuation for each world as follows:

$$\mathrm{v}_w : \mathrm{v}_w(A) = \mathrm{v}(w, A)$$

We can think of v_w as the assignment of truth-values on the supposition or assumption that w is the actual world. And these functions will be precisely the admissible valuations of the language, with satisfaction defined accordingly:

» A function v is an *admissible valuation* of the language $\mathcal{L}_K$ iff there is an $\mathcal{L}_K$-model $\langle \mathcal{W}, \mathcal{R}, \mathrm{v}\rangle$ and a member w of $\mathcal{W}$ such that $\mathrm{v} = \mathrm{v}_w$. The valuation v satisfies sentence A iff $\mathrm{v}(A) = 1$.

SEMANTIC PROPERTIES AND RELATIONS

The important semantic properties and relations are defined as usual by (Def 3.5)–(Def 3.8). In particular, where $\mathcal{M} = \langle \mathcal{W}, \mathcal{R}, \mathrm{v}\rangle$ is an $\mathcal{L}_K$ model, we also say that $\mathcal{M}$ *satisfies* A *at* w iff $\mathrm{v}_w(A) = 1$. Similarly, where $\mathcal{X}$ comprises $\mathcal{L}_K$-sentences, we say that $\mathcal{M}$ *satisfies* $\mathcal{X}$ *at* w iff $\mathcal{M}$ satisfies A at w, for every $A \in \mathcal{X}$.

Where $\mathcal{M}$ and A are as above, we shall say that $\mathcal{M}$ *satisfies* A iff $\mathcal{M}$ satisfies A at *every* $w \in \mathcal{W}$. (In other words, if A is satisfied at every world of $\mathcal{W}$, then we drop explicit reference to worlds and say only that $\mathcal{M}$ satisfies A.)

One may read '$\mathrm{v}_w(A) = 1$' and '$\mathrm{v}_w(A) = 0$' as 'A is true at w under v' and 'A is false at w under v', respectively. Given this terminology, *semantic consequence* (or implication) is truth-preservation over all worlds of all $\mathcal{L}_K$-models; we will write $\Vdash_K$ for the consequence relation in $\mathcal{L}_K$.

One notable feature of $\mathcal{L}_K$ is that $\sim\Diamond A$ and $\Box\sim A$ are equivalent in $\mathcal{L}_K$, as are $\sim\Box A$ and $\Diamond\sim A$. To say that A and B are equivalent in $\mathcal{L}_K$ is to say that no two admissible $\mathcal{L}_K$-valuations differ with respect to the values assigned to A and B. In other words, if A is false at some world of some model, then B is also false at that world, and if A is true at some world of some model, then so too is B. That $\sim\Box A$ and $\Diamond\sim A$ are equivalent may be seen thus, where each step falls directly out of the clauses on admissible $\mathcal{L}_K$-valuations:

$$
\begin{aligned}
\mathrm{v}_w(\sim\Box A) = 1 \quad & \text{iff} \quad \mathrm{v}_w(\Box A) = 0 \\
& \text{iff} \quad \text{for some } w' \text{ s.t. } \langle w, w'\rangle \in \mathcal{R},\ \mathrm{v}_{w'}(A) = 0 \\
& \text{iff} \quad \text{for some } w' \text{ s.t. } \langle w, w'\rangle \in \mathcal{R},\ \mathrm{v}_{w'}(\sim A) = 1 \\
& \text{iff} \quad \mathrm{v}_w(\Diamond\sim A) = 1
\end{aligned}
$$

[10] That set, of course, is $\{w \in \mathcal{W} : \mathrm{v}(w, A) = 1\}$, which we can conveniently denote as $\mathrm{v}_{\mathcal{M}}(A)$, for a given model $\mathcal{M} = \langle \mathcal{W}, \mathcal{R}, \mathrm{v}\rangle$. We will return to this notion in an exercise and make use of it more extensively in a later chapter.

Similarly, by replacing 'some' with 'all' and '□' with '◊' in the above proof, the equivalence of $\sim\Diamond A$ and $\Box{\sim}A$ may likewise be established:

$$\begin{aligned} v_w(\sim\Diamond A) = 1 \quad & \text{iff} \quad v_w(\Diamond A) = 0 \\ & \text{iff} \quad \text{for all } w' \text{ s.t. } \langle w, w'\rangle \in \mathcal{R},\ v_{w'}(A) = 0 \\ & \text{iff} \quad \text{for all } w' \text{ s.t. } \langle w, w'\rangle \in \mathcal{R},\ v_{w'}(\sim A) = 1 \\ & \text{iff} \quad v_w(\Box{\sim}A) = 1 \end{aligned}$$

As a result of these equivalences, one can enjoy a smaller set of connectives without losing the expressive power of $\mathcal{L}_K$; one can simply take either □ or ◊ as primitive and, using ~, introduce the other as an abbreviation.

Another notable feature of $\mathcal{L}_K$ is that, given the clauses on admissible $\mathcal{L}_K$-valuations in §5.3, if w accesses no worlds (i.e., if there is no w' s.t. $\langle w, w'\rangle \in \mathcal{R}$) then every sentence of the form $\Diamond A$ is false at w while every sentence of the form $\Box A$ is (vacuously) true at w. (If w accesses no worlds, then *a fortiori* there is no world w' s.t. $\langle w, w'\rangle \in \mathcal{R}$ and $v_{w'}(A) = 0$, in which case $v_w(\Box A) = 1$.) This is significant, at least in as much as one interprets $\mathcal{L}_K$ as a model of alethic modality. We will return to this point after discussing *counterexamples*.

COUNTEREXAMPLES

Let $\mathcal{M} = \langle \mathcal{W}, \mathcal{R}, v\rangle$ be an $\mathcal{L}_K$ model; let $\mathcal{X}$ comprise $\mathcal{L}_K$-sentences; and let A be an $\mathcal{L}_K$-sentence. Moreover, let $\langle \mathcal{X}, A\rangle$ be an $\mathcal{L}_K$-argument (where $\mathcal{X}$ comprises the premises and A is the conclusion). We say that $\mathcal{M}$ is an *$\mathcal{L}_K$-counterexample* or *counter-model* to $\langle \mathcal{X}, A\rangle$ iff $\mathcal{M}$ satisfies $\mathcal{X}$ at w but $\mathcal{M}$ does not satisfy A at w, for some $w \in \mathcal{W}$.[11] So, $\mathcal{X} \Vdash_K A$ iff there is no counterexample to $\langle \mathcal{X}, A\rangle$.

Likewise, where $\mathcal{M}$ and A remain as above, we say that $\mathcal{M}$ is a counterexample to A iff $\mathcal{M}$ does not satisfy A at w for some $w \in \mathcal{W}$. In other words, a counterexample to A is an $\mathcal{L}_K$-model that provides us with an admissible valuation that assigns 0 to A at some world. So, A is a valid sentence of $\mathcal{L}_K$ iff there is no counterexample to A.

By way of example consider any $\mathcal{L}_K$-sentence of the form

$$\Box A \supset A \tag{5.1}$$

Is there a counterexample to (5.1)? Yes:

$$\begin{aligned} \mathcal{W} &= \{w_0\} \\ \mathcal{R} &= \emptyset \\ v_{w_0}(A) &= 0 \end{aligned}$$

[11] We will henceforth drop the explicit reference to $\mathcal{L}_K$ unless more than one language is under discussion.

In this case, we have exactly one world, namely w_0. A is false at w_0 under ν. Moreover, since w_0 has access to no worlds (given that $\mathcal{R}$ is empty), there are no worlds accessible to w_0 at which A is false, in which case, by the semantics for $\Box$A, we have it that $\Box$A is true at w_0. But, then, the antecedent of (5.1) is true at w_0 and its consequent false at w_0. Hence, given the $\mathcal{L}_K$ clauses for $A \supset B$, it follows that (5.1) is false at w_0. Therefore, there is a counterexample to (5.1). The same counterexample applies to the argument from $\Box$A to A. Accordingly, we have it that $\Box A \nVdash_K A$. As we discuss below, these results make it difficult to read $\Box$ as 'Necessarily' or $\Diamond$ as 'Possibly', given this semantics. Rather, these connectives belong to a general sort of which 'Necessarily' and 'Possibly' (as well as 'It ought to be that' and 'It is permitted that', and so forth) are special examples.

EXERCISES 5.3.1

1 Give an $\mathcal{L}_K$-counterexample to $\Box A \supset A$ in which $\mathcal{R} \neq \emptyset$.

2 Give an $\mathcal{L}_K$-counterexample to $\Box A \supset \Diamond A$ in which $\mathcal{R} \neq \emptyset$.

3 Either prove or give counterexamples in the language $\mathcal{L}_K$ for the following:

1. $\Box(A \supset B) \supset (\Box A \supset \Box B)$
2. $\Box(A \vee \Box B) \supset (\Box A \vee \Box B)$
3. $(\Diamond A \wedge \Box B) \supset \Diamond(A \wedge \Box B)$
4. $A \supset \Box\Diamond A$
5. $\Box\Diamond A \supset A$

4 Show that in general an admissible valuation ν_w of $\mathcal{L}_K$ does not have a base. (See §3.3, Def 3.2, page 27.)

5 Define for each $\mathcal{L}_K$-model $\mathcal{M} = \langle \mathcal{W}, \mathcal{R}, \nu \rangle$ the function

$$\nu_{\mathcal{M}}(A) = \{w \in \mathcal{W} : \nu(w, A) = 1\}$$

This is a valuation; and while it is not in the class of admissible valuations of $\mathcal{L}_K$, it is closely related to them. Show that:

1. $A \Vdash B$ iff $\nu_{\mathcal{M}}(A) \subseteq \nu_{\mathcal{M}}(B)$, in every model $\mathcal{M}$ of $\mathcal{L}_K$.
2. A is valid in $\mathcal{L}_K$ iff $\nu_{\mathcal{M}}(A) = \mathcal{W}$, for every model $\mathcal{M}$ of $\mathcal{L}_K$.
3. $\nu_{\mathcal{M}}(A \wedge B) = \nu_{\mathcal{M}}(A) \cap \nu_{\mathcal{M}}(B)$.
4. $\nu_{\mathcal{M}}({\sim}A) = \mathcal{W} - \nu_{\mathcal{M}}(A)$.

6 Let $\mathcal{M} = \langle \mathcal{W}, \mathcal{R}, v \rangle$ be an $\mathcal{L}_K$-model. Show that $\langle 2^{\mathcal{W}}, \mathbb{C}, \odot \rangle$ is a base for the valuation $v_{\mathcal{M}}(A) = \{w : v(w, A) = 1\}$, where $2^{\mathcal{W}}$ is $\wp(\mathcal{W})$ and $\odot$ associates an operation on sets with each connective:

$$\begin{aligned} \odot_{\wedge}(\mathcal{X}, \mathcal{Y}) &= \mathcal{X} \cap \mathcal{Y} \\ \odot_{\sim}(\mathcal{X}) &= \mathcal{W} - \mathcal{X} \\ \odot_{\Box}(\mathcal{X}) &= \{w : \mathcal{R}(w) \subseteq \mathcal{X}\} \end{aligned}$$

where $\mathcal{R}(w) = \{w' : w\mathcal{R}w'\}$.

5.4 AMENDING $\mathcal{R}$: EXTENSIONS OF $\mathcal{L}_K$

As in §5.2 the languages of this chapter are underwritten by a common syntax. What differentiates the languages is their respective semantics. In this section we introduce the various languages, explaining how they arise out of $\mathcal{L}_K$ (in a sense illustrated below).

The target languages are *extensions of* $\mathcal{L}_K$. Where $\mathcal{L}$ and $\mathcal{L}'$ are languages with syntax S we say that:

DEFINITION 5.1 $\mathcal{L}'$ is an *extension* of $\mathcal{L}$ exactly if any $\mathcal{L}'$-model is an $\mathcal{L}$-model.

Accordingly, where $\Vdash_{\mathcal{L}}$ and $\Vdash_{\mathcal{L}'}$ are the (semantic) consequence relations of $\mathcal{L}$ and $\mathcal{L}'$, respectively, we say that

DEFINITION 5.2 $\Vdash_{\mathcal{L}'}$ is an *extension* of $\Vdash_{\mathcal{L}}$ just in case $\mathcal{X} \Vdash_{\mathcal{L}'} A$ if $\mathcal{X} \Vdash_{\mathcal{L}} A$ (where A is any S-sentence and $\mathcal{X}$ any class of such sentences).

With such terminology in hand we can now specify the (technical) meaning of 'normal' in 'normal modal logic' or 'normal modal language'. Specifically, a language is a *normal* modal language iff it is an extension of $\mathcal{L}_K$. Similarly, a consequence relation, $\Vdash$, is a *normal modal consequence relation* iff $\Vdash$ is an extension of $\Vdash_K$.

Each of the languages to be discussed in this chapter is a normal modal language; each is an extension of $\mathcal{L}_K$. Indeed, the differences between the various normal modal languages arise from restrictions on the $\mathcal{L}_K$-models—specifically, restrictions on the accessibility relation, $\mathcal{R}$.

EXERCISES 5.4.1

1 Show that $\Vdash_{\mathcal{L}'}$ is an extension of $\Vdash_{\mathcal{L}}$ if $\mathcal{L}'$ is an extension of $\mathcal{L}$. Discuss the question whether the converse must also hold in general.

2 Show that the relation *is an extension of* is reflexive and transitive.

THE LANGUAGE $\mathcal{L}_K^r$

Amending the accessibility relation involved in $\mathcal{L}_K$ gives rise to the various normal modal languages. Such amending is not without philosophical motivation. Consider, again, (5.1): $\Box A \supset A$. Suppose that we are interested in reading the box as *it is necessarily the case that....* Presumably, if it is necessarily the case that cats are wise, then cats are wise, and similarly for any sentence: If A is necessarily true, then A is true. If this is right then $\mathcal{L}_K$ does not adequately model alethic modality; alethic modality requires that (5.1) be true—logically true.

How might we modify the semantics of $\mathcal{L}_K$ to yield a language in which (5.1) has no counterexamples? A natural answer turns to $\mathcal{R}$. Let $\mathcal{M} = \langle \mathcal{W}, \mathcal{R}, v \rangle$ be any $\mathcal{L}_K$-model. Where $\mathcal{R} \in \mathcal{M}$ we shall say that

» $\mathcal{M}$ is *reflexive* iff $\mathcal{R}$ is reflexive;

» $\mathcal{M}$ is *symmetric* iff $\mathcal{R}$ is symmetric;

» $\mathcal{M}$ is *transitive* iff $\mathcal{R}$ is transitive;

We also call $\mathcal{R}$ *serial* iff for every $w \in \mathcal{W}$ there is some w' in $\mathcal{W}$ (not necessarily distinct from w) s.t. $w\mathcal{R}w'$. In turn, we say

» $\mathcal{M}$ is *serial* iff $\mathcal{R}$ is serial.

By way of answering the question concerning (5.1) we prove:

FACT 5.1 *$\mathcal{M}$ satisfies $\Box A \supset A$ if $\mathcal{M}$ is reflexive.*

PROOF FACT 5.1 Suppose that $\mathcal{M}$ is reflexive and that v and w_0 are in $\mathcal{M}$.[12] Suppose that $v_{w_0}(\Box A) = 1$. Given the conditions on box claims it follows that for any $w \in \mathcal{W}$ s.t. $\langle w_0, w \rangle \in \mathcal{R}$, $v_w(A) = 1$. Since $\mathcal{R}$ is reflexive, we have it that $\langle w_0, w_0 \rangle \in \mathcal{R}$ and, so, that $v_{w_0}(A) = 1$, which is what we wanted to show. Given that w_0 was arbitrary, we conclude that for *any* w in $\mathcal{M}$, if $v_w(\Box A) = 1$ then $v_w(A) = 1$ (given that $\mathcal{M}$ is reflexive). Hence, if $\mathcal{M}$ is reflexive, then $\mathcal{M}$ satisfies $\Box A \supset A$.[13] QED

Fact 5.1 is important if, as many think, alethic modality requires that $\Box p \supset p$ be valid—where, once again, the box is read *it is necessarily the case that*. One way of *ensuring* that (5.1) is valid is to *restrict* our attention to a *proper* subset of $\mathcal{L}_K$-models—specifically, the reflexive ones. Doing so gives

[12] For convenience we say that w *is in* $\mathcal{M}$, by which we mean that $w \in \mathcal{W}$ where $\mathcal{W} \in \mathcal{M}$. We will follow this practice throughout the book.

[13] We will eventually omit some of the steps in such proofs—assuming, for example, that the reader understands the role of "arbitrary objects" in proving generalizations, and the various steps involved in so-called conditional proof, etc.. That said, we will use some of these earlier proofs to give the reader a feel for the requisite methods of proof.

rise to an extension of $\mathcal{L}_K$, namely, the language $\mathcal{L}_K^{r}$ (as we will call it). 'T' is the standard name for the given language; however, we will reserve 'T' for the tableaux system for the language $\mathcal{L}_K^{r}$. The superscripted 'r' in '$\mathcal{L}_K^{r}$' is our (heuristic) device to indicate that $\mathcal{L}_K^{r}$ extends $\mathcal{L}_K$ by restricting its models to *reflexive* $\mathcal{L}_K$-models.[14]

To summarize the features that distinguish the different normal modal languages we look for *characteristic sentences*. These are sentences that are valid in the corresponding languages and their extensions but not valid in the languages "before" them (the ones of which they are proper extensions). So, for example, (5.1) is the characteristic sentence (form) for $\mathcal{L}_K^{r}$. Sentences of the form (5.1) are valid in $\mathcal{L}_K^{r}$ and its extensions but not in $\mathcal{L}_K$ or $\mathcal{L}_K^{ser}$. The importance of characteristic sentences will appear in Part IV, where we discuss alternative formulations of the normal modal logics. For now, because it is useful to keep such characteristic sentences in mind, we simply list the ones covered thus far (see Exercise 3.1 of §5.3.1, page 59):

» Characteristic $\mathcal{L}_K$ sentence: $\Box(A \supset B) \supset (\Box A \supset \Box B)$

» Characteristic $\mathcal{L}_K^{r}$ Sentence: $\Box A \supset A$

That the characteristic sentence of $\mathcal{L}_K$ is valid in $\mathcal{L}_K^{r}$ (an extension of $\mathcal{L}_K$) should not be a surprise. Intuitively, as the set of models decreases the set of valid sentences increases, because there are fewer counterexamples. Any "potential counterexample" in $\mathcal{L}_K^{r}$ is a potential counterexample in $\mathcal{L}_K$, but there are more such potential counterexamples in $\mathcal{L}_K$ than there are in $\mathcal{L}_K^{r}$. Hence, if a sentence A escapes counterexamples in $\mathcal{L}_K$, then it surely escapes counterexamples in $\mathcal{L}_K^{r}$, and likewise escapes counterexamples in any extension of $\mathcal{L}_K$. This relation between $\mathcal{L}_K$ and its extensions is important to keep in mind. For now, we turn to another extension of $\mathcal{L}_K$.

THE LANGUAGE $\mathcal{L}_K^{ser}$

Our next considered language is generated in the same way: amending $\mathcal{L}_K$'s accessibility relation, $\mathcal{R}$. Such amending need not be free of philosophical motivation. Suppose, for example, that one's concern is deontic discourse and that one intends to read the box and diamond as *it is morally obligatory that* and *it is morally permissible that*, respectively. In this case, presumably one wants a language in which the following is valid:

$$\Box A \supset \Diamond A. \tag{5.2}$$

[14]The notation is also intended to suggest that $\mathcal{L}_K^{r}$ "arises from" $\mathcal{L}_K$ by imposing the condition of reflexivity. Throughout the book we continue to use superscripts in the way indicated, which sits nicely with the *absence* of any superscript in '$\mathcal{L}_K$', indicating that there are no (relevant) restrictions on $\mathcal{L}_K$.

After all, if something is morally obligatory then (presumably) it is morally permissible.

Have we covered a language in which (5.2) is valid? Consider $\mathcal{L}_K$. Is (5.2) valid in $\mathcal{L}_K$? No, as the following $\mathcal{L}_K$-counterexample shows:

$$\begin{aligned} \mathcal{W} &= \{w_0\} \\ \mathcal{R} &= \emptyset \\ \nu_{w_0}(p) &= 1 \end{aligned}$$

So, $\mathcal{L}_K$ won't do the trick.

What about $\mathcal{L}_K^r$? Is (5.2) valid in $\mathcal{L}_K^r$? Yes. To see this, let $\mathcal{M}$ be an $\mathcal{L}_K^r$-model (and hence reflexive), where $\nu \in \mathcal{M}$ and $\mathcal{W} \in \mathcal{M}$. We want to show that $\mathcal{M}$ satisfies $\Box A \supset \Diamond A$, that is, that $\nu_w(\Box A \supset \Diamond A) = 1$ for all $w \in \mathcal{W}$. We can do this by showing that, for arbitrary w, if $\nu_w(\Box A) = 1$ then $\nu_w(\Diamond A) = 1$. Accordingly, let w_0 be in $\mathcal{W}$ and suppose that $\nu_{w_0}(\Box A) = 1$. Then for all w s.t. $w_0 \mathcal{R} w$, $\nu_w(A) = 1$. Given that $\mathcal{R}$ is reflexive, we have it that $w_0 \mathcal{R} w_0$ and, so, $\nu_{w_0}(A) = 1$. But, then, w_0 is a world that is possible relative to w_0 (i.e., accesible to itself) and is s.t. A is true (at w_0); hence, $\nu_{w_0}(\Diamond A) = 1$. Given that each of w_0 and $\mathcal{M}$ was arbitrary, we conclude that $\Box A \supset \Diamond A$ is true at all worlds of all $\mathcal{L}_K^r$-models: $\Vdash_{\mathcal{L}_K^r} \Box A \supset \Diamond A$.

So, (5.2) is valid in $\mathcal{L}_K^r$, and (presumably) this is what one wants if one interprets the box and diamond in deontic terms. The trouble is that (presumably) one does *not* want (5.1) to be valid when thus interpreted; sometimes a person fails to love her neighbor even though she is morally obligated to do so. If this is right, then $\mathcal{L}_K^r$ does not represent deontic notions accurately.

How can $\mathcal{L}_K$ be modified so as to yield the validity of (5.2) but not (5.1)? By way of answering this question we prove the following fact, where $\mathcal{M}$ is any $\mathcal{L}_K$-model:

FACT 5.2 $\mathcal{M}$ *satisfies* $\Box A \supset \Diamond A$ *if $\mathcal{M}$ is serial.*

PROOF FACT 5.2 Let ν and w_0 be in $\mathcal{M}$. Given that $\mathcal{R}$ is serial we have it that for some $w \in \mathcal{W}$ (call it 'w_1'), $\langle w_0, w_1 \rangle \in \mathcal{R}$. Now, suppose that $\nu_{w_0}(\Box A) = 1$. Then $\nu_w(A) = 1$ for all $w \in \mathcal{W}$ s.t. $\langle w_0, w \rangle \in \mathcal{R}$, in which case $\nu_{w_1}(A) = 1$. By the semantics for diamond-claims (see §5.3), if $\langle w_0, w_1 \rangle \in \mathcal{R}$ and $\nu_{w_1}(A) = 1$, then $\nu_{w_0}(\Diamond A) = 1$. So, $\nu_{w_0}(\Diamond A) = 1$, which is what we wanted to show. As w_0 was arbitrary we conclude that for any $w \in \mathcal{W}$, if $\nu_w(\Box A) = 1$ then $\nu_w(\Diamond A) = 1$. Hence, provided that $\mathcal{M}$ is serial, $\mathcal{M}$ satisfies $\Box A \supset \Diamond A$. QED

Another fact is worth mentioning:

FACT 5.3 $\mathcal{M}$ *is serial if $\mathcal{M}$ is reflexive.*

PROOF FACT 5.3 If $\mathcal{R}$ is reflexive on $\mathcal{W}$, then every $w \in \mathcal{W}$ is accessible to itself and, hence, given that $\mathcal{W}$ is non-empty, every w is accessible to *some* world or other. (If every world accesses itself, then every world accesses *some* world or other.) QED

How, then, do we modify $\mathcal{L}_K$ so as to ensure the validity of (5.2) but not (5.1)? Fact 5.2 gives the answer: We restrict our $\mathcal{L}_K$-models to *serial* ones; in doing so, we get the language $\mathcal{L}_K^{ser}$.[15] We note:

» Characteristic $\mathcal{L}_K^{ser}$ Sentence: $\Box A \supset \Diamond A$

$\mathcal{L}_K^{ser}$ is an extension of $\mathcal{L}_K$ but it is *not* an extension of $\mathcal{L}_K^{r}$. That said, given Fact 5.3, $\mathcal{L}_K^{r}$ is an extension of $\mathcal{L}_K^{ser}$, and indeed it is a *proper extension* of $\mathcal{L}_K^{ser}$. To say that $\mathcal{L}'$ is a *proper* extension of $\mathcal{L}$ is to say that any $\mathcal{L}'$-model is an $\mathcal{L}$-model, but *not* vice versa.

THE LANGUAGE $\mathcal{L}_K^{rt}$

Suppose that instead of necessity or moral duty one's concern is epistemology, and in particular *knowledge*. In this case, one might (informally) interpret the box as *it is known that*.[16] With this in mind, presumably one wants a language in which each of (5.1) and (5.2) are valid sentences. After all, if A is known, then A is true—the upshot of (5.1). Likewise, if A is known then the negation of A is not known—the upshot of (5.2).[17]

A natural candidate for representing our ideal knower is $\mathcal{L}_K^{r}$, given that each of (5.1) and (5.2) is logically true in $\mathcal{L}_K^{r}$. One might think, however, that for any A an *ideal* knower knows that she knows A. If this is correct, then one will want a language in which the following is logically true:

$$\Box p \supset \Box\Box p. \tag{5.3}$$

(5.3) is *not* logically true in $\mathcal{L}_K^{r}$, as the following counterexample shows:

$$\begin{aligned}
\mathcal{W} &= \{w_0, w_1, w_2\} \\
\mathcal{R} &= \{\langle w_0, w_0\rangle, \langle w_1, w_1\rangle, \langle w_2, w_2\rangle, \langle w_0, w_1\rangle, \langle w_1, w_2\rangle\} \\
v_{w_0}(p) &= 1 \\
v_{w_1}(p) &= 1 \\
v_{w_2}(p) &= 0
\end{aligned}$$

---

[15] Again, 'D' is the traditional name for the relevant logic, and we use the superscripted 'ser' to indicate the relevant restriction on $\mathcal{L}_K$-models.

[16] The diamond can be (informally) read in terms of its box-equivalent: $\Diamond A$ is read in terms of $\sim\Box\sim A$. For example, if A is 'There are other inhabited planets' then $\Diamond A$ will be 'It is not known that it is not such that there are other inhabited planets', which could be paraphrased as 'It is possible, for all we know, that there are other inhabited planets'.

[17] Our informal readings of (5.1) and (5.2) are slightly loose here, as we have (in effect) treated knowledge as a predicate rather than an operator, but for present purposes we favor readability over "strict speech". (As an optional exercise you might give the "strict reading" of (5.1) and (5.2); the exercise is not as easy as it first appears!)

The question is: What modification of $\mathcal{L}_K^r$ will ensure that each of (5.1)–(5.3) is logically true? The answer, as in previous cases, calls for *restriction*. By way of answering the question we prove the following fact, where $\mathcal{M}$ is any $\mathcal{L}_K$-model:

FACT 5.4 *$\mathcal{M}$ satisfies $\Box A \supset \Box\Box A$ if $\mathcal{M}$ is transitive.*

PROOF FACT 5.4 Suppose that $\mathcal{M}$ is transitive, v and w_0 are in $\mathcal{M}$, and that $v_{w_0}(\Box A) = 1$. Suppose, for reductio, that $v_{w_0}(\Box\Box A) \neq 1$. Then for some $w \in \mathcal{W}$ (call it 'w_1') $w_0\mathcal{R}w_1$ and $v_{w_1}(\Box A) \neq 1$, in which case there is some $w \in \mathcal{W}$ (call it 'w_2') s.t. $w_1\mathcal{R}w_2$ and $v_{w_2}(A) \neq 1$. But, then, we have it that $w_0\mathcal{R}w_1$ and $w_1\mathcal{R}w_2$, in which case, *given transitivity*, $w_0\mathcal{R}w_2$. But, now, since $v_{w_0}(\Box A) = 1$ and $w_0\mathcal{R}w_2$ we have it that $v_{w_2}(A) = 1$, in which case we have that $v_{w_2}(A) = 1$ *and* $v_{w_2}(A) \neq 1$. This is ruled out, given that v is a function. Given that w_0 was arbitrary, we conclude that for any w in $\mathcal{M}$, if $v_w(\Box A) = 1$ then $v_w(\Box\Box A) = 1$. (In other words, $\mathcal{M}$ satisfies $\Box A \supset \Box\Box A$, given that $\mathcal{M}$ is transitive.)[18] QED

If we restrict our attention only to *transitive* $\mathcal{L}_K^r$-models—and, hence, only to *reflexive and transitive* $\mathcal{L}_K$-models—we get the language $\mathcal{L}_K^{rt}$. We note:

» Characteristic $\mathcal{L}_K^{rt}$ Sentence:[19] $\Box A \supset \Box\Box A$

$\mathcal{L}_K^{rt}$ is a (proper) extension of $\mathcal{L}_K^r$, which is a (proper) extension of $\mathcal{L}_K^{ser}$. This fact, together with Fact 5.4, ensures that $\mathcal{L}_K^{rt}$ is a language in which each of (5.1)–(5.3) is valid.

THE LANGUAGE $\mathcal{L}_K^{rst}$

The last of our target normal modal languages, like the others, is achieved by amending $\mathcal{R}$. Specifically, the language $\mathcal{L}_K^{rst}$ is gained by restricting our attention to only the *symmetric* $\mathcal{L}_K^{rt}$-models—and, so, restricting attention to only the reflexive, symmetric and transitive $\mathcal{L}_K$-models. Some philosophers have thought that $\mathcal{L}_K^{rst}$ best represents alethic modality; they have thought that if A is possibly true, then it is necessarily the case that A is possibly true. If this is correct, then the following ought to be valid:

$$\Diamond A \supset \Box\Diamond A. \qquad (5.4)$$

Whether such thinking is ultimately correct is not particularly germane, for present purposes. Our focus, for present purposes, are a few special features of $\mathcal{L}_K^{rst}$.

[18] We will henceforth drop the explicit justification invoking arbitrary worlds, etc.. We will assume that the reader now has a sufficient feel for proving such results.

[19] Note, however, that this sentence is valid even if one considers *irreflexive* but transitive K-models.

Before turning to the target features of $\mathcal{L}_K^{rst}$ we should first note that (5.4) is not valid in $\mathcal{L}_K^{rt}$ (and, hence, not valid in any language of which $\mathcal{L}_K^{rt}$ is an extension), as the following counterexample shows:

$$\begin{aligned} \mathcal{W} &= \{w_0, w_1\} \\ \mathcal{R} &= \{\langle w_0, w_0\rangle, \langle w_1, w_1\rangle, \langle w_0, w_1\rangle\} \\ v_{w_0}(A) &= 1 \\ v_{w_1}(A) &= 0 \end{aligned}$$

On this specification $\mathcal{R}$ is reflexive and (vacuously) transitive. $\Diamond A$ is true at w_0, since there is at least one w_0-accessible world (viz., w_0) at which A is true. But there are no w_1-accessible worlds at which A is true; hence, $\Diamond A$ is false at w_1, in which case $\Box\Diamond A$ is false at w_0, since not every w_0-accessible world is one at which $\Diamond A$ is true.

Given that $\mathcal{L}_K^{rst}$ is an extension of $\mathcal{L}_K^{rt}$ the foregoing counterexample shows that $\mathcal{L}_K^{rst}$ is a *proper* extension of $\mathcal{L}_K^{rt}$.

THE LANGUAGE $\mathcal{L}_{UA}$

A notable feature concerns the role of $\mathcal{R}$ in $\mathcal{L}_K^{rst}$. Suppose that instead of restricting our attention to only symmetric $\mathcal{L}_K^{rt}$-models we defined a language (on the syntax S_{mpl}) thus: A *model* is a *pair*, $\langle \mathcal{W}, v\rangle$, where $\mathcal{W}$ is a non-empty set of worlds and v is a function from $\mathcal{S} \times \mathcal{W}$ to $\{1, 0\}$. (So, again, v assigns a "truth value" to each sentence at each world.) In turn, the *admissible* valuations are defined as before *except* for the clauses governing the box and diamond, which are now given thus:

$$\begin{aligned} v_w(\Diamond A) = 1 \quad &\text{iff} \quad v_{w'}(A) = 1, \text{ for some } w' \in \mathcal{W} \\ v_w(\Box A) = 1 \quad &\text{iff} \quad v_{w'}(A) = 1, \text{ for all } w' \in \mathcal{W} \end{aligned}$$

Call the resulting language '$\mathcal{L}_{UA}$', where the subscripted 'UA' may be read *universal access*. There is no explicitly invoked "access" relation in the semantics for $\mathcal{L}_{UA}$ but, given the semantics, one can (if one wishes) think of the worlds as enjoying "universal access"—each world "accesses" every world. So, we could equivalently define $\mathcal{L}_{UA}$-models to be triples, $\langle \mathcal{W}, \mathcal{R}, v\rangle$, where $\mathcal{R}$ is a universal access relation.

The question is this: What is the relation between $\mathcal{L}_K^{rst}$ and $\mathcal{L}_{UA}$? More to the point: Is $\mathcal{L}_K^{rst}$ an extension of $\mathcal{L}_{UA}$? Is $\mathcal{L}_{UA}$ an extension of $\mathcal{L}_K^{rst}$? How are the respective consequence relations related to each other?

FACT 5.5 *The valid arguments and sentences in $\mathcal{L}_K^{rst}$ are precisely the valid arguments and sentences in $\mathcal{L}_{UA}$.*

We leave the proof as an optional exercise.

ITERATED MODALITIES

Another notable feature of $\mathcal{L}_K^{rst}$ (and, in turn, $\mathcal{L}_{UA}$) concerns so-called *iterated modalities*, which are S_{mpl}-sentences containing sequences of modal operators, sequences of the box and diamond: $\Diamond\Box p$, $\Box\Box p$, $\Box\Box\Diamond p$, and so on. Specifically, every iterated modality is equivalent (in $\mathcal{L}_K^{rst}$) to a sentence containing only one modal operator. This result is due to the following so-called *reduction laws*, each of which is logically true in $\mathcal{L}_K^{rst}$:

$$\Diamond A \equiv \Box\Diamond A \tag{5.5}$$

$$\Box A \equiv \Diamond\Box A \tag{5.6}$$

$$\Diamond A \equiv \Diamond\Diamond A \tag{5.7}$$

$$\Box A \equiv \Box\Box A \tag{5.8}$$

The upshot of these equivalences is that in $\mathcal{L}_K^{rst}$ one may (validly) delete all but the last modal operator of a sentence—where the far left operator is the first, the far right the last—and thereby have a logically equivalent sentence. So, for example, the rather complicated-looking

$$\Box\Diamond\Diamond\Box\Box\Box\Diamond\Box p$$

is logically equivalent in $\mathcal{L}_K^{rst}$ to the rather friendlier-looking

$$\Box p$$

Another upshot of the given equivalences is that there are only six non-equivalent *modalities* in $\mathcal{L}_K^{rst}$, where (for present purposes) a *modality* is any unbroken sequence (including the empty sequence) of S_{mpl}-monadic operators—an unbroken sequence of $\sim$, $\Diamond$ and $\Box$.[20] Given the noted equivalences, the six non-equivalent $\mathcal{L}_K^{rst}$-modalities are

$$p,\ \sim p,\ \Diamond p,\ \sim\Diamond p,\ \Box p,\ \sim\Box p$$

We leave proofs of (5.6)–(5.8) as an exercise.

EXERCISES 5.4.2

1 Show that $\Box(A \supset B) \supset (\Box A \supset \Box B)$ is valid (i.e., that every instance of the given "schema" is logically true) in all extensions of $\mathcal{L}_K$ canvassed in this chapter.

---

[20] Of course, $\sim$ is not a modal operator, at least in the current semantics; however, $\sim\Diamond\sim$ and $\sim\Box\sim$ are "modalities" in a very intuitive sense—the former may be read (in alethic modal logic) 'it is necessary that...' and the latter 'it is possible that...'. Hughes and Cresswell [51] provide further discussion.

2 Specify the (canvassed) languages in which $\Box p \wedge \Box\sim p$ and $\Box(p \wedge \sim p)$ are satisfiable. Specify the (canvassed) languages in which neither $\Box p \wedge \Box\sim p$ nor $\Box(p \wedge \sim p)$ is satisfiable.

3 Specify the (canvassed) languages in which $\Diamond(p \vee \sim p)$ is merely contingent.

4 Give a 3-world $\mathcal{L}_K^{rt}$-counterexample to (5.4). (A counterexample is an n-world counterexample if $\mathcal{W}$ comprises exactly n worlds.)

5 Another well-known normal modal language is $\mathcal{L}_K^{rs}$, which arises from $\mathcal{L}_K^{r}$ by restricting the models to *symmetric* ones. The characteristic sentence of $\mathcal{L}_K^{rs}$ is $A \supset \Box\Diamond A$ and the corresponding logic is called 'B' (the "Brouwersche" logic).

1. Show that $\mathcal{L}_K^{rs}$ is an extension of $\mathcal{L}_K^{r}$.
2. Show that $\mathcal{L}_K^{rs}$ is a *proper* extension of $\mathcal{L}_K^{r}$ (and, hence, a proper extension of $\mathcal{L}_K$).
3. Show that $\mathcal{L}_K^{rt}$ is *not* an extension of $\mathcal{L}_K^{rs}$.
4. Show that $\mathcal{L}_K^{rst}$ is a proper extension of $\mathcal{L}_K^{rs}$.
5. Give a direct (non-reductive) proof of Fact 5.4.
6. What philosophical motivation might motivate $\mathcal{L}_K^{rs}$? What notions might be modeled by the box and diamond in $\mathcal{L}_K^{rs}$?

6 Prove the equivalences (5.6)–(5.8).

7 In alethic modal logic $\mathcal{R}$ is informally translated in terms of *relative possibility*. How might $\mathcal{R}$ be translated in deontic modal logic? How might it be translated in epistemic logic?

5.5 TABLEAUX FOR NORMAL MODAL LOGICS

Modal tableaux differ from CPL tableaux in two basic respects: the *nodes* and *rules of resolution*. The differences, while significant, are predictable. Indeed, the differences reflect the basic *semantic* difference between CPL and modal languages: relativity to *worlds* (or, more neutrally, "points"). Whereas CPL-valuations assign a "truth value" directly to sentences, modal valuations assign a "truth value" to *sentences at worlds*. These semantic differences guide the construction of our otherwise semantic-free proof theory; they guide the construction of our tableaux. As we shall see, these differences also have the incidental consequence that, unlike for CPL, a tableau construction may be unending (yielding, if effect, an infinite branch).

We will use $\mathcal{L}_{\mathsf{K}}$ to illustrate. Tableaux for the other normal modal languages follow the same basic pattern. The logical system (tableaux rules system) for $\mathcal{L}_{\mathsf{K}}$ will be called K, which is its traditional name in the literature. The (syntactic) logical consequence relation defined by the tableau rules will be denoted as $\vdash_{\mathsf{K}}$.

TABLEAUX FOR K

Tableaux for K look much like tableaux for CPL. The difference (in appearance) is at the nodes. By way of illustration consider a CPL-tableau for the sentence: $p \supset (q \vee p)$. (You know what one looks like; so we won't display one here.) By contrast a typical K-tableau for the given sentence looks like this:

$$\boxed{\sim(p \supset (q \vee p))\ ,\ w_0}$$
$$|$$
$$p\ ,\ w_0$$
$$\boxed{\sim(q \vee p)\ ,\ w_0}$$
$$|$$
$$\sim q\ ,\ w_0$$
$$\sim p\ ,\ w_0$$
$$\otimes$$

The difference, as above, is at the nodes; but the difference, as we said, has a natural (semantic) reading.[21] An intuitive reading of the given CPL-tableau reads its leaf as '$\sim p$ is true' (under a valuation represented by the branch), and similarly for its other nodes. Likewise, an intuitive reading of the given K-tableau reads its leaf as '$\sim p$ is *true at* w_0' (under a valuation represented by the branch), and similarly for its other nodes. So, the "big" difference reflects the difference in semantics: relativity to worlds.

What about the *accessibility* relation in $\mathcal{L}_{\mathsf{K}}$? How, if at all, does this enter modal tableaux? By way of answering this question we consider a different example. Assume, for reductio, that $\Box(A \supset B) \supset (\Box A \supset \Box B)$ is not logically true in $\mathcal{L}_{\mathsf{K}}$, in which case some admissible $\mathcal{L}_{\mathsf{K}}$-valuation satisfies its negation at some world (call it 'w_0'). Now, just as with CPL tableaux, we begin to construct a tree to represent our (assumed) valuation. In particular, we represent that the negation is true at w_0 at the root, which in this case is our (single sentence) initial list:

$$\sim(\Box(p \supset q) \supset (\Box p \supset \Box q))\ ,\ w_0$$

This sentence is a negated (material) conditional which, given the semantics for $\supset$ in $\mathcal{L}_{\mathsf{K}}$, is true at w_0 iff its antecedent is true at w_0 and its consequent is false at w_0. Accordingly, no new "branching possibilities" open up;

[21] Of course, one needs to remember that the tableaux are strictly formal—mere mechanical, semantic-free devices. Still, their semantic motivation is a useful heuristic guide to their otherwise "meaningless" behavior.

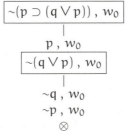

we stay on the same branch, which is now represented thus:

$$\boxed{\sim(\Box(p \supset q) \supset (\Box p \supset \Box q))\ ,\ w_0}$$
$$|$$
$$\Box(p \supset q)\ ,\ w_0$$
$$\sim(\Box p \supset \Box q)\ ,\ w_0$$

If, as the second line has it, $\Box(p \supset q)$ is true at w_0, then $p \supset q$ is true at every w_0-accessible world. For now, given that we have only w_0 and no reason to think that w_0 is itself w_0-accessible, we turn to the third line, which contains another negated (material) conditional. This line is treated just as above; it yields the *continued path*

$$\Box p\ ,\ w_0$$
$$\sim\Box q\ ,\ w_0$$

In effect, the first line "says" that p is true at every w_0-accessible world; but we still have no reason to think that there are any w_0-accessible worlds; so, we turn to the second line, which (alas) affords a w_0-accessible world. After all, $\sim\Box q$ is true at w_0 exactly if there is some w_0-accessible world (call it 'w_1') at which $\sim q$ is true; and there is some w_0-accessible world at which $\sim q$ is true exactly if $\Diamond\sim q$ is true at w_0. So, node $\langle\sim\Box q\ ,\ w_0\rangle$ tells us that $\Diamond\sim q$ is true at w_0, which, in turn, tells us that w_0 accesses some world (call it 'w_1') at which $\sim q$ is true. We represent these two claims by *three* nodes: $\langle\Diamond\sim q\ ,\ w_0\rangle$, $\langle w_0 R w_1\rangle$, $\langle\sim q\ ,\ w_1\rangle$. The second node, namely $\langle w_0 R w_1\rangle$, records the fact that w_1 is a w_0-accessible world; it captures the (semantic) idea that $w_0 \mathcal{R} w_1$. Putting the foregoing steps together we have

$$\boxed{\sim(\Box(p \supset q) \supset (\Box p \supset \Box q))\ ,\ w_0}$$
$$|$$
$$\Box(p \supset q)\ ,\ w_0$$
$$\boxed{\sim(\Box p \supset \Box q)\ ,\ w_0}$$
$$|$$
$$\Box p\ ,\ w_0$$
$$\boxed{\sim\Box q\ ,\ w_0}$$
$$|$$
$$\boxed{\Diamond\sim q\ ,\ w_0}$$
$$|$$
$$w_0 R w_1$$
$$\sim q\ ,\ w_1$$

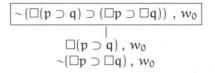

Four of the lines have been *boxed-up*, as each of them has been fully processed. Two of the un-boxed lines are $\Box(p \supset q)$ and $\Box p$, each of which is true at w_0 (under the valuation represented by the given branch). As above, this tells us that $(p \supset q)$ and p are true at every w_0-accessible world; *a fortiori* each is true at w_1, since we have it that w_1 is w_0-accessible. So:

$$\begin{array}{c} p \supset q\ ,\ w_1 \\ p\ ,\ w_1 \end{array}$$

The first line is a (material) conditional, which introduces "branching possibilities", represented, as in CPL-tableaux, thus:

$$\begin{array}{ccc} & \vdots & \\ & \diagup\ \diagdown & \\ {\sim}p\ ,\ w_1 & & q\ ,\ w_1 \end{array}$$

Appending this to the previous branch yields an end to the matter:

$$\begin{array}{ccc}
& \boxed{{\sim}(\Box(p \supset q) \supset (\Box p \supset \Box q))\ ,\ w_0} & \\
& | & \\
& \Box(p \supset q)\ ,\ w_0 & \\
& \boxed{{\sim}(\Box p \supset \Box q)\ ,\ w_0} & \\
& | & \\
& \Box p\ ,\ w_0 & \\
& \boxed{{\sim}\Box q\ ,\ w_0} & \\
& | & \\
& \boxed{\Diamond{\sim}q\ ,\ w_0} & \\
& | & \\
& w_0Rw_1 & \\
& {\sim}q\ ,\ w_1 & \\
& \boxed{p \supset q\ ,\ w_1} & \\
& p\ ,\ w_1 & \\
& \diagup\ \diagdown & \\
{\sim}p\ ,\ w_1 & & q\ ,\ w_1 \\
\otimes & & \otimes
\end{array}$$

This ends the matter as each branch contains nodes of the forms $\langle A, w_i\rangle$ and $\langle {\sim}A, w_i\rangle$. The upshot is that any $\mathcal{L}_K$-valuation satisfying the initial list is one that assigns both 1 and 0 to the same sentence (e.g., p or q) at some world (e.g., w_1), something no *admissible* $\mathcal{L}_K$-valuation can do. As with CPL tableaux, we use the *closed-off* symbol to record that a branch is "inconsistent".[22]

[22] Although we are motivating and illustrating the tableaux from a semantic perspective we should recall that, strictly speaking, tableaux are purely formal, devoid of "meaning". Accordingly, a branch is *inconsistent* only in a syntactic sense: the branch contains a node at which $\langle A, w_i\rangle$ occurs and a node at which $\langle {\sim}A, w_i\rangle$ occurs.

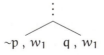

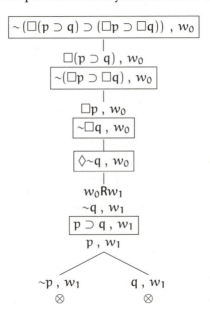

RESOLUTION RULES FOR K

The resolution rules for extensional (truth-functional) connectives present little drama. K-rules for $\wedge$, $\supset$, $\sim$, $\equiv$ and $\vee$ are precisely the CPL-rules except that instead of applying directly to sentences the K-rules apply to lines of the following form, where $i \in \{0, 1, 2, 3, \ldots\}$:

$$A\ ,\ w_i$$

In particular, the rules for extensional connectives run as follows:[23]

K-RULES FOR EXTENSIONAL CONNECTIVES:

$\boxed{(A \supset B), w_i}$	$\boxed{(A \vee B), w_i}$	$\boxed{\sim(A \wedge B), w_i}$
$\sim A, w_i \qquad B, w_i$	$A, w_i \qquad B, w_i$	$\sim A, w_i \qquad \sim B, w_i$
$\boxed{\sim(A \supset B), w_i}$	$\boxed{\sim(A \vee B), w_i}$	$\boxed{(A \wedge B), w_i}$
A, w_i $\sim B, w_i$	$\sim A, w_i$ $\sim B, w_i$	A, w_i B, w_i
$\boxed{(A \equiv B), w_i}$	$\boxed{\sim(A \equiv B), w_i}$	$\boxed{\sim\sim A\ ,\ w_i}$
$A, w_i \qquad \sim A, w_i$ $B, w_i \qquad \sim B, w_i$	$A, w_i \qquad \sim A, w_i$ $\sim B, w_i \qquad B, w_i$	$A\ ,\ w_i$

Before giving the K-rules for *modal* operators we first give their (semantic) motivation, which runs as follows:

» Box-Sentences: (*Box-sentences* are those and only those that *begin* with the box!) If $\Box A$ is true at w_i, then A is true at every w_j s.t. $w_i \mathcal{R} w_j$. So, if we have $\langle \Box A\ , w_i \rangle$ and $\langle w_i R w_j \rangle$ on a branch, then we may infer that A is true at w_j (on that branch); that is, we may write '$A\ , w_j$' on the given branch.

» Negated Box-Sentences: If $\sim\Box A$ is true at w_i, then there is some w_i-accessible world at which $\sim A$ is true, which is to say that $\Diamond\sim A$ is true at w_i. So, if we have '$\sim\Box A\ , w_i$' on a branch, then we may infer that $\Diamond\sim A$ is true at w_i (on that branch); that is, we may write '$\Diamond\sim A\ , w_i$' on the given branch.

---

[23]Each of the rules retains its corresponding CPL-rule name. We trust that no confusion will result from this systematic ambiguity.

» Diamond-Sentences: Suppose that $\Diamond A$ is true at w_i. Then there is some w_i-accessible world at which A is true. Accordingly, if we have $\langle \Diamond A , w_i \rangle$ on a branch, then we may infer two things:

  » *Some* world is w_i-accessible. [We record this fact by using a *new name* for the w_i-accessible world (a name, 'w_j', such that 'w_j' occurs nowhere "earlier" on the given branch) and write '$w_i R w_j$' on the branch.]

  » A is true at our "new" w_i-accessible world. [We record this fact by writing 'A , w_j' on the given branch.]

» Negated Diamond-Sentences: If ${\sim}\Diamond A$ is true at w_i, then there is no w_i-accessible world at which A is true, which is to say that every w_i-accessible world is one at which ${\sim}A$ is true, which, in turn, is to say that $\Box{\sim}A$ is true at w_i. So, if we have $\langle {\sim}\Diamond A , w_i \rangle$ on a branch, then we may infer that $\Box{\sim}A$ is true at w_i (on that branch); that is, we may write '$\Box{\sim}A , w_i$' on the given branch.

The foregoing remarks motivate the K-rules for modal operators; the official rules are below, where boldface type is used to indicate a *new name* (a name, as above, appearing nowhere before on the given branch). The following rules, from left to right, are named 'Box (Pos)', 'Box (Neg)', 'Diamond (Pos)' and 'Diamond (Neg)', respectively:

K-RULES FOR MODAL CONNECTIVES:

$\Box A , w_i$	$\boxed{{\sim}\Box A , w_i}$	$\boxed{\Diamond A , w_i}$	$\boxed{{\sim}\Diamond A , w_i}$
$w_i R w_j$	|	|	|
|	$\Diamond{\sim}A , w_i$	$w_i R \mathbf{w}_j$	$\Box{\sim}A , w_i$
A , w_j		A , w_j	

Note that Box (Pos), the K-rule for box-sentences, does not allow boxing-up; the reason is that one and the same box-sentence may be resolved *multiple times*.[24] We will note this again in the conventions governing K-tableaux but, for now, the slogan is: *Don't box-up box-sentences!*

Before turning to the conventions governing K-tableaux we note that definitions of 'closed branch', 'closed tree' and so on are exactly as in CPL-tableaux except for the requisite modification to accommodate "worlds". Accordingly, we say:

[24] The fact that any box sentence may be resolved multiple times, plus the provision that resolving a diamond sentence introduces a new name, together account for the appearance of unending branches (as we shall see below).

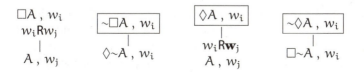

» A branch is *closed* iff there are two nodes on the branch such that $\langle A, w_i \rangle$ occurs by itself at one node and $\langle {\sim}A, w_i \rangle$ by itself at the other, for some $A \in \mathcal{S}$ and some $i \in \{0, 1, 2, 3, \ldots\}$.

» A *tree is closed* iff every branch (of the given tree) is closed.

In turn, a branch is open iff it is not closed; and a tree is open iff it is not closed.

For purposes of defining (proof-theoretic) K-validity we need the definition of a *finished tree*. To facilitate the definition we shall say, for any $A \in \mathcal{S}$ and $i \in \{0, 1, 2, 3, \ldots\}$, that $\langle A, w_i \rangle$ (occurring by itself on a node of a branch) is a *sentence-world-pair*; and that $\langle A, w_i \rangle$ is an *atomic-world-pair* iff $A \in \mathcal{A}$ (A is atomic); and that $\langle {\sim}A, w_i \rangle$ is a *negation-atomic-world-pair* iff $A \in \mathcal{A}$. With this in hand we say:

» A tree is *finished* iff the tree is closed or no further resolution rules are applicable.

We note that the *initial list* of a tree is to be understood as per CPL-tableaux. (See §4.3.) Other conventions governing K-tableaux are likewise similar to those in CPL-tableaux, but there are a few new ones, which we present explicitly:

CONVENTIONS GOVERNING K-TABLEAUX

» Starting-Off: Every sentence of a tree's initial list is to be "paired" with w_0. (In other words, we conventionally agree to start the trees at "world zero".)

» Closing-Off: Let b be any branch of any K-tree. We write the closed-off sign, namely '⊗', below the tip of b iff a sentence-world-pair of the form $\langle A, w_i \rangle$ occurs (alone) at one node of b and, for the same sentence A, a sentence-world-pair of the form $\langle {\sim}A, w_i \rangle$ occurs (alone) at another node of b.

» Boxing-Up: We box-up a line of branch b iff the line's K-rule has been applied to the line *and* the line does *not* contain a box-sentence (i.e., a box-sentence-world-pair, as it were).[25] Along this vein we repeat: *Do not box-up box-sentences!* The reason for this is that new world-names may appear later, in which case the K-rule for Box-sentences should be applied again.

[25] We leave it to the reader to give a precise definition of *a line's K-rule*. [Hint: First define every line as a φ-sentence-world-pair, for connective φ. Then say (for example) that Hook (Pos) is a node's K-rule iff the node is a ⊃-sentence-world-pair, and so on. Do similarly for *negated*-φ-sentence-world-pairs. (The terminology is clumsy, we admit. Fortunately, we won't have frequent need for it.)

With these conventions in hand we note that *proof-theoretic* K-*validity* (or proof-theoretic K-consequence) is defined as per (Def 4.1). Where $A \in \mathcal{S}$ and $\mathcal{X} \subseteq \mathcal{S}$ we use '$\mathcal{X} \vdash_K A$' as shorthand for 'A is a proof-theoretic K-consequence of $\mathcal{X}$'. Given (Def 4.1) we have it that $\mathcal{X} \vdash_K A$ iff there is a closed tree the initial list of which comprises the elements of $\mathcal{X}$ and $\langle {\sim}A, w_0 \rangle$.

By way of example let us test the characteristic $\mathcal{L}_K^r$-sentence in K (i.e., test it using a K-tableau). We begin our initial list thus:

$${\sim}(\Box p \supset p)\ ,\ w_0$$

Given Hook (Neg) we write

$$\boxed{{\sim}(\Box p \supset p)\ ,w_0}$$
$$|$$
$$\Box p\ ,w_0$$
$${\sim}p\ ,w_0$$

The only line left to resolve is the second, which is a box-sentence, but the only way to resolve it requires an additional w_0-accessible world, which we do not have on the branch. (Indeed, the only way to get "new worlds" is via Diamond (Pos), as careful attention to the K-rules indicates.) Accordingly, the tree above is not only finished; it also remains *open*.

As with CPL-tableaux a finished, open tree is telling: it affords an easy way to construct a counterexample to the original sentence (in this case, the characteristic $\mathcal{L}_K^r$-sentence). The "climbing" procedure in §4.3 (see page 40) is still in effect, except that we make requisite modifications to accommodate "worlds" and $\mathcal{R}$. Specifically, we now climb as follows:

COUNTEREXAMPLES VIA CLIMBING A BRANCH

» Beginning the climb:
  » Start at the tip of any open branch, b.
  » Ignore all boxed-up sentences in b.
» Constructing $\mathcal{W}$
  » For any i, if 'w_i' occurs on b, let w_i be in $\mathcal{W}$.
» Constructing $\mathcal{R}$
  » For any i and j, let $\langle w_i, w_j \rangle$ be in $\mathcal{R}$ iff '$w_i R w_j$' occurs on b. (Otherwise, $\mathcal{R} = \emptyset$.)
» Contructing v (where $A \in \mathcal{A}$, i.e. *atomic*)[26]

[26] v is extended to all sentences via constraints on admissible valuations.

> » If $\langle A, w_i \rangle$ occurs as a node of b, let $v_{w_i}(A) = 1$.

> » If $\langle \sim A, w_i \rangle$ occurs as node of b, let $v_{w_i}(A) = 0$.

Applying these instructions to the K-tableau above (page 75), yields the following $\mathcal{L}_K$-counterexample to the characteristic $\mathcal{L}_K^r$-sentence:

$$\begin{aligned}
\mathcal{W} &= \{w_0\} \\
\mathcal{R} &= \emptyset \\
v_{w_0}(p) &= 0
\end{aligned}$$

Of course, the existence of $\mathcal{L}_K$-counterexamples to the characteristic $\mathcal{L}_K^r$-sentence is hardly news at this stage; indeed, this particular counterexample has already been discussed. The point of the above example is merely to illustrate that the "climbing" method of constructing counterexamples is available in K-tableaux (and any modal tableaux, for that matter).

A feel for K-tableaux can be gained via exercises. For now, we note (without proof) that $\vdash_K$ is strongly sound and complete with respect to $\Vdash_K$.[27] Accordingly, one may use K as a reliable test for logical truth and consequence in $\mathcal{L}_K$.

5.6   Amending R-Rules: Extensions of K

Just as extensions of $\mathcal{L}_K$ are achieved by amending $\mathcal{R}$, so too extensions of K (i.e., extensions of $\vdash_K$) are achieved by amending the resolution rules. We achieve tableaux for our other normal modal logics by mirroring the restrictions imposed on $\mathcal{R}$. Specifically, we add rules governing R as it occurs in tableaux.

Example. The difference between $\mathcal{L}_K$ and $\mathcal{L}_K^r$ is that the latter, unlike the former, imposes a restriction on $\mathcal{R}$, namely, that $\mathcal{R}$ be reflexive. This restriction is easily mirrored by augmenting the K-tableaux-rules: add that one may write '$w_i R w_i$' on any branch in which $\langle A, w_i \rangle$ occurs, for any sentence-world-pair. By adding to the set of K-rules we mirror the restriction on $\mathcal{R}$. (This is how things normally go with rules: adding more of them reduces freedom!) With such a rule at hand our previous tableau (page 75) would close:

$$\boxed{\sim(\Box p \supset p), w_0}$$
$$|$$
$$\Box p, w_0$$
$$\sim p, w_0$$
$$w_0 R w_0$$
$$p, w_0$$
$$\otimes$$

---

[27]See further §12.2.

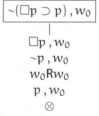

With the new R-rule the second line, combined with Box (Pos), yields the fifth line which, given the third line, calls for the closed-off sign (i.e., closes the branch).

So, specifying the official rules for our other normal modal logics is straightforward: While retaining *all* K-rules (and conventions) we proceed to specify additional rules governing R.[28] Moreover, the various definitions specified for K-tableaux (e.g., *finished tree*, etc.) remain in effect, and *proof-theoretic consequence* for the various normal modal logics is defined as per (Def 4.1). Accordingly, we proceed to specify the remaining (target) tableaux rules by focusing only on the additional rules governing R.

TABLEAUX FOR T

The normal model logic T corresponds to $\mathcal{L}_K^r$. The official rules for T-tableaux comprise all K-rules (and conventions) and the following rule governing R, namely *Reflexivity* [abbreviated '(Ref)']:

$$\begin{array}{c} A\,, w_i \\ | \\ w_i R w_i \end{array}$$

This rule is intended to mirror the reflexivity of $\mathcal{R}$ in $\mathcal{L}_K^r$. In effect, the rule instructs one to write '$w_i R w_i$' on any (open) branch on which '$A\,, w_i$' occurs, for any sentence-world-pair. Adding (only) this rule to K yields T, which is sound and complete wrt $\mathcal{L}_K^r$.

TABLEAUX FOR D

Logical system D (for 'deontic logic'), with consequence relation $\vdash_D$, corresponds to $\mathcal{L}_K^{ser}$. The official rules for D-tableaux comprise all K-rules (and conventions) and the following rule governing R, namely *Serial* [abbreviated '(Ser)']:

$$\begin{array}{c} \ldots w_i \ldots \\ | \\ w_i R \mathbf{w}_j \end{array}$$

This rule requires explanation; it is intended, of course, to mirror the restrictions imposed on $\mathcal{R}$ in $\mathcal{L}_K^{ser}$, namely, that $\mathcal{R}$ be serial. What requires explanation is the new notation, in particular '$\ldots w_i \ldots$'. (The boldface notation carries its previous meaning: new name.) In effect, the rule instructs one to write '$w_i R \mathbf{w}_j$' on any open branch in which a "world-name" occurs, *provided* that there is no previous R-line (as it were) in which 'w_i' occurs as the left component. ('w_i' is the left component of the R-line '$w_i R w_j$'.) The rule is easy to remember: Just remember that (Ser) mirrors a *serial* relation on worlds, which means that every world accesses *some world* (or

[28]Note that when we say that the conventions of K-tableaux are retained, we intend to include the "climbing" method for constructing counterexamples.

other). With that in mind, (Ser) is straightforward: If 'w_i' occurs on an open branch but is not the left component of an R-line, then, in accord with (Ser), write '$w_i R\mathbf{w}_j$' on that branch—where '$\mathbf{w}_j$' is a new world-name. Examples are given in the exercises (page 81).

Adding only (Ser) to K yields D, which is sound and complete with respect to $\mathcal{L}_K^{ser}$. We pause to note, however, that even for finite initial lists some D-tableaux are *infinite*.[29] The result is that D is not a so-called *decidable* test for satisfiability in $\mathcal{L}_K^{ser}$. We shall not discuss the issue of decidability here; instead, we give an example of the "problem" at hand and also an example of infinite counterexamples.

Suppose that one wishes to use D to test whether $\Box p$ is logically true in $\mathcal{L}_K^{ser}$.[30] As per the D-rules and conventions, one proceeds to construct the root which, in this case, comprises only $\langle {\sim}\Box p, w_0 \rangle$ as node. In turn, one applies Box (Neg), which yields the node $\langle \Diamond{\sim} p, w_0 \rangle$. At this stage, one may apply (Ser) or Diamond (Pos). A general rule of thumb (and this applies to all modal tableaux) suggests applying Diamond (Pos) at the first opportunity, and so we will, which results in the following (unfinished) tree:[31]

$$\boxed{{\sim}\Box p\ ,\ w_0}$$
$$|$$
$$\boxed{\Diamond{\sim}p\ ,\ w_0}$$
$$|$$
$$w_0 R\mathbf{w}_1$$
$${\sim}p\ ,\ w_1$$

As our branch remains open we proceed to the next available rule, which in this case is (Ser). But now the "danger" is evident: (Ser) instructs one to write '$w_i R w_j$' for every world-name 'w_i' that appears on the branch and is not the left component of any R-line (on the branch). But, then, as a moment's reflection shows, we "immediately" get an infinitely long *open*

[29] We say that a tableaux is infinite iff it has at least one infinitely long branch. (Given König's Lemma (see §10) a tableau cannot grow infinitely wider by growing more and more finite branches; if a tableau has infinitely many branches then at least one of them will be infinite.) Moreover, we say that a model is *infinite* iff $\mathcal{W}$ is infinite; otherwise, it is said to be *finite*.

[30] Admittedly, the scenario may be much like Humpty Dumpty's demand to have the difference of 356and 1 "done on paper" so that he could double-check its accuracy. Still, the example nicely illustrates the target phenomenon, to which we return.

[31] The reason for this has to do with Diamond (Pos)'s introduction of a *new name*. The idea, as with so-called '∃-introduction rule' in classical predicate logic, is that by introducing one's "new names" first one tends to save time. (This rule of thumb will become obvious after one does a few tableaux in the exericses.)

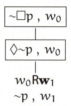

branch:

$$\boxed{\sim\Box p\ ,\ w_0}$$
$$|$$
$$\boxed{\Diamond\sim p\ ,\ w_0}$$
$$|$$
$$w_0 R w_1$$
$$\sim p\ ,\ w_1$$
$$|$$
$$w_1 R \mathbf{w}_2$$
$$w_2 R \mathbf{w}_3$$
$$w_3 R \mathbf{w}_4$$
$$\vdots$$

Infinite D-tableaux will always result if the tree does not close; this is just the nature of (Ser). Indeed, if one attempted to apply (Ser) before any other rule, one would launch oneself into an infinite tree—even if the initial list is unsatisfiable! (Hence, another rule of thumb: Apply (Ser) only after all other available moves have been made!)

That said, not all is gloomy. The method of "climbing" still affords an easy (albeit infinite) counterexample to $\Box p$. An examination of the tree reveals the following $\mathcal{L}_{K}^{ser}$-counterexample to $\Box p$ generated by the usual steps:

$$\begin{aligned} \mathcal{W} &= \{w_0, w_1, w_2, w_3, \ldots\} \\ \mathcal{R} &= \{\langle w_0, w_1\rangle, \langle w_1, w_2\rangle, \langle w_2, w_3\rangle, \ldots\} \\ \nu_{w_i}(p) &= 0, \text{ for any } i \in \mathbb{N}, \end{aligned}$$

This counterexample[32] can also be represented diagrammatically as follows, where (in the current context) '$A, w_i \longrightarrow A, w_j$' indicates that w_i has access to w_j (i.e., that $\langle w_i, w_j\rangle \in \mathcal{R}$), and '$A^{[0]}, w_i$' indicates that A is false at w_i:

$$p^{[0]}, w_0 \longrightarrow p^{[0]}, w_1 \longrightarrow p^{[0]}, w_3 \longrightarrow p^{[0]}, w_4 \longrightarrow \ldots$$

So, infinite tableaux still reveal counterexamples; it is just that the revelation takes longer. That said, sometimes matters are quite difficult, and one soon learns that the "method of conjecture" is often one's best recourse in trying to find counterexamples in D (or other systems affording infinite tableaux). Indeed, with respect to $\Box p$ simple reflection, rather than D-tableaux, yields a quick and *finite* counterexample: falsifying $\Box p$ at a world w_i requires only a w_i-accessible world at which p is false; and to ensure

[32]Note that, as per the climbing method, $\nu_{w_0}(p)$ may be either 0 or 1.

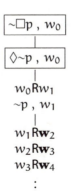

that our model is an $\mathcal{L}_K^{ser}$-model we need only ensure that every world accesses some world. As is easy to verify the following *finite* counterexample does the trick:

$$\begin{aligned} \mathcal{W} &= \{w_0\} \\ \mathcal{R} &= \{\langle w_0, w_0 \rangle\} \\ v_{w_0}(p) &= 0 \end{aligned}$$

In this model every world (viz., w_0) accesses some world; so, the model is serial. Moreover, p is false at some w_0-accessible world (viz., w_0), in which case $\Box p$ is false at w_0.

TABLEAUX FOR S4

Normal modal logic S4 corresponds in the by now familiar way to $\mathcal{L}_K^{rt}$. The official rules for S4-tableaux comprise all T-rules (and conventions) and the following rule governing R, namely *Transitivity* [abbreviated '(Trans)']:

$$\begin{array}{c} w_i R w_j \\ w_j R w_k \\ | \\ w_i R w_k \end{array}$$

This rule is intended to mirror the transitivity of $\mathcal{R}$ in $\mathcal{L}_K^{rt}$. In effect, the rule instructs one to write '$w_i R w_k$' on any (open) branch on which both '$w_i R w_j$' and '$w_j R w_k$' occur. Adding (only) this rule to T (or, equivalently, adding only Transitivity and Reflexivity to K) yields S4, which is sound and complete with respect to $\mathcal{L}_K^{rt}$.

We note that the "danger" of infinite tableaux arises in S4. The culprit in this system is not (Ser); it is (in effect) the combination of Diamond (Pos), Box (Pos), (Ref), and (Trans). This is brought out in exercises (page 81, exercises 5.6.1).

TABLEAUX FOR S5

The most famous and, in a sense, simplest normal modal logic is S5, which corresponds equally to language $\mathcal{L}_K^{rst}$ and $\mathcal{L}_{UA}$. The official rules for S5-tableaux comprise all S4-rules (and conventions) and the following rule governing R, namely *Symmetry* [abbreviated '(Sym)']:

$$\begin{array}{c} w_i R w_j \\ | \\ w_j R w_i \end{array}$$

This rule is intended to mirror the symmetry of $\mathcal{R}$ in $\mathcal{L}_K^{rst}$. In effect, the rule instructs one to write '$w_j R w_i$' on any open branch on which '$w_i R w_j$'

occurs. Adding only this rule to S4 yields S5, which is sound and complete with respect to $\mathcal{L}_{\mathsf{K}}^{rst}$.

We note that UA-tableaux rules, which inductively define the logical consequence relation $\vdash_{\mathsf{UA}}$, provide an equivalent tableaux system.[33] The official rules for UA comprise all *extensional* K-rules (and conventions), Diamond (Neg), Box (Neg), and the following versions of Diamond (Pos) and Box (Pos):

$$\frac{\boxed{\Diamond A\,,w_i}}{A\,,\mathbf{w}_j} \qquad\qquad \frac{\begin{array}{c}\Box A\,,w_i\\ \ldots w_j \ldots\end{array}}{A\,,w_j}$$

These rules replace the K-versions of Box (Pos) and Diamond (Neg); they are intended to mirror the "universal access relation" enjoyed in $\mathcal{L}_{\mathsf{UA}}$. The Diamond rule instructs one to write '$A\,,\mathbf{w}_j$' (new name 'w_j') on any (open) branch in which '$\Diamond A\,,w_i$' occurs. The Box rule instructs one to write '$A\,,w_j$' on any (open) branch in which '$\Box A\,,w_i$' occurs, for *any* j such that 'w_j' occurs on the branch. Adding these rules, in addition to Box (Neg) and Diamond (Neg), to the extensional K-rules yields UA, which is sound and complete with respect to $\mathcal{L}_{\mathsf{K}}^{rst}$.

EXERCISES 5.6.1

1 For each of the following specify the canvassed tableaux system(s) in which it is (proof-theoretically) valid. [Hint: In the absence of tell-tale signs of a "higher" system a good strategy is to begin at K and see what is required to close the tableau.]

1. $\Diamond(p \vee q) \supset (\Diamond p \vee \Diamond q)$
2. $(\Box p \vee \Box q) \equiv \Box(\Box p \vee \Box q)$
3. $\sim\Diamond\sim p \supset (q \vee \Box p)$
4. $\Box(\Box(p \equiv q) \supset r) \supset (\Box(p \equiv q) \supset \Box r)$
5. $\Diamond(p \supset q) \equiv (\Box p \supset \Diamond q)$
6. $\Box\sim p \supset \Box(p \supset q)$
7. $\Diamond p \supset \Diamond\Diamond p$
8. $\Box\sim p \supset \Box(p \supset \sim q)$
9. $(\Box p \wedge (p \supset q)) \supset q$
10. $(\Box(p \supset q) \wedge \sim q) \supset \sim p$

[33]That is: anything that is proof-theoretically valid in S5 is proof-theoretically valid in UA and vice versa.

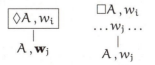

11. $(\Box p \wedge p) \supset \Diamond p$

2 With respect to the following sentences:

$$\sim(\Box\Diamond p \supset \Diamond\Box p) \tag{5.9}$$

$$\sim(\Diamond p \supset \Diamond\Box p) \tag{5.10}$$

1. Construct an S4-tableau with initial list comprising only (5.9). Do the same for (5.10). (Your tableaux, if done correctly, will be infinite.)
2. Use your tableaux to give infinite $\mathcal{L}_K^{rt}$-counterexamples to $(\Box\Diamond p \supset \Diamond\Box p)$ and $(\Diamond p \supset \Diamond\Box p)$.
3. Give *finite* $\mathcal{L}_K^{rt}$-counterexamples to $(\Box\Diamond p \supset \Diamond\Box p)$ and $(\Diamond p \supset \Diamond\Box p)$.
4. Where the initial list of an S5-tableau comprises only (5.9), is the tableau infinite? (What about the case involving (5.10)?)

3 Prove each of the following in the modal logic of your choice but indicate why you did not choose a weaker logic:

1. $\Diamond\Box{\sim}A \supset {\sim}\Box\Diamond A$
2. ${\sim}\Diamond(A \vee B) \supset ({\sim}\Diamond A \wedge {\sim}\Diamond B)$
3. $\Diamond(A \vee B) \supset (\Diamond A \vee \Diamond B)$
4. $\Box A \supset (\Diamond B \supset \Diamond(A \wedge B))$
5. $\Diamond A \supset \Diamond\Diamond A$
6. $\Diamond\Box\Diamond A \supset \Diamond A$
7. $\Box(A \vee \Box B) \supset (\Box A \vee \Box B)$
8. $(\Diamond A \wedge \Box B) \supset \Diamond(A \wedge \Box B)$
9. $A \supset \Box\Diamond A$
10. $\Box\Diamond A \supset A$

4 In modal models certain argument forms are valid precisely if the access relation has certain properties. Discuss the relationship between the following properties of $\mathcal{R}$ in $\mathcal{M} = \langle \mathcal{W}, \mathcal{R}, v \rangle$ and the listed "axioms".

» DIRECTEDNESS: $\mathcal{R}$ is *directed* just in case if $w\mathcal{R}u$ and $w\mathcal{R}t$ then there is a world z such that $u\mathcal{R}z$ and $t\mathcal{R}z$, for all worlds w, u, t.

» TRANSITIVITY: $\mathcal{R}$ is *transitive* just in case if $w\mathcal{R}u$ and $u\mathcal{R}t$ then $w\mathcal{R}t$, for all worlds w, u, t.

» ENDPOINT EXISTENCE: $\mathcal{R}$ *has endpoints* iff for every world w there is a world u such that $w\mathcal{R}u$ and, for all worlds t, if $u\mathcal{R}t$ then $u = t$.

(Can you give examples of relations that have the first or third property so as to illustrate why these names are appropriate?)

» GEACH AXIOM: If $\Diamond\Box A$ then $\Box\Diamond A$. (If it is possible that A is necessary then A is necessarily possible.)

» MCKINSEY AXIOM: If $\Box\Diamond A$ then $\Diamond\Box A$. (If A is necessarily possible then it is possible that A is necessary.)

5 Define '$A \dashv B$' to mean $\Box(A \supset B)$ and '$A \dashv B$' to mean $(A \dashv B) \wedge (B \dashv A)$, and read these as expressing the relations of *strict implication* and *strict equivalence*, respectively.

1. In CPL we can prove that for any three sentences, at least two must be materially equivalent. Show that in the canvassed normal modal logics, it cannot be proved that for any n sentences at least $n - 1$ must be strictly equivalent.
2. Suppose that a rule or axiom to the following effect were added to K: that for any 5 sentences at least 4 must be strictly equivalent. What sort of condition on the access relation or set of worlds might this imply or require?

6 Let us define a new language, called $\mathcal{L}_K^t$, which is defined only over *transitive* $\mathcal{L}_K$-models. (The logical system for this language is standardly called 'K4'.) In turn, let us define a K^t-tableaux system by retaining all K-rules and conventions and adding only the rule *Transitivity* (Tran).

1. Is $\mathcal{L}_K^{rt}$ an extension of $\mathcal{L}_K^t$? – a proper extension?
2. Is $\mathcal{L}_K^t$ an extension of $\mathcal{L}_K^{rt}$? – a proper extension?
3. Is $\Box A \supset \Box\Box A$ logically true in $\mathcal{L}_K^t$? (If so, prove it! If not, prove that!)
4. Prove that $\Diamond\Diamond A$ is not logically true—that is, that not every instance is logically true—in either $\mathcal{L}_K^{rt}$ or $\mathcal{L}_K^t$.
5. Use a K^t-tableau to test whether $(\Diamond p \supset \Diamond\Box p)$ is logically true in $\mathcal{L}_K^t$. [Proceed to use the method to construct an infinite counterexample. (Your tableau, if done correctly, will be infinite.)]

FURTHER READING

In addition to Kripke's papers mentioned above, useful textbooks include Chellas' [20], Rod Girle's [37], Hughes and Cresswell's [51], and Priest's [79]. A more advanced discussion, in addition to many classic references, may be found in Bull and Segerberg's [17].

"Contrariwise", continued Tweedledee,
"if it was so, it might be;
and if it were so, it would be;
but as it isn't, it ain't.
That's logic."
– Lewis Carrol, *Through the Looking Glass*

Chapter 6
Variations on a Theme

Variations of normal modal logic may be capable of representing complex intricacies of our modal discourse. When C. I. Lewis formulated the first series of modern modal logics, his S4 and S5 were so named because they followed his S1–S3, none of which we can accommodate with just the resources of the preceding chapter. Much of Lewis' motivation pertained to the difficulties of capturing the role or roles of 'if... then' in natural language—a motive shared by quite a few other writers in philosophical logic. We shall touch on some of the variations of normal modal logic, including Lewis' own S2, which is a *non-normal* modal logic, and also the quite distinct logic of "counterfactual" conditionals and intuitionistic logic.

6.1 Non-Normal Modal Logic

In Chapter 5 we presented various normal modal languages each of which is an extension of the basic language $\mathcal{L}_K$. In this section we discuss languages of which $\mathcal{L}_K$ is a proper extension: non-normal languages.[1]

A useful way to think of the relation between normal languages and the non-normal ones discussed here is in terms of logical truths. Let $\mathcal{T}_\mathcal{L}$ comprise the logical truths of $\mathcal{L}$ and $\mathcal{T}_{\mathcal{L}'}$ the logical truths of $\mathcal{L}'$, where $\mathcal{L}$ and $\mathcal{L}'$ share a common syntax. Then $\mathcal{L}$ is *weaker* than $\mathcal{L}'$ iff $\mathcal{T}_\mathcal{L} \subset \mathcal{T}_{\mathcal{L}'}$. On this way of talking each of the (non-normal) languages discussed in this chapter is weaker than $\mathcal{L}_K$ and, hence, weaker than all its extensions.

Much of the groundwork for the target non-normal languages was laid in the previous chapter, and so our presentation will be somewhat swifter. Still, we pause from the start to give some (slightly non-standard) philosophical motivation for the target languages.[2]

[1] We shall say that any modal language (or logic) which is not an extension of $\mathcal{L}_K$ (or its underlying logic) is a non-normal language (logic). While $\mathcal{L}_K$ is a proper extension of each non-normal language canvassed in this chapter, there are also non-normal languages (logics) of which $\mathcal{L}_K$ is not an extension.

[2] We should emphasize that the following motivation is not historically accurate, as non-normal semantics were originally created as a mere technical device for giving world-semantics

ON WAYS THINGS COULDN'T BE

There are many ways our world could have been, including the way our world actually is: The Red Sox could have retained Babe Ruth; Fermat's last theorem could have remained without (known) proof; and kangaroos could've been called 'Tasmanian devils'. If talk of such "ways" provides grounds for talk of possible worlds, then perhaps such talk likewise provides grounds for talk of *im*possible worlds.

Are there *ways things could not be*? Suppose, as many philosophers do, that English sentences of the form $\sim A \vee A$ are logically true.[3] Presumably, every logical truth is necessarily true, in which case, letting the box represent (alethic) necessity, $\Box(\sim A \vee A)$ is true (at our actual world). The question is: Could $\Box(\sim A \vee A)$ be false? Presumably not. Any way of falsifying $\Box(\sim A \vee A)$ is a way things could *not* be—assuming, as we are, that $\sim A \vee A$ is necessarily true.

Another example: Suppose that *every* sentence were possible. "That couldn't be!", one is likely to say. And, indeed, standard thinking agrees. Letting the diamond represent (alethic) possibility, if *everything* were possible then $\Diamond A$ would be true for all sentences A, including $(p \wedge \sim p)$! So, one way things couldn't be is one in which $\Diamond A$ is true for all A.

Notice that if you were going along with this last bit of reasoning (without unbearable intellectual strain) then you were in fact supposing something impossible. If you thought 'if all things were possible then it would be possible that $p \wedge \sim p$', then you were in fact reasoning from an impossible antecedent. So, you can reason about ways that things couldn't be![4] The idea, then, is that "ways" talk goes both ways (as it were): If *ways things could be* represent possible worlds, then *ways things couldn't be* represent *im*possible worlds, the latter being "entities" of a recalcitrant bent, including some where (alethic) diamond claims are one and all true while (alethic) box claims are one and all false.

The question, for now, concerns the effect of taking such recalcitrant "ways" seriously in our semantics for modal propositional languages. The answer, of course, depends on how the semantics are constructed. In this chapter we shall present a standard way of incorporating "impossible worlds" due to Kripke [61]. They will be impossible worlds of the very simple sort that we just discussed; they are unlike the possible worlds only in that *all* claims of necessity are false there and all possibility claims true. Kripke called such "worlds" *non-normal worlds*, and we shall follow suit.

---

for so-called Lewis logics weaker than S4.

[3]Whether this principle, traditionally called *Excluded Middle*, is logically true is controversial. In subsequent chapters we shall discuss languages in which it fails.

[4]While this does not establish that there really are such entities as *ways things couldn't be*, it shows that this sort of discourse does have its own logic; some reasoning in it is correct and some incorrect.

SYNTAX

The syntax of each non-normal modal language is the same as in the normal languages, namely S_{mpl}. (See §5.2.) The difference emerges at the semantic level, to which we now turn. We shall discuss a language we call '$\mathcal{L}_{NN}$'. A *non-normal modal language* is an extension of $\mathcal{L}_{NN}$.

BASIC NON-NORMAL SEMANTICS

$\mathcal{L}_{NN}$ interprets S_{mpl} by way of a structure, $\langle \mathcal{W}, \mathcal{N}, \mathcal{R}, \nu \rangle$, where $\mathcal{W}$, $\mathcal{R}$ and ν are as per normal modal logic (see §5.3) and $\mathcal{N} \subseteq \mathcal{W}$ (with $\mathcal{N} \neq \emptyset$). Intuitively, $\mathcal{N}$ comprises "normal worlds" and $\mathcal{W} - \mathcal{N}$ comprises "non-normal worlds". As with normal languages, ν assigns a truth value to each sentence at each world (including non-normal worlds, if there are any).

$\mathcal{L}_{NN}$-models are simply structures of the sort above. The chief difference between normal and non-normal models arises with modal sentences (box- and diamond-sentences) at *non-normal worlds*: at any non-normal world every box-sentence is false and every diamond sentence true. We call a model $\mathcal{M} = \langle \mathcal{W}, \mathcal{N}, \mathcal{R}, \nu \rangle$ *normal* if $\mathcal{W} - \mathcal{N}$ is empty, and *non-normal* otherwise. We require of an $\mathcal{L}_{NN}$-model that

» ν obeys the clauses in §5.3 (page 56), if $w \in \mathcal{N}$

» If $w \in \mathcal{W} - \mathcal{N}$, then ν obeys the clauses in §5.3 for all *extensional* connectives and, with respect to the modal operators, is such that $\nu_w(\Box A) = 0$ and $\nu_w(\Diamond A) = 1$.

We note that, as in normal modal languages, $\sim\Box A$ and $\Diamond\sim A$ are equivalent in $\mathcal{L}_{NN}$, as are $\sim\Diamond A$ and $\Box\sim A$. That these equivalences hold may be shown along previous lines. (We leave the proofs as exercises.)

SEMANTIC PROPERTIES AND RELATIONS

Admissible valuations of $\mathcal{L}_{NN}$ are the functions ν_w defined by

$$\nu_w(A) = \nu(w, A)$$

where $w \in \mathcal{N}$ with model $\mathcal{M} = \langle \mathcal{W}, \mathcal{N}, \mathcal{R}, \nu \rangle$. We count only the *normal* worlds in specifying the admissible valuations; hence, where A is an $\mathcal{L}_{NN}$-sentence, $\mathcal{X}$ a set of such sentences, and $\mathcal{M}$ any $\mathcal{L}_{NN}$-model,

» A is a *consequence* of $\mathcal{X}$ in $\mathcal{L}_{NN}$ (abbreviated: $\mathcal{X} \Vdash_{NN} A$) iff for any *normal* world w, $\mathcal{M}$ satisfies A at w if $\mathcal{M}$ satisfies $\mathcal{X}$ at w.

» A is a *valid sentence* in $\mathcal{L}_{NN}$ iff $\emptyset \Vdash_{NN} A$.

In other words, logical truth in $\mathcal{L}_{NN}$ is truth-preservation over all normal worlds of all non-normal models.

COUNTEREXAMPLES

Given the definition of *validity* and *consequence* in $\mathcal{L}_{NN}$, and in particular the restriction to normal worlds, counterexamples are likewise restricted to normal worlds. In particular, a *counterexample* to A in $\mathcal{L}_{NN}$ is an $\mathcal{L}_{NN}$-model in which $v_w(A) = 0$, for some $w \in \mathcal{N}$.

By way of example consider the sentence

$$\Box(A \supset \Box({\sim}B \vee B)) \tag{6.1}$$

That $\nVdash_{NN} \Box(A \supset \Box({\sim}B \vee B))$ is shown by the counterexample:

$$\begin{aligned} \mathcal{W} &= \{w_0, w_1\} \\ \mathcal{N} &= \{w_0\} \\ \mathcal{R} &= \{\langle w_0, w_1 \rangle\} \\ v_{w_1}(A) &= 1 \end{aligned}$$

In this case there are exactly two worlds, one being normal (viz., w_0) and the other non-normal. Since w_1 is non-normal, $\Box({\sim}B \vee B)$ is false at w_1. Given that A is true at w_1, $A \supset \Box({\sim}B \vee B)$ is false at w_1. Hence, there is some w_0-accessible world (viz., w_1) at which $A \supset \Box({\sim}B \vee B)$ is false, in which case (6.1) is false at w_0 and, so, false at a *normal* world. This serves as an $\mathcal{L}_{NN}$-counterexample to (6.1).[5]

NECESSITATION AND NON-NORMALITY

Before turning to the other target languages we pause to note one more feature of non-normality. Non-normal worlds, as above, are recalcitrant: they treat every box-sentence as false. As we discussed at the outset, such worlds may be called 'impossible worlds'. The "recalcitrance" of non-normal worlds is especially apparent in the failure of *the rule of necessitation* (sometimes 'Necessitation'), which holds in all normal modal languages:

» NECESSITATION: If $\Vdash_{\mathcal{L}} A$ then $\Vdash_{\mathcal{L}} \Box A$

This principle is true for all *normal* $\mathcal{L}$ but false for any non-normal $\mathcal{L}$.[6] Take each claim in turn:

» NORMAL: Suppose that $\Vdash_{\mathcal{L}} A$, for any normal $\mathcal{L}$. Then A is true at all worlds of all $\mathcal{L}$-models, in which case A is true at every w-accessible world of every $\mathcal{L}$-model, for any $w \in \mathcal{W}$. But, then, by normal clauses for box-sentences, $\Box A$ is true at all worlds of all normal models.

---

[5] We have left $v_{w_0}(A)$ and $v_{w_0}(B)$ unspecified given that either value (i.e., 1 or 0) will do the trick in each case.

[6] Similarly, the following principle is likewise correct in normal modal *logical systems* but fails in the non-normal ones: If $\vdash A$ then $\vdash \Box A$. This principle is also called the *rule of necessitation*.

» Non-normal: Let A be any tautology of $\mathcal{L}_{\mathsf{CPL}}$. Then A is true at all worlds of any non-normal model, in which case A is true at all normal worlds of any non-normal model, and hence $\Box$A is true at all normal worlds of any non-normal model; hence, $\Vdash_{\mathcal{L}} \Box A$, for any non-normal $\mathcal{L}$. To show that $\nVdash_{\mathcal{L}} \Box\Box A$ for all *non-normal* $\mathcal{L}$ it suffices to have a model in which $\Box\Box$A is false at some *normal* world w. This may be done by letting w access a non-normal world.

The failure of Necessitation is perhaps the most striking feature of the non-normal semantics we are discussing. What to make of this failure is something that we leave to the reader's reflection.

Amending $\mathcal{R}$

Not every $\mathcal{L}_{\mathsf{NN}}$-model contains non-normal worlds. For example, let $\mathcal{W} = \mathcal{N}$, in which case there are no non-normal worlds; indeed, we have a normal model. What sort of normal model? The answer depends on properties of $\mathcal{R}$. In particular, if $\mathcal{W} = \mathcal{N}$ and there are no restrictions imposed on $\mathcal{R}$, then we have an $\mathcal{L}_{\mathsf{K}}$-model; and if $\mathcal{W} = \mathcal{N}$ and $\mathcal{R}$ is reflexive, then we have an $\mathcal{L}_{\mathsf{K}}^{\mathsf{r}}$-model; and so on. Accordingly, normal models can be regarded as special cases of non-normal models, and all admissible $\mathcal{L}_{\mathsf{K}}$-valuations are admissible $\mathcal{L}_{\mathsf{NN}}$-valuations. Thus, the fact that normal models are special cases of non-normal models yields an immediate result with respect to $\mathcal{L}_{\mathsf{NN}}$ and $\mathcal{L}_{\mathsf{K}}$: the latter is an extension of the former. After all, if A is true at all normal worlds of all *non-normal* models (i.e., $\Vdash_{\mathsf{NN}} A$), then *a fortiori* A is true at all worlds of all normal models, which, as in §5, means that $\Vdash_{\mathsf{K}} A$.

While $\mathcal{L}_{\mathsf{K}}$ is an extension of $\mathcal{L}_{\mathsf{NN}}$ the converse does not hold; this follows from the fact that (6.1) is logically true in the former but not the latter. (That (6.1) is logically true in $\mathcal{L}_{\mathsf{K}}$ is left as an exercise.) Hence, $\mathcal{L}_{\mathsf{K}}$ is a *proper* extension of $\mathcal{L}_{\mathsf{NN}}$.

Given that every normal modal language is an extension of $\mathcal{L}_{\mathsf{K}}$, it follows from above that every such language is an extension of $\mathcal{L}_{\mathsf{NN}}$, and since $\mathcal{L}_{\mathsf{K}}$ is a proper extension of $\mathcal{L}_{\mathsf{NN}}$, it follows that each normal language is likewise a *proper* extension of $\mathcal{L}_{\mathsf{NN}}$.

Different non-normal languages may be constructed by amending $\mathcal{R}$ along familiar lines. For present purposes we briefly mention one, which corresponds to one of the various so-called *Lewis logics* (after C.I. Lewis).

The Language $\mathcal{L}_{\mathsf{NN}}^{\mathsf{r}}$

We achieve the language $\mathcal{L}_{\mathsf{NN}}^{\mathsf{r}}$ by amending $\mathcal{R}$. Specifically, we define admissible $\mathcal{L}_{\mathsf{NN}}^{\mathsf{r}}$-models to be all and only *reflexive* $\mathcal{L}_{\mathsf{NN}}$-models. 'S2' is the standard name for the corresponding logical system.

Why might one impose this restriction? One fairly obvious motivation is at hand: namely, the "intuition" that *strict material modus ponens* ought to hold:

$$A, \Box(A \supset B) \Vdash B \qquad\qquad (6.2)$$

Reading the box in (6.2) as *alethic* modality (necessity), the "intuition" is just this: that if A is true at w and $(A \supset B)$ is true at all (w-accessible) worlds, then B ought to be true at w. If one has this "intuition" then $\mathcal{L}_{NN}$ will appear to be inadequate, at least as a language for alethic modality; the reason is that (6.2) is not valid in $\mathcal{L}_{NN}$. (See exercises below.) What is required, as in the corresponding normal case (viz., $\mathcal{L}_K$), is reflexivity. With this constraint material modus ponens is valid: If A is true at w, $A \supset B$ is true at all (w-accessible) worlds, *and* $\langle w, w \rangle \in \mathcal{R}$, then B is true at w.

We note that $\mathcal{L}_K^r$ is an extension of $\mathcal{L}_{NN}^r$ and, as above, it is a proper extension given, for example, (6.1), which holds in $\mathcal{L}_K$ and therefore in $\mathcal{L}_K^r$. We also note that the characteristic $\mathcal{L}_K^r$ sentence is logically true in $\mathcal{L}_{NN}^r$. The proof is left as exercise.

Tableaux

Tableaux procedures for non-normal logics may be constructed in the pattern of our previous (normal) modal tableaux; the big difference concerns Dia (Pos). We leave the construction of such tableaux to the interested reader.

Exercises 6.1.1

1 Prove the validity of (6.2), of the characteristic $\mathcal{L}_K^r$ sentence, and of the characteristic $\mathcal{L}_K$ sentence in $\mathcal{L}_{NN}^r$. Are they valid in $\mathcal{L}_{NN}$?

2 Prove the validity of $\Box(A \vee \sim A) \vee \Diamond(A \wedge \sim A)$ in $\mathcal{L}_{NN}$ or provide a counterexample.

3 Prove the validity in $\mathcal{L}_{NN}^r$ of

  » Becker's Rule: $\Box(\Box A \supset \Box B)$ is valid if $\Box(A \supset B)$ is valid.

4 Prove the validity in $\mathcal{L}_{NN}^r$ of Lewis' original

  » Consistency Postulate: $\Diamond(A \wedge B) \supset \Diamond A$.

5 What is the effect of defining validity in terms of truth-preservation over *all* worlds of (say) all $\mathcal{L}_{NN}^r$-models. (Hint: $\mathcal{L}_{NN}^r$ will be an extension of your new language, and similarly for the corresponding logical system. Why?)

6.2   Paradoxes of Material Implication

C.I. Lewis [62, 63, 64] marks the beginning of modern modal logic. Lewis was not chiefly concerned with modeling necessity or any of the other modal notions discussed in §5; his chief concern centered on *conditionals*.[7] Specifically, Lewis recognized an *implicative* conditional, one that purports to express logical implication. On one hand, Lewis acknowledged a "weak" sense of 'implies' which, he thought, is expressed by the material conditional (the hook) formulated in the pioneering work of Russell and Whitehead [105]. On the other hand, Lewis thought that the material conditional was too weak to express 'implies' in the strong, logical sense; the hook, Lewis thought, fails to accurately model 'If...then...' in the strong, logical sense.[8] What bothered Lewis are the so-called *paradoxes of material implication*, some of which are:

1. $A \supset (B \supset A)$
2. $\sim A \supset (A \supset B)$
3. $(A \supset B) \vee (B \supset A)$

Reading (1)–(3) in terms of (logical) implication, which was Lewis' target reading, we get, respectively:

» A true statement is implied by *any* statement.

» A false statement implies *any* statement.

» For any two statements, one of them implies the other.

These claims were at odds with Lewis' pretheoretic "intuitions" about logical implicative conditionals.[9]

Lewis' proposed cure for the dissatisfaction was *the strict conditional*, which Lewis represented as $\prec$ (sometimes called *the fishhook*). Lewis introduced the fishhook as a new primitive; however, given S_{mpl} we may introduce it as a defined connective in terms of the box:

» DEFINITION: $A \prec B$ stands for $\Box(A \supset B)$

Each of (1)–(3) fails to be logically true in $\mathcal{L}_K^{rst}$ when the hook is replaced by its "intensional" big brother, the fishhook. One way of seeing this is via S5-tableaux. We leave the tableaux to the reader; however, here is a

7Lewis's preferred logic of (alethic) modality is S2. It was an effort to provide world-semantics for the Lewis logics weaker than S4 that led Kripke [61] to the construction of non-normal languages (and their various non-normal worlds).

8Whether there *is* any such strong, logical implicative sense of 'If...then...' has been challenged by some philosophers. A useful discussion of the issues may be found in Anderson and Belnap's [1].

9Lewis was not alone in such dissatisfaction. As Hughes and Cresswell note [51], Hugh MacColl voiced similar dissatisfaction.

counterexample to $A \multimap (B \multimap A)$: the sentence $p \multimap (q \multimap p)$ is false at w_1.

$$\begin{aligned} \mathcal{W} &= \{w_1, w_2\} \\ \mathcal{R} &= \mathcal{W} \times \mathcal{W} \\ \nu_{w_1}(p) &= 1 \\ \nu_{w_2}(q) &= 1 \\ \nu_{w_2}(p) &= 0 \end{aligned}$$

Similar counterexamples may be given for (2)–(3). (These are left as exercise.) What is important to recall is that $\mathcal{L}_K^{rst}$ is an extension of every canvassed (normal and non-normal) language; hence, since (1)–(3) fail to be logically true in $\mathcal{L}_K^{rst}$ they thereby fail to be logically true in the weaker languages. This is as Lewis wanted.

Lewis' strict implication (the fishhook) resolves the initial "paradoxes" of the material conditional; however, some [1, 2] have argued that it leaves residual problems. For example, let $\perp$ be any necessary falsehood—false at all worlds. Then

4. $\perp \multimap B$

is valid in $\mathcal{L}_{NN}$ and, hence, in all of its extensions (viz., all the modal languages we have canvassed). The apparent problem here is that "intuitively" it seems incorrect to say that *any* statement is implied by *any* necessary falsehood. For example, in the target sense of 'implies', *that 2+2=5* does not imply *that the Red Sox will win the World Series.*[10] When properly understood (the thinking goes) an implicative conditional is true only if there is some connection—often called 'relevance'—between antecedent and consequent.

(4), among others, is what is known as a *paradox of strict implication*. Such "paradoxes" gave rise to what is called *relevance logic* (or, in Australasia, *relevant logic*). We will not dwell on these "paradoxes" at this stage; however, we will return to relevance logic in later chapters.

EXERCISES 6.2.1

1 Specify $\mathcal{L}_K^{rst}$-counterexamples to the fishhook versions of (2) and (3) of §6.2 (page 91). Infer that each is invalid in the languages of which $\mathcal{L}_K^{rst}$ is an extension.

2 Show that, where $\perp$ is any unsatisfiable sentence, $\perp \multimap B$ is logically true in $\mathcal{L}_{NN}$, for any B. Infer that the schema is valid for all (canvassed) normal and non-normal languages.

[10] We assume with most philosophers that mathematical claims are necessarily false if false. (Different examples may be given should this assumption need to be rejected.)

3 Prove the following for the fishhook in $\mathcal{L}_K$.

» $A \multimap B \Vdash (A \wedge C) \multimap B$

» $A \multimap B, B \multimap C \Vdash A \multimap C$

» $\Vdash A \multimap (B \vee \sim B)$

6.3 Logic of Conditionals

Other apparent problems face the hook and fishhook if they are taken to symbolize indicative or subjunctive conditionals in English. As one may easily check (exercise) the following claims are true:

» $A \supset B \Vdash_{CPL} (A \wedge C) \supset B$

» $A \supset B, B \supset C \Vdash_{CPL} A \supset C$

The former is standardly called *Antecedent Strengthening* (sometimes *Weakening* because strengthening the antecedent weakens the conditional as a whole) and the latter *Transitivity*. The fishhook-versions of Antecedent Strengthening and Transitivity also hold in $\mathcal{L}_{NN}$. Accordingly, Antecedent Strengthening and Transitivity hold for all of the canvassed modal languages.

The apparent trouble with Antecedent Strengthening and Transitivity is that they seem *not* to hold for various conditionals in English.[11] Consider, for example, the following inferences:

a. *Antecedent Strengthening*:

i. If the Red Sox have the best record at the end of the regular season, then the Red Sox will be in the playoffs.

i. Therefore, if the Red Sox have the best record at the end of the regular season *and* the playoffs are cancelled (due to strike), then the Red Sox will be in the playoffs.

b. *Transitivity*:

i. If the Red Sox win, their opponents will be upset.

ii. If their opponents try to lose and succeed, the Red Sox will win.

iii. Hence, if the opponents try to lose and succeed, they will be upset.

If the given conditionals are modeled by the hooks ($\supset$ or $\multimap$) then they are valid, but "intuitively" they are not valid, as they go from true (or at least possibly true) premises to false conclusions.[12]

[11]We give well-known examples of indicative conditionals below, but so-called subjunctive or counterfactual conditionals also provide many examples.

[12]Nelson Goodman [39, Ch. 1].

Ceteris Paribus CONDITIONALS

Responses to the inferences of §6.3 often invoke a hidden *ceteris paribus* clause, which is Latin for 'other things being equal'. The idea is that premise (a.i), for example, is elliptical for a longer conditional:

a.i′ If the Red Sox have the best record at the end of the regular season *and* there is no strike *and* . . . , then the Red Sox will be in the playoffs.

What fills the ellipsis in (a.i′) is a long conjunction of other relevant conditions determined (in part) by the circumstances (or world) in which (a.i) is asserted and the antecedent of (a.i). What are those other relevant conditions? All we know about them is that they are conditions that hold in this world, but are in general not nearly all that is true there. For example, if the antecedent is not true then that fact is not included. But this is enough to show that the conditional in question has a strict conditional (represented by our fishhook) as counterpart:

> There is a certain true proposition p such that the antecedent of (a.i) conjoined with p strictly implies the consequent of (a.i).

We can now see that modus ponens holds for this conditional; for in any world in which the antecedent is also true, as well as that certain proposition p, the consequent will be true.

Logic of Conditionals, due originally to Robert Stalnaker [93] and David Lewis [65], arose in response to the problems raised by Antecedent Strengthening and (among others) Transitivity. In Part IV we will discuss some of the conditional logics and languages. For now, we pause only to note that not all familiar principles go by the wayside in (standard) conditional logic. While Transitivity and (among others) Antecedent Strengthening are rejected, two minimal constraints on a genuine conditional remain (where $\Rightarrow$ is our "ceteris paribus conditional"):

» *Modus Ponens.* $A, A \Rightarrow B \Vdash B$.

» *Weak Conditional Proof.* If $A \Vdash B$, then $C \Rightarrow A \Vdash C \Rightarrow B$.

EXERCISES 6.3.1

1 Relying on the "ceteris paribus" reading of the conditional, demonstrate (informally) that the principles of Modus Ponens and Weak Conditional Proof must hold.

2 How crucial to your reasoning above is the assumption that the content of the "certeris paribus" (the factors that are being held constant or assumed "equal") depends only on the antecedent of the conditional and the actual world? Could it depend on other factors in normal or everyday discourse?

6.4 INTUITIONISTIC LOGIC

Intuitionistic logic is historically tied to the philosophy of mathematics called 'intuitionism', initially developed by L.E.J. Brouwer [16]. After briefly motivating intuitionistic logic we turn to the language proper, followed by a suitable tableaux system. Our remarks about intuitionism rely mostly on Brouwer's student, Arend Heyting [46], although we do not attempt to stick closely to Heyting's position. As will quickly appear, both 'if...then' and 'not' have new and different roles in this logic.

TRUTH AS PROOF

A perennial source of philosophical curiosity is mathematics. According to mathematical realists, mathematical truths are "made true" by a mind-independent realm, in just the same way that common empirical truths are "made true" by the empirical world. Intuitionists reject this view of mathematical truth; they maintain that the truth of a mathematical statement consists in nothing more nor less than the existence of a proof—sometimes *construction*, *demonstration*—of the statement. Heyting maintains that the language of mathematics is best understood in terms of *proof conditions*, as opposed to the traditional *truth conditions*. Proofs, in this context, are "mental constructions" of some sort, where these, unlike the entities enjoyed by realists, are very much mind-dependent.

PROOF CONDITIONS

The proposed proof conditions specify what counts as a canonical proof of each sentence, assuming we know what counts as a proof of atomic sentences. The standard proof conditions, due to Heyting, run as follows, where, *nota bene*, $\perp$ is any unsatisfiable sentence—an "absurd sentence".

» A proof of $A \wedge B$ consists of a proof of A and a proof of B.

» A proof of $A \vee B$ consists of a proof of A or a proof of B.

» A proof of $A \supset B$ consists of a procedure for transforming any proof of A into a proof of B.

» A proof of $\sim A$ consists of a procedure for transforming any proof of A into a proof of $\perp$.

These informal proof conditions immediately motivate a salient departure from classical logic: namely, that some instances of $A \vee \sim A$ should fail to be "true" (fail to be verified), at least in as much as—at the current state of mathematical knowledge—not every instance of $A \vee \sim A$ has a proof. A standard example:

0. There is a sequence of twenty-two '5's in the decimal expansion of π.

As things currently stand, there is no proof of (o) and there is no proof of its negation. Hence, the disjunction of (o) and its negation has no proof (at least as things currently stand). Accordingly, $A \vee {\sim}A$ (Excluded Middle) should fail in intuitionistic logic—and it does, as will be clear below.[13]

Note well that negation is conceived of quite differently here. A proof of ${\sim}A$ is a proof that $A \supset \bot$, and the best way to understand ${\sim}A$ in intuitionistic logic is to think of it as $A \supset \bot$. That has an effect on double negation: ${\sim\sim}A$ amounts to $(A \supset \bot) \supset \bot$, and for the intuitionist that does not imply A. If it is quite impossible to prove that a supposition that A leads to absurdity, it may still also be quite impossible to prove that A.

Before turning to the language proper we pause to note what may already be evident: that while intuitionistic logic emerged within mathematics it is also naturally motivated by various philosophical accounts of truth. In particular, any account of truth according to which *truth is verification* motivates the logic. We leave this to the reader's reflection.

THE LANGUAGE $\mathcal{L}_I$

Heyting originally formulated intuitionistic logic as an axiom system; however, in keeping with the semantic slant of this book, we will present the *language of intuitionism* in terms of "possible worlds", following the work of Kripke [60], and present a suitable tableaux system, which falls out of the semantics. (We present an alternative formulation in Part IV.)

Syntax

The syntax of $\mathcal{L}_I$ is simply that of S_{cpl}, but there are significant differences in the semantics, to which we now turn.

Semantics

An $\mathcal{L}_I$*-model* is an $\mathcal{L}_K^{rt}$-structure, $\langle \mathcal{W}, \mathcal{R}, \nu \rangle$, where $\mathcal{R}$ is a reflexive, transitive binary relation on $\mathcal{W}$, and ν maps worlds and sentences of $\mathcal{L}_I$ into $\{1, 0\}$. The *admissible valuations* will once again be the functions $\nu_w(A)$ defined as before: ν_w *satisfies* A iff $\nu_w(A) = 1$.

At the formal level, the "nature" of $\mathcal{W}$'s elements is immaterial; however, in the current context it is useful to think of them as *stages of knowledge* or *stages of information*, and so we will let s, s', and s_i (for any $i \in \mathbb{N}$) be our "worlds", our elements of $\mathcal{W}$. Along this line, it is useful to think of $\mathcal{R}$ as the *possible development of knowledge* relation; that is, $\langle s, s' \rangle \in \mathcal{R}$ iff s' is a possible development (or extension) of s, where s and s' are stages of knowledge. From this angle, the reflexivity and transitivity of $\mathcal{R}$ are natural constraints: if s' is a possible development of what is known at stage s, and s'' is a possible development of what is known at stage s', then s'' is a possible development of what is known at stage s. Similarly for reflexivity:

[13] We may add that there may also be sentences such that neither they nor their negations are provable, even in principle.

for any stage of knowledge, s, it seems natural to say that s is a possible development of what is known at s, because what is actual is possible. In this case, it may be useful to think in dynamic terms: $\langle s, s' \rangle \in \mathcal{R}$ iff it is possible to "get to" stage s' from s, in which reflexivity seems eminently plausible.

Not only are reflexivity and transitivity motivated by the informal "possible stages of knowledge" metaphor but so too is the following so-called *heredity condition*:

$$\text{For all } \textit{atomic } A,\ v_{s'}(A) = 1 \text{ if } \langle s, s' \rangle \in \mathcal{R} \text{ and } v_s(A) = 1$$

If p is true at s, and s' is a possible development of the information at s, then p is true s'—nothing is lost or forgotten as time passes.[14]

MODELS: Heuristics in hand, we proceed to specify $\mathcal{L}_I$-models. An $\mathcal{L}_I$-model $\mathcal{M}$ is an $\mathcal{L}_K^{rt}$-structure such that

1. the heredity condition is satisfied; and
2. v is such that
   (a) $v_s(A \wedge B) = 1$ iff $v_s(A) = v_s(B) = 1$
   (b) $v_s(A \vee B) = 1$ iff $v_s(A) = 1$ or $v_s(B) = 1$
   (c) $v_s({\sim}A) = 1$ iff $v_{s'}(A) = 0$, for all s' s.t. $\langle s, s' \rangle \in \mathcal{R}$
   (d) $v_s(A \supset B) = 1$ iff $v_{s'}(A) = 0$ or $v_{s'}(B) = 1$, for all s' s.t. $\langle s, s' \rangle \in \mathcal{R}$.

Note that negation is now *intensional*; whether ${\sim}A$ is true at s depends not only on s but on what is happening elsewhere, so to speak. This is a significant departure from classical negation; the effect is that negation now behaves like a box-claim, quantifying over all (accessible) stages of knowledge, as it were.

With $\perp$ defined as $p \wedge {\sim}p$ for the first atomic sentence p, we note that $v_s(\perp) = 0$ for all s (since $\mathcal{R}$ is reflexive).

Not only negation but also the conditional is intensional in this language; in fact, the hook here plays the role of the fishhook discussed above. If the antecedent is false, the conditional can still be either true or false. Moreover, negation is clearly equated with the implication of "absurdity", as ${\sim}A$ is equivalent to $A \supset \perp$. At first sight disjunction is classical, for at any given stage of knowledge a disjunction is true iff one of its disjuncts is

[14] One might say that the "extending stages of knowledge" metaphor motivates a heredity condition for *all* elements of $\mathcal{S}$, not just the atomics. With an eye on simplifying the I-tableaux system (which is none the less complete) we restrict the heredity condition to atomic sentences. In fact, the heredity condition is satisfied for all sentences in these models.

true. But we must keep in mind that on this conception there is absolutely no way to prove or know or have as true any disjunction unless one knows, has proven, or has as true at least one of those disjuncts. This means that the Intuitionist does not in general recognize the validity of "reductio ad absurdum" proofs, which are a staple of classical reasoning.

TABLEAUX FOR $\mathcal{L}_\mathsf{I}$

Consider sentence-world-pairs in previous modal tableaux. In such tableaux a node of the form $\langle{\sim}A, w_i\rangle$ represented the falsity of A at w_i (under some given valuation). This no longer holds, since the semantics allow A to be untrue at a stage without ${\sim}A$ thereby being true at the given stage.

For the foregoing reason lines of I-tableaux will be of the following forms:[15]

$$A,\oplus(s_i) \qquad A,\ominus(s_i)$$

Informally, one may read these as 'A is true at s_i' and 'A is not true at s_i', respectively. For ease of reference we will call $\oplus$ and $\ominus$ *value markers*. With this modification in hand the tableau system, namely I, arises naturally from the semantics. We proceed to resolution rules.

Resolution Rules for I

The resolution rules fall out of the various semantic clauses. As before, boldface indicate the introduction of a *new* name.

RESOLUTION (CONNECTIVE) RULES FOR I:

$$\begin{array}{c}\boxed{(A\vee B),\oplus(s_i)}\\ \swarrow \quad \searrow\\ A,\oplus(s_i) \quad B,\oplus(s_i)\end{array} \qquad \begin{array}{c}\boxed{(A\vee B),\ominus(s_i)}\\ |\\ A,\ominus(s_i)\\ B,\ominus(s_i)\end{array} \qquad \begin{array}{c}{\sim}A,\oplus(s_i)\\ s_iRs_j\\ |\\ A,\ominus(s_j)\end{array}$$

$$\begin{array}{c}\boxed{(A\wedge B),\oplus(s_i)}\\ |\\ A,\oplus(s_i)\\ B,\oplus(s_i)\end{array} \qquad \begin{array}{c}\boxed{(A\wedge B),\ominus(s_i)}\\ \swarrow \quad \searrow\\ A,\ominus(s_i) \quad B,\ominus(s_i)\end{array} \qquad \begin{array}{c}\boxed{{\sim}A,\ominus(s_i)}\\ |\\ s_iR\mathbf{s}_j\\ A,\oplus(s_j)\end{array}$$

$$\begin{array}{c}(A\supset B),\oplus(s_i)\\ s_iRs_j\\ \swarrow \quad \searrow\\ A,\ominus(s_j) \quad B,\oplus(s_j)\end{array} \qquad \begin{array}{c}\boxed{(A\supset B),\ominus(s_i)}\\ |\\ s_iR\mathbf{s}_j\\ A,\oplus(s_j)\\ B,\ominus(s_j)\end{array}$$

[15] R-lines remain as before, except for the change from 'w' to 's'

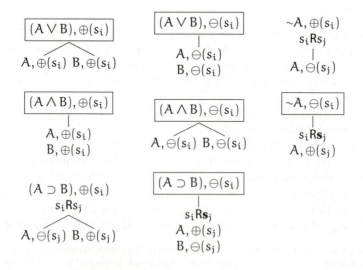

In addition to the connective rules we also require R-rules, so that the tableaux remain faithful to the semantic clauses on $\mathcal{R}$. The rules for reflexivity and transitivity, namely (Ref) and (Trans), remain as before. We need a rule corresponding to the *heredity* condition; the following is obvious:

» For any *atomic* A, if both $\langle A, \oplus(s_i)\rangle$ and $\langle s_i R s_j\rangle$ occur on (open) branch b, then write '$A\ ,\ \oplus(s_j)$' on b (for all $j \neq i$).

Such a rule is a non-branching rule, applying (note well) only to *atomic* sentence-stage-pairs—nodes at which only an atomic sentence occurs (with the "value marker" and stage-name).

While $\wedge$ and $\vee$ remain the same, note that the $\supset$-rules mimic the behavior of $\Box(A \supset B)$. Suppose, for example, that $\nu_{s_i}(A \supset B) = 1$ and $\langle s_i, s_j\rangle \in \mathcal{R}$, for some s_j. Then, given the clauses on $\supset$, either $\nu_{s_j}(A) = 0$ or $\nu_{s_j}(B) = 1$. Accordingly, the $\supset$-Pos rule (the positive rule for $\supset$) is a branching rule. A linear, non-branching rule is $\supset$-Neg, which applies to sentences of the form $\sim(A \supset B)$. Suppose that $\nu_{s_i}(\sim(A \supset B)) = 1$. Then there is some s_i-accessible stage s_j (that is, $\langle s_i, s_j\rangle \in \mathcal{R}$) such that $\nu_{s_j}(A) = 1$ and $\nu_{s_j}(B) = 0$.

Similarly, the $\sim$-rules mimic the behavior of $\Box\sim$ in previous modal languages. Suppose, for example, that $\nu_{s_i}(\sim A) = 1$ and, for some s_j, $\langle s_i, s_j\rangle \in \mathcal{R}$. Then, $\nu_{s_j}(A) = 0$, given the semantic clauses on $\sim$. Likewise, if $\nu_{s_i}(\sim A) = 0$ then there is some s_i-accessible stage, s_j, such that $\nu_{s_j}(A) = 1$. All of this falls out of the semantic clauses, which are motivated by the Heyting's proof conditions.

Proof-Theoretic Definitions

Requisite proof-theoretic notions—*finished tree*, consequence, and so on—are defined almost exactly as per usual. What is important to note is that *initial lists* (or trunks) are slightly different in I-tableaux than in previous tableaux. In I-tableaux the last node of one's initial list need not be a negation; instead, it is a sentence-value-marker pair, where the value marker is $\ominus$. So, for example, if one is testing the argument from premises $A_1, \ldots, A_n$ to B, one's initial list looks like this:

$$\begin{array}{c} A_1\ ,\oplus \\ \vdots \\ A_n\ ,\oplus \\ B\ ,\ominus \end{array}$$

Except for this difference I-tableaux "run" as per previous tableaux; however, the given difference requires a corresponding (though obvious) change in definitions of 'finished tree', and so on. We leave the definitions as exercise.

Counterexamples

$\mathcal{L}_I$-counterexamples, defined in the usual way, may be read off I-tableaux via the "climbing" method. Construction of $\mathcal{W}$ and $\mathcal{R}$ remains precisely as before. The familiar steps for constructing v are slightly modified to accommodate the corresponding modified tableaux; in particular, for any atomic A, $v_{s_i}(A) = 1$ iff $\langle A, \oplus(s_i)\rangle$ occurs on the given open branch b; otherwise, $v_{s_i}(A) = 0$.[16]

EXERCISES 6.4.1

1 Show that $\Vdash_{cpl}$ is a *proper extension* of $\Vdash_I$. [Hint: Are there restrictions you can impose on $\mathcal{L}_I$-models to get, in effect, admissible $\mathcal{L}_{cpl}$-valuations from them?]

2 Prove that the following are intuitionistically valid:

1. $\sim A \Vdash A \supset \bot$.
2. $A \supset \bot \Vdash \sim A$.
3. $A \supset B \Vdash (A \wedge C) \supset B$.
4. $A \Vdash \sim\sim A$.
5. *Strong Conditional Proof.*

   If $\mathcal{X}, A \Vdash B$ then $\mathcal{X} \Vdash A \supset B$.

   Compare with *Weak* Conditional Proof in the preceding section.

3 Give counterexamples in $\mathcal{L}_I$ to

1. $\Vdash A \vee \sim A$
2. $\sim\sim A \Vdash A$

4 Although intuitionists do not recognize the general validity of *reductio ad absurdum* proofs, their interpretation of negation allows for a special case (proofs of negated statements). Show the intuitionistic validity of

1. $A \supset B, A \supset \sim B \Vdash \sim A$
2. $A \wedge \sim A \Vdash B$
3. $\Vdash \sim(A \wedge \sim A)$ ("Principle of Non-Contradiction")

and the invalidity of

4. $\sim A \supset B, \sim A \supset \sim B \Vdash A$.

[16] Recall that S4, where (Ref) and (Trans) govern R, affords infinite tableaux. Not surprisingly, the same situation arises with I, and these may be handled in the previous fashion.

5 One crucial difference between CPL and Intuitionistic logic is that

» PEIRCE'S FORMULA: $((A \supset B) \supset A) \supset A$

is classically but not intuitionistically valid. Display a model that shows the intuitionistic invalidity of Peirce's Formula. Also: How would the Intuitionist respond to the following argument from a classical logician? (Several responses are in order.)

> Suppose Peirce's Formula is not true. Then A is false while $(A \supset B) \supset A$ is true. But given that A is false, the latter's antecedent must be false too, so A is true and B is false. Now we have a contradiction, so the Formula must be true, by Reductio ad Absurdum.
>
> Just to press the point, we have demonstrated that the supposition that the Formula is false is absurd. But it must be either true or false, and the absurd cannot be true. Therefore, the formula is true.

6 TENSE LOGIC. Construct a language that has the following resources. The "worlds" in a model are times (instants in time), ordered in the usual way (they can be numbers, standing for dates, and be ordered by the relation $<$, standardly interpreted). A valuation begins by assigning to each atomic sentence the set of times at which it is true. (Think of an atomic statement being something like 'The car is wet'.) For any statement A there is a statement PA which is true at a given time precisely if A is true at some time before then. Read 'P' as *It was the case at some past time that*. Introduce similar connectives that can be read, for example, as *It has always been true* and *It will be the case at some future time that*. Compare to modal connectives in normal modal logic. How are the properties of the relation $<$ reflected in the valid argument patterns in this language?

7 CALCULUS OF SYSTEMS. Referring back to Exercises 3.6.1 on deductive systems, we can define *system union* as

» $\mathcal{X} \Cup \mathcal{Y} = Cn(\mathcal{X} \cup \mathcal{Y})$.

Consider also the *system complement* defined by

» $\ominus\mathcal{X}$ is the set of all sentences A such that if v does not satisfy $\mathcal{X}$ then it satisfies A,

where 'v' ranges over the admissible valuations of language $\mathcal{L}$. Discuss analogues to principles such as Excluded Middle and Non-Contradiction, as well as

1. If $\mathcal{X} \subseteq \mathcal{Y}$ then $\ominus\mathcal{Y} \subseteq \ominus\mathcal{X}$

2. $\ominus(\mathcal{X} \Cup \mathcal{Y}) = \ominus\mathcal{X} \cap \ominus\mathcal{Y}$

Discuss the relations between this calculus of systems and intuitionistic logic.

FURTHER READING

Hughes and Cresswell [51] provide further discussion of non-normal modal logic (and much else). Graham Priest [79] provides tableaux procedures for the non-normal logics we mentioned; he also provides adequacy results for the procedures.

Good sources for intuitionistic logic are Dummett's [27] and van Dalen's [26]. Beyond the classic sources on conditional logic mentioned in the text (Lewis, Stalnaker), see discussion and references in Chellas' [20]. General resources for such topics are Goble's [38] and Jacquette's [53].

Greg Restall [84] discusses the metaphor of "ways things couldn't be" and Priest [78] explores the suggestion that non-normal worlds are worlds where logical laws fail.

My love is of a birth as rare
As 'tis for object strange and high:
It was begotten by Despair
Upon Impossibility.
– Andrew Marvell

Part III

Paradox

Chapter 7
AROUND TRUTH AND FALSITY

In this chapter we make the move from two-valued languages to many-valued languages, which will be the focus of the subsequent three chapters. Our initial example of a many-valued logic is one that is also an example of a (very simple) so-called *relevance* logic: FDE, the logic of tautological entailment. After a few informal remarks we turn to a brief, abstract description of many-valued languages, followed by simple but (we hope) illuminating examples.

7.1 FOUR CORNERS OF TRUTH

Classical Western thought divides statements into two categories: The True and The False. Classical Indian thought (or, at least, classical Indian logic) recognized four categories: The True, The False, The Both, The Neither.[1]

Taking the four possibilities seriously one immediately sees a problem with standard classical semantics.[2] Let $\mathcal{S}$ comprise the sentences of $\mathtt{S_{cpl}}$, and let ν be a classical (admissible) valuation on $\mathtt{S_{cpl}}$. The apparent problem with classical semantics is two-fold:

a) ν is a function into $\{1, 0\}$

b) the domain of ν is $\mathcal{S}$

These features of classical semantics are problematic if we wish to take all four possibilities seriously; for (a) rules out The Both while (a) and (b) together rule out The Neither. If we wish to recognize the four possibilities in our semantics, then (a) and (b) need to be modified.

---

[1]This is the classification given by the early (pre-sixth century) logician Sanjaya, according to P. T. Raju [82]. Sanjaya coined the term 'four corners', which is discussed below.

[2]By 'classical logic' (semantics, etc.) we mean classical *Western* logic, as reviewed in §4.

NON-FUNCTIONAL VALUATIONS

One way to achieve the requisite modification is to use *non-functional* relations. In particular, let R be such that $R \subseteq \mathcal{S} \times \{1, 0\}$, which immediately yields four possibilities:

1) A is related to The True (A is true only):

$$\langle A, 1\rangle \in R$$
$$\langle A, 0\rangle \notin R$$

2) A is related to The False (A is false only):

$$\langle A, 1\rangle \notin R$$
$$\langle A, 0\rangle \in R$$

3) A is related to The Both (A is both true and false):

$$\langle A, 1\rangle \in R$$
$$\langle A, 0\rangle \in R$$

4) A is related to The Neither (A is neither true nor false):

$$\langle A, 1\rangle \notin R$$
$$\langle A, 0\rangle \notin R$$

Such a set R can thus be regarded as a new sort of valuation. We can go on from here to specify what count as admissible valuations and satisfaction, and then investigate the semantic consequence relation more or less as before. But this modified notion of valuation, making it a non-functional relation, would be quite a change in our basic conceptions, and so it will be convenient to see how we can achieve the same effect in a less radically different way.

FUNCTIONAL VALUATIONS

A more familiar way of accommodating the four possibilities[3] retains *functions*. In particular, let v be a function from $\mathcal{S}$ into $\wp(\{1, 0\})$, the powerset of $\{1, 0\}$, which comprises $\{1\}$ (Truth), $\{0\}$ (Falsity), $\{1, 0\}$ (Both) and $\emptyset$ (Neither). We immediately get our four possibilities:

1) A is is true only ($v(A) = \{1\}$):

$$1 \in v(A)$$
$$0 \notin v(A)$$

[3] due to J. Michael Dunn [29, 30, 31]

2) A is false only ($v(A) = \{0\}$):

$$1 \notin v(A)$$
$$0 \in v(A)$$

3) A is both true and false ($v(A) = \{1, 0\}$):

$$1 \in v(A)$$
$$0 \in v(A)$$

4) A is neither true nor false ($v(A) = \emptyset$):

$$1 \notin v(A)$$
$$0 \notin v(A)$$

With valuations in hand the next step, as before, is to specify admissible valuations; however, we will once again skip this matter here and briefly discuss one further (but equivalent) way of accommodating our four possibilities.

Four Values: Four Corners

Another (equivalent) approach lets our truth values be $\mathcal{V} = \{1, 0, \mathsf{b}, \mathsf{n}\}$, where the elements carry their intended meaning (truth, falsity, both, neither). Valuations, then, are simply functions from $\mathcal{S}$ into $\mathcal{V}$. With this in hand our four possibilities immediately arise:

1) $v(A) = 1$

2) $v(A) = 0$

3) $v(A) = \mathsf{b}$

4) $v(A) = \mathsf{n}$

These four possibilities may be usefully pictured as a so-called lattice:

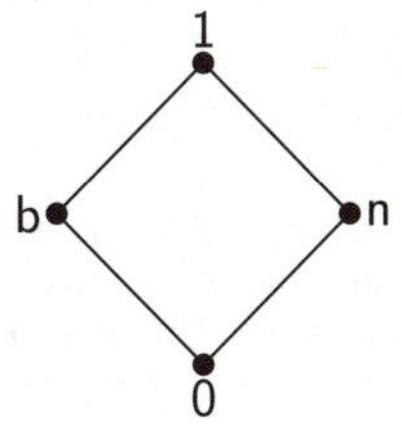

Figure 7.1: Four Corners of Truth

Following the Indian tradition, one may think of this lattice as *the four corners of truth*. The structure of the diagram means to indicate that b and n are in some sense *less* than 1, while 0 is *less* than all the others. This allows us to speak of "greatest lower bound" (glb) and "least upper bound" (lub) of sets of elements in the lattice. Intuitively: If you're going up the lines then the glb of x and y is the highest "node" (as it were) from which you can reach both x and y. (Examples: the glb of 1 and 0 is 0, which is also the glb of n and b. The glb of x and x is x, for any x.) Similarly, if you're going down the lines then the lub of x and y is the lowest "node" from which you can reach both x and y. (Examples: the lub of 1 and 0 is 1, which is also the lub of n and b. The lub of x and x is x, for any x.)[4]

7.2 MANY-VALUED LANGUAGES

Thus far, we have merely given a few different ways to accommodate the four "possibilities" arising from truth and falsity; we have not specified any languages in which this idea is made concrete (as it were). We will give one such language in §7.3. For now, we give a brief, abstract characterization of *many-valued languages* in general.

THE BASIC STRUCTURE

To begin, we recall the notion of a *base* defined by Def 3.2. Valuation v has base $\mathcal{B} = \langle \mathcal{V}, \mathbb{C}, \odot \rangle$ exactly if v assigns an element of $\mathcal{V}$ to each sentence, and $\odot$ assigns an n-ary operator $\odot_\varphi \in \mathbb{C}$ to each n-ary connective φ such that for all sentences $A_1, \ldots, A_n$,

$$v(\varphi(A_1, \ldots, A_n)) = \odot_\varphi(v(A_1), \ldots, v(A_n)).$$

In a many-valued language all valuations have a common base. The elements of $\mathcal{V}$ are the "truth values". In addition, in all the cases we shall study, $\mathcal{V}$ has a subset $\mathcal{D}$ of so-called *designated* elements. Satisfaction, in turn, is defined by

$$v \textit{ satisfies } A \text{ iff } v(A) \in \mathcal{D}.$$

Accordingly, $\mathcal{D} \subset \mathcal{V}$, where $\mathcal{V} - \mathcal{D}$ comprises the so-called *undesignated values* (sometimes 'anti-designated'). We will call the larger structure $\langle \mathcal{V}, \mathcal{D}, \mathbb{C}, \odot \rangle$ a *matrix*.[5] By omitting the second element of a matrix we have a *base for*

[4] Dunn [29] showed how to use this so-called De Morgan lattice to specify various languages, including the one discussed in §7.3. For example, a natural decision is to let $\wedge$ be the so-called *greatest lower bound* (glb) and $\vee$ the *least upper bound* (lub). Negation, in turn, may likewise be defined in terms of the lattice. We will briefly return to this topic in §7.3.

[5] In this part of the book we will frequently use '$\wedge$', '$\sim$' and the like to name *both* the connective (in the syntax) and the operator corresponding to the connective, when that cannot cause confusion.

valuations, and that second element then determines what constitutes satisfaction. In classical semantics, for example, we have[6]

$$\begin{aligned}\mathcal{V} &= \{1,0\}\\ \mathbb{C} &= \{\sim,\wedge,\vee,\supset,\equiv\}\\ \mathcal{D} &= \{1\}\\ \nu &: \mathcal{S}\longrightarrow\mathcal{V}\end{aligned}$$

But as we have just seen, in other languages $\mathcal{V}$ and $\mathcal{D}$ may be much larger.

Semantic Properties and Relations

The important semantic properties and relations are defined as usual. The difference is that we now invoke $\mathcal{D}$ to define satisfaction. Therefore, with respect to consequence we can equivalently say that $\mathcal{X} \Vdash A$ just in case $\nu(A) \in \mathcal{D}$ if $\nu(B) \in \mathcal{D}$, for every $B \in \mathcal{X}$ (and any admissible ν). In other words, A is a consequence of (is implied by) $\mathcal{X}$ just in case A is designated if every element of $\mathcal{X}$ is designated.

DESIGNATION?

How, exactly, should one understand the notion of designation? For purposes of doing logic, it is sufficient to understand the designated values as above: they are a subset of one's "truth values" and are such that designation is to be preserved in valid inferences.

That said, it may be useful to think of designated values as different ways of being true. For example, given our four corners of truth we might think that there are two ways of being true: 1 and b. The former value represents *true only* while the latter represents *true and false*. Since being true *and* false is a way of being true, we might well include both 1 and b in our designated values.[7]

Our aim is not to wade into deep metaphysical waters. For current purposes, one may think of having a designated value primarily as the status to be preserved in valid inferences; but in as much as validity is "truth-preservation" and one has more than one sort of value being preserved in valid inferences, one may also think of designated values as different ways of being true—whatever, in the end, the details of such "ways" turn out to be.

FIDDLING WITH FOUR POSSIBILITIES

If, as above, we think of languages in terms of a structure, $\langle\mathcal{V},\mathcal{D},\mathbb{C},\nu\rangle$, we immediately see room for "fiddling". In particular, given some syntax, one

---

[6] with a great deal of redundancy represented with respect to $\mathbb{C}$

[7] Of course, the same consideration seems to go the other way: being true *and* false is a way of being false, in which case one might want b in one's undesignated values.

may fiddle with each element of the (semantic) structure and thereby wind up with a different language.

We say that a language is n-valued iff $\mathcal{V}$ comprises (exactly) n elements. In turn, we say (following standard convention) that an n-valued language is *many-valued* iff $n \geq 3$. (Moreover, a language is said to be *finitely many-valued* iff $\mathcal{V}$ is finite.)

For the most part, the many-valued languages that we shall discuss arise from fiddling with the four "possibilities" discussed in §7.1.[8] The given fiddling usually concerns either $\mathcal{V}$ or $\mathcal{D}$, as will be evident. As usual, such fiddling need not be without philosophical motivation, and we will briefly discuss some motivation in due course. For now, we turn to a specific example of a many-valued language.

7.3 THE LANGUAGE $\mathcal{L}_{\mathsf{FDE}}$

The language $\mathcal{L}_{\mathsf{FDE}}$ we are about to introduce is called *the language of tautological entailment* or of *first degree entailment*; it is a simple example of the family of so-called *relevance logics*.[9] Its most remarkable non-classical feature is that contradictions do not just imply anything, nor does just anything at all imply a given tautology. Thus the "paradoxes of strict implication", as well as some paradoxes of material implication, are avoided. $\mathcal{L}_{\mathsf{FDE}}$ recognizes all four possibilities mentioned in §7.1 and is often characterized via the first two approaches discussed in §7.1. We will use the third of the above approaches, but we should emphasize that any of the approaches (suitably specified) yield the same language.

SYNTAX

The syntax of $\mathcal{L}_{\mathsf{FDE}}$ is simply S_{cpl}, although to simplify matters we will treat $\supset$ and $\equiv$ as *defined* connectives in the usual way.

SEMANTICS

It will already be clear that a matrix is going to play much the same role as a (possible worlds) model did for a modal language. By specifying a particular valuation for which the matrix includes the base we obtain a model for our language. To be precise: An $\mathcal{L}_{\mathsf{FDE}}$-structure is a structure $\mathcal{M} = \langle \mathcal{V}, \mathcal{D}, \mathbb{C}, v \rangle$,

[8] The exception is the so-called continuum-many language of Łukasiewicz, which is discussed in a subsequent chapter.

[9] We will examine the logical system traditionally called 'first degree entailment' in Part IV. We also use the name for our tableaux system in this chapter.

where

$$\begin{array}{rcl} \mathcal{V} & = & \{1, b, 0, n\} \\ \mathbb{C} & = & \{\sim, \wedge, \vee\} \\ \mathcal{D} & = & \{1, b\} \\ \nu & : & \mathcal{S} \longrightarrow \mathcal{V} \end{array}$$

As with other canvassed languages, whether an $\mathcal{L}_{\mathsf{FDE}}$-structure is an $\mathcal{L}_{\mathsf{FDE}}$-model turns on the behavior of ν.[10] There are two standard ways of specifying admissible $\mathcal{L}_{\mathsf{FDE}}$-models; we sketch both approaches, focusing mainly on the second.

Four Corners

Using the four corners of truth (figure 7.1, page 107) we may specify *admissible* $\mathcal{L}_{\mathsf{FDE}}$-valuations as those (and only those) $\mathcal{L}_{\mathsf{FDE}}$-valuations in accordance with the following, where *least upper bound* and *greatest lower bound* are understood relative to the four corners of truth:

$\nu(A \wedge B)$ is the greatest lower bound of $\nu(A)$ and $\nu(B)$

$\nu(A \vee B)$ is the least upper bound of $\nu(A)$ and $\nu(B)$

With respect to negation the clauses run thus:

$$\nu(\sim A) = \begin{cases} 1 & \text{if } \nu(A) = 0 \\ b & \text{if } \nu(A) = b \\ n & \text{if } \nu(A) = n \\ 0 & \text{if } \nu(A) = 1 \end{cases}$$

In this case, negation is sometimes said to be an *order-inverting map* with b and n as its fixed points.[11]

Operator Diagrams

A more familiar but none the less equivalent way of specifying admissible $\mathcal{L}_{\mathsf{FDE}}$-valuations utilizes *operator diagrams*: Admissible $\mathcal{L}_{\mathsf{FDE}}$-valuations are those (and only those) $\mathcal{L}_{\mathsf{FDE}}$-valuations that "accord with" the following diagrams:

[10] It also turns on the elements of $\mathbb{C}$ but we shall brush over this for now, leaving a more detailed discussion to Part IV.

[11] That negation is an order-inverting map means that, the fixed points aside, it toggles values in the given structure (the four corners, which forms a so-called lattice); so, negation toggles 1 and 0 but otherwise "stays put" at b and n.

$\sim$	
1	0
b	b
n	n
0	1

$\wedge$	1	b	n	0
1	1	b	n	0
b	b	b	0	0
n	n	0	n	0
0	0	0	0	0

$\vee$	1	b	n	0
1	1	1	1	1
b	1	b	1	b
n	1	1	n	n
0	1	b	n	0

Informally, by 'accord with the diagrams' we mean that ν conforms to the functions specified in the diagrams. So, for example, if ν accords with the given diagrams, then $\nu(\sim A) = 1$ iff $\nu(A) = 0$, and similarly for assignments to $A \wedge B$ and so on.[12]

FACT 7.1 *There is an admissible $\mathcal{L}_{FDE}$ valuation which assigns an undesignated value to all sentences of $\mathcal{L}_{FDE}$.*

Fact 7.1 may be intuitively obvious: Consider the assignment by ν of n to all atomic sentences. A look at the operator tables should quickly convince us that any sentence made up by means of the given connectives will also receive value n. A rigorous proof can be given by means of "strong induction", which we shall introduce in Part IV.

7.4 TRUTH AND CONSEQUENCE

Before turning to tableaux we pause to observe that, in view of the fact just noted, there are no logical truths in $\mathcal{L}_{FDE}$. This is not to say that there are no valid arguments in $\mathcal{L}_{FDE}$; there are, as the exercises (page 118) make clear. The upshot:

» *Logical truth and consequence come apart!*

In $\mathcal{L}_{CPL}$ the valid arguments correspond to valid conditional sentences; that is not so here. This is a feature common in a variety of standard many-valued languages, as we will discuss in subsequent chapters.

For now, we note that the given divergence is not terribly surprising in $\mathcal{L}_{FDE}$, especially given the informal motivation involving "four corners of truth". Logical truths are sentences that are designated *come what may*, as it were. If, as the given motivation goes, every sentence may be *neither true nor false* (an undesignated "possibility"), then it's not the case that, come what may, some sentence is designated, and so $\mathcal{L}_{FDE}$ enjoys no logical truths. We leave the proof that $\nVdash_{FDE} A$ as an exercise, and turn briefly to FDE-tableaux.

7.5 FDE TABLEAUX

A tableaux system for $\mathcal{L}_{FDE}$, which we will call 'FDE', falls out of the foregoing semantics. As with Intuitionistic logic we will employ *value markers*:

[12]The diagrams specify each $\odot_\varphi \in \mathbb{C}$, the operators corresponding to the connectives $\varphi \in \mathcal{C}$. So, ν is said to *accord with the diagrams* iff for each n-ary connective $\varphi \in \mathcal{C}$ and its corresponding n-ary operator $\odot_\varphi \in \mathbb{C}$, $\nu(\varphi(A_1, \ldots, A_n)) = \odot_\varphi(\nu(A_1), \ldots, \nu(A_n))$.

$\oplus$ and $\ominus$. Nodes of our FDE-tableaux are of the forms $\langle A, \oplus \rangle$ and $\langle A, \ominus \rangle$, which may be informally read as 'A is designated' and 'A is undesignated', respectively. Note that such tableaux-lines do *not* determine a unique semantic value: that A is designated implies only that $\nu(A) = 1$ or $\nu(A) = \mathsf{b}$. (Similarly, that A is undesignated implies only that $\nu(A) = 0$ or $\nu(A) = \mathsf{n}$.) Fortunately, suitable rules for constructing counterexamples will avoid the apparent "underdetermination" (as it were).

Before giving the resolution rules for FDE we pause to give their motivation. Begin with conjunction. Let ν be an admissible valuation. There are two (general) possibilities:

$$\nu(A \wedge B) \in \mathcal{D} \quad \text{or} \quad \nu(A \wedge B) \notin \mathcal{D}$$

Suppose the former. Then each of $\nu(A)$ and $\nu(B)$ is in $\mathcal{D}$, as given by the $\wedge$-diagram. On the other hand, suppose that $\nu(A \wedge B) \notin \mathcal{D}$. Then either $\nu(A) \notin \mathcal{D}$ or $\nu(B) \notin \mathcal{D}$.[13] Hence, if a conjunction is designated, then so too are its conjuncts; if it is undesignated, then so too is (at least) one of its conjuncts.

With an eye on Carrot (Neg), suppose that $\nu({\sim}(A \wedge B)) \in \mathcal{D}$. Then either $\nu({\sim}A) \in \mathcal{D}$ or $\nu({\sim}B) \in \mathcal{D}$.[14] On the other hand, suppose that $\nu({\sim}(A \wedge B)) \notin \mathcal{D}$. Then $\nu({\sim}A) \notin \mathcal{D}$ and $\nu({\sim}B) \notin \mathcal{D}$.[15]

So goes $\wedge$ and (the motivation for) its corresponding rules. Disjunction runs along similar lines. For each of $A \vee B$ and ${\sim}(A \vee B)$ there are two possibilities: designated and undesignated. The FDE-rules fall out of the semantics that govern these possibilities.

Negation is likewise straightforward. With ν as above, suppose that $\nu({\sim}{\sim}A) \in \mathcal{D}$. Then $\nu({\sim}{\sim}A) = 1$ or $\nu({\sim}{\sim}A) = \mathsf{b}$. Suppose the former. A glance at the ${\sim}$-diagram reveals that $\nu({\sim}B)$ is 1 iff $\nu(B)$ is 0. Hence, since $\nu({\sim}{\sim}A) = 1$ it follows that $\nu({\sim}A) = 0$, in which case $\nu(A) = 1$ and, hence, $\nu(A) \in \mathcal{D}$. On the other hand, suppose that $\nu({\sim}{\sim}A) = \mathsf{b}$. The ${\sim}$-diagram immediately reveals that $\nu({\sim}B)$ is b iff $\nu(B)$ is b, in which case $\nu({\sim}A) = \mathsf{b}$ and, hence, $\nu(A) = \mathsf{b}$, whence $\nu(A) \in \mathcal{D}$. This takes care of *designated* double-negations. The idea is that if ${\sim}{\sim}A$ is designated then so too is A, just as in classical logic.

[13]Proof: If $\nu(A \wedge B) \notin \mathcal{D}$, then $\nu(A \wedge B) = 0$ or $\nu(A \wedge B) = \mathsf{n}$. A glance at the $\wedge$-diagram (or brief reflection on the "four corners", where $\wedge$ is the glb) reveals that $\nu(A \wedge B) = 0$ only if $\nu(A) = \mathsf{n}$ or $\nu(B) = 0$ (or vice versa); either way, $\nu(A) \notin \mathcal{D}$ or $\nu(B) \notin \mathcal{D}$.

[14]Proof: $\nu({\sim}(A \wedge B))$ is either 1 or b. Suppose the former. Then $\nu(A \wedge B) = 0$, in which case, as above, either $\nu(A) = \mathsf{n}$ or $\nu(B) = 0$ (or vice versa), in which case either $\nu({\sim}A) = 1$ or $\nu({\sim}B) = 1$, which implies that $\nu({\sim}A) \in \mathcal{D}$ or $\nu({\sim}B) \in \mathcal{D}$. Suppose, now, that $\nu({\sim}(A \wedge B))$ is b. Then $\nu(A \wedge B) = \mathsf{b}$, in which case either $\nu(A) = \mathsf{b}$ or $\nu(B) = \mathsf{b}$, and hence either $\nu({\sim}A) = \mathsf{b}$ or $\nu({\sim}B) = \mathsf{b}$, from which it follows that $\nu({\sim}A) \in \mathcal{D}$ or $\nu({\sim}B) \in \mathcal{D}$. (Henceforth, we will, for the most part, skip such proofs; however, you should make sure that you can prove claims that strike you as suspicious or otherwise demanding of proof.)

[15]Proof is left as exercise, but it falls immediately out of the given operator diagrams.

As for *undesignated* double-negations, suppose that $\nu({\sim}{\sim}A) \notin \mathcal{D}$. Then $\nu({\sim}{\sim}A) = 0$ or $\nu({\sim}{\sim}A) = \mathsf{n}$. As the ~-diagram (or four corners) indicates, either option quickly yields that $\nu(A) \notin \mathcal{D}$. Hence, if ~~A is undesignated, then so too is A, just as in classical logic.

FDE RESOLUTION RULES

The FDE-rules retain previous names; however, each name—for example, 'Carrot (Pos)', and so on—now denotes a pair of rules, one for *designated* sentences and the other *undesignated.*[16]

FDE RESOLUTION RULES FOR $\wedge$

$(A \wedge B), \oplus$ — one branch: $A, \oplus$; $B, \oplus$

$(A \wedge B), \ominus$ — two branches: $A, \ominus$ | $B, \ominus$

${\sim}(A \wedge B), \oplus$ — two branches: ${\sim}A, \oplus$ | ${\sim}B, \oplus$

${\sim}(A \wedge B), \ominus$ — one branch: ${\sim}A, \ominus$; ${\sim}B, \ominus$

FDE RESOLUTION RULES FOR $\vee$

$(A \vee B), \oplus$ — two branches: $A, \oplus$ | $B, \oplus$

$(A \vee B), \ominus$ — one branch: $A, \ominus$; $B, \ominus$

${\sim}(A \vee B), \oplus$ — one branch: ${\sim}A, \oplus$; ${\sim}B, \oplus$

${\sim}(A \vee B), \ominus$ — two branches: ${\sim}A, \ominus$ | ${\sim}B, \ominus$

FDE RESOLUTION RULES FOR ~

${\sim}{\sim}A, \oplus$ — one branch: $A, \oplus$

${\sim}{\sim}A, \ominus$ — one branch: $A, \ominus$

[16] When necessary, the given ambiguity may be resolved by inserting 'designated' or 'undesignated' into the name.

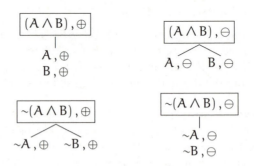

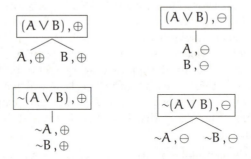

We note that the *initial list* of a tree is to be understood along the lines of I-tableaux:

$$\begin{array}{c} A_1\,,\oplus \\ A_2\,,\oplus \\ \vdots \\ A_n\,,\oplus \\ B\,,\ominus \end{array}$$

where, for example, one is testing whether $\{A_1, A_2, \ldots, A_n, B\}$ is satisfiable in $\mathcal{L}_{\mathsf{FDE}}$ or, in turn, testing the inference from $A_1, A_2, \ldots, A_n$ to B, for any sentences A_i and B.

NOTE: While the usual definitions (open tree, and so on) apply we note that a branch b is *closed* iff $\langle A, \oplus \rangle$ occurs at node n of b and $\langle A, \ominus \rangle$ occurs at n' of b, where $n \neq n'$.[17] Other conventions governing FDE-tableaux are also similar to those in earlier procedures, including the *closing off* symbol, which is inserted just when a branch closes.

COUNTEREXAMPLES

A counterexample to A in $\mathcal{L}_{\mathsf{FDE}}$ is an admissible $\mathcal{L}_{\mathsf{FDE}}$-valuation according to which A is undesignated. Likewise, a counterexample to the claim

$$\{A_1, A_2, \ldots, A_n\} \Vdash_{\mathsf{FDE}} B$$

is an admissible $\mathcal{L}_{\mathsf{FDE}}$-valuation according to which B is undesignated but each A_i is designated.

CLIMBING AN FDE-TREE

One may construct counterexamples by the usual climbing method; however, there are now a few extra steps that are involved. The crucial stage concerns the construction of ν, which proceeds in two steps.[18] The steps run as follows.

Constructing ν

Let n and n' be nodes of our (chosen) open branch, and A any *atomic* sentence (i.e., element of $\mathcal{A}$).

1. STEP ONE: Establishing designation and undesignation.

---

[17]Why shouldn't a branch close if it contains nodes of the forms $\langle A, \oplus \rangle$ and $\langle \sim A, \oplus \rangle$, or $\langle A, \ominus \rangle$ and $\langle \sim A, \ominus \rangle$? This question bears on the next chapter.

[18]It is worth noting that had we characterized $\mathcal{L}_{\mathsf{FDE}}$ via (for example) the non-functional approach described in §7.1, the climbing method for FDE-tableaux could be followed just as in previous systems. For example, constructing R is straightforward: For any element A of $\mathcal{A}$, if open branch b has $\langle A, \oplus \rangle$ at a node, let $\langle A, 1 \rangle \in R$, and if $\langle \sim A, \oplus \rangle$ occurs at a node, let $\langle A, 0 \rangle \in R$. That's it! We leave the full *non-functional* specification of $\mathcal{L}_{\mathsf{FDE}}$ as an exercise.

(a) If $\langle A, \oplus \rangle$ occurs on n, let $v(A) \in \mathcal{D}$. If $\langle {\sim}A, \oplus \rangle$ occurs on n, let $v({\sim}A) \in \mathcal{D}$.

(b) If $\langle A, \ominus \rangle$ occurs on n, let $v(A) \notin \mathcal{D}$. If $\langle {\sim}A, \ominus \rangle$ occurs on n, let $v({\sim}A) \notin \mathcal{D}$.

2. STEP TWO: Establishing v's relevant values (after step one is finished):

   (a) If v is such that $v(A) \in \mathcal{D}$ *and* $v({\sim}A) \in \mathcal{D}$, let $v(A) = \mathsf{b}$.

   (b) If v is such that $v(A) \notin \mathcal{D}$ *and* $v({\sim}A) \notin \mathcal{D}$, let $v(A) = \mathsf{n}$.

   (c) Assume that not both $v(A) \in \mathcal{D}$ and $v({\sim}A) \in \mathcal{D}$. Then:

      i. If $v(A) \in \mathcal{D}$, let $v(A) = 1$.
      ii. If $v({\sim}A) \in \mathcal{D}$, let $v(A) = 0$.

   (d) Assume that not both $v(A) \notin \mathcal{D}$ and $v({\sim}A) \notin \mathcal{D}$. Then:

      i. If $v(A) \notin \mathcal{D}$, let $v(A) = 0$.
      ii. If $v({\sim}A) \notin \mathcal{D}$, let $v(A) = 1$.

The steps may seem complicated but, on reflection, each is straightforward. The idea, in short, is that $v(A) = \mathsf{b}$ iff $v({\sim}A) = \mathsf{b}$, and $v(A) = \mathsf{n}$ iff $v({\sim}A) = \mathsf{n}$. Hence, if an open branch b has $\langle A, \oplus \rangle$ at n and $\langle {\sim}A, \oplus \rangle$ at n', then the value of A is designated and, in particular, b. Likewise, if b has $\langle A, \ominus \rangle$ at n and $\langle {\sim}A, \ominus \rangle$ at n', then the value of A is undesignated and, in particular, n. If neither of these situations arises, then we may safely take a "classical stance", assigning 1 or 0 depending on the given value marker.[19]

PROOF-THEORETIC CONSEQUENCE

Proof-theoretic consequence may be defined as usual: $\mathcal{X} \vdash_{\mathsf{FDE}} B$ iff there is a closed tree the initial list of which comprises $\langle A_i, \oplus \rangle$ and $\langle B, \ominus \rangle$, for each $A_i \in \mathcal{X}$. We leave the other relevant definitions as exercise.

EXAMPLES

Familiarity with FDE-tableaux may be achieved via exercises but, by way of brief illustration, we give one example. Consider the claim

$$\{(r \wedge {\sim}q), ({\sim}p \vee q)\} \vdash_{\mathsf{FDE}} {\sim}p.$$

[19] This "stance" needn't be made; one could just as reliably assign b and n in response to the appropriate markers—provided, again, that not both $\langle A, \oplus \rangle$ and $\langle {\sim}A, \oplus \rangle$ (similarly for $\ominus$) occur on b.

A tableau for this claim is as follows:

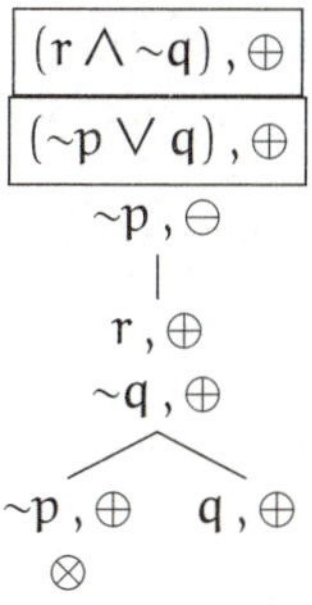

By climbing the open branch we get a counterexample in which $v(q) = b$ and $v(p) = v(r) = 1$. This shows that the original claim is false; it also shows (indirectly) that *disjunctive syllogism*, namely, the inference from $A \vee B$ and $\sim B$ to A, is not valid in $\mathcal{L}_{\mathsf{FDE}}$. (Just modify the example by omitting r. More directly, let $v(A) = 0$ and $v(B) = b$.)

Similarly, the given counterexample shows that *material modus ponens*, namely, the inference from A and $A \supset B$ to B, is not valid in $\mathcal{L}_{\mathsf{FDE}}$. (If $A \supset B$ is defined as $\sim A \vee B$, and A implies $\sim\sim A$, then material modus ponens is a special case of disjunctive syllogism.)

These "failures" are characteristic of *relevance logic*, of which FDE is a basic (and, in effect, conditional-free) example. We will return to the topic of relevance logic in Part IV.

We pause to note that FDE is sound and complete with respect to $\mathcal{L}_{\mathsf{FDE}}$, and so one may verify claims about semantic consequence via the tableaux procedure. While we do not prove these results here, we offer proofs for a similar system in Part IV.

Philosophical Issues

We began this chapter with a few hand-waving remarks about "four possibilities" emerging from truth and falsity. A pressing philosophical question is whether there is any good reason to take such "possibilities" seriously. For example, is there any reason to think that the English language itself affords the four (so-called) possibilities? Are there alternative (informal) interpretations of the four values posited in $\mathcal{L}_{\mathsf{FDE}}$?

Without trying to settle them, the next chapter touches on some of the given philosophical issues. For now, the important thing is to gain familiarity with $\mathcal{L}_{\mathsf{FDE}}$, given that subsequent languages arise (in effect) from fiddling with the basic elements of $\mathcal{L}_{\mathsf{FDE}}$-valuations. With this in mind, we close with a handful of exercises intended to yield the requisite familiarity.

EXERCISES 7.5.1

1 Characterize $\mathcal{L}_{\mathsf{FDE}}$ in terms of the non-functional valuations sketched in §7.1.

2 True or false? (These are so-called *De Morgan Laws.*)

1. $\sim(p \vee q) \vdash_{\mathsf{FDE}} \sim p \wedge \sim q$.
2. $\sim(p \wedge q) \vdash_{\mathsf{FDE}} \sim p \vee \sim q$

3 For each of the following claims prove that it is true, or give a counterexample. Construct tableaux for each claim.

1. $A \wedge \sim A \Vdash_{\mathsf{FDE}} B$
2. $A \Vdash_{\mathsf{FDE}} B \vee \sim B$
3. $A \Vdash_{\mathsf{FDE}} B \supset B$
4. $A \vee B \Vdash_{\mathsf{FDE}} (A \wedge (A \supset B)) \supset B$
5. $A, A \supset B \Vdash_{\mathsf{FDE}} B$
6. $A \Vdash_{\mathsf{FDE}} (A \supset B) \vee (B \supset A)$
7. $A \Vdash_{\mathsf{FDE}} A \equiv A$

FURTHER READING

For more advanced discussion of FDE and variations of the "four corners" see especially Dunn's and Hardegree's [28] and Restall's [85]. Discussion of the Indian tradition to which we alluded may be found in Raju's [82] and Horn's [49]. We will return to FDE in Part IV.

With humans this is impossible;
but with God all things are possible.
– St. Matthew, *Matthew 19:21*

Chapter 8
Gaps, Gluts, and Liars

This chapter considers a few popular many-valued languages that arise from fiddling with the four possibilities discussed in §7.3. Instead of merely waving at "four possibilities of truth" we will motivate the various languages by a perennial philosophical problem: the Liar paradox.

Not all of the given languages were in fact motivated by the Liar. Indeed, Łukasiewicz, who pioneered many-valued languages, formulated so-called Ł3 to deal with the problem of future contingents.[1] None the less, the Liar continues to provide inspiration in contemporary philosophical logic and it serves as a convenient (and, we hope, interesting) peg on which to hang the canvassed languages.

8.1 The Liar Paradox

Informally, a *paradox* (deriving from the Greek for *beyond or above belief*) is an argument with apparently true premises, apparently valid reasoning, and an apparently false (or untrue) conclusion.[2] One version of the liar paradox arises from the following sentence:

The first displayed sentence in §8.1 is false.

Call the displayed sentence 'l'. l is a sentence that says of itself—or, at any rate, may be used to say of itself—(only) that it is false. If what l says is true, then l is false; and if l is false, then what l says is true. Given that l is either true or false, it follows that l is both! A contradiction.[3]

"But what if l is *neither* true *nor* false?" the reader will reply. And now the race for many-valued logics has truly begun!

---

[1]See §1 for brief discussion. Emil Post [74] also pioneered many-valued logic, though not with an eye squarely on philosophy.

[2]Further distinctions are frequently made but, for our purposes, the given account is sufficient. Quine [81] gives a standard distinction between *paradoxes* and *antinomies*, where the latter are (in some sense) more serious.

[3]For present purposes, we can think of a contradiction as the conjunction of a sentence and its negation. (We will pass over the important but thorny question: What is it for B to be the negation of A? Gabbay and Wansing [36] and Wansing [103] provide papers on this topic.)

The driving question is: What does the Liar teach us? We will look at three different answers to this question. We leave the reader to judge which (if any) of the three is best.

8.2 Truth Value Gaps

The first answer posits so-called *truth value gaps*. A sentence which is neither true nor false is said to be *gappy*, the idea being that it falls into a gap between truth and falsity.[4] What the Liar teaches us, according to the first answer, is that some sentences are gappy; in particular, l is gappy, and so l is neither true nor false. With this lesson in mind, the problematic contradiction is avoided: if l itself is neither true nor false, then we are left only with the curious (but not contradictory) biconditional that l is true iff l is false.

On the going answer we have "discovered" only one non-classical category into which our (meaningful, declarative) sentences fall: the *gap* between Truth and Falsity. Accordingly, we are led only to a three-valued semantics: Truth, Falsity, and Neither (aka, Gappy).

The question is: How are these three values distributed over *compound* sentences? For example, which of these three values is assigned to the conjunction of (say) True and Gappy? What about True and False? What about Gappy and False? Moreover, how are the values distributed over disjunctions? And what about negation? Is a sentence false iff its negation is true?

We will now explore one specific response to these questions that completes this first answer and makes it precise. With respect to the foregoing questions we take here a "classical stance", as it were. For example, if we have a conjunction one conjunct of which is False, then we say that the conjunction itself is False, irrespective of the other conjunct. Likewise, if we have a disjunction one disjunct of which is True, then we say that the disjunction itself is True, irrespective of the other disjunct. With respect to negation we retain the "classical" idea that a negation is True iff its negatum is False. In this respect, the standard account of falsity (viz., truth of negation) is preserved.

The Language $\mathcal{L}_{K_3}$

The going response motivates a language standardly called '$\mathcal{L}_{K_3}$'.[5] As you may notice, one way the language can be constructed is by fiddling with

---

[4]The terminology of "gaps" and (as below in §8.3) "gluts" is from Kit Fine [33].

[5]Strictly speaking, the language is frequently called 'K_3' but we shall reserve this name for the given tableaux system. The semantics for this language are also frequently called *Strong Kleene*, after Kleene [56]. (We will mention the corresponding *weak Kleene* semantics in due course.) Kleene's main concern was not the Liar; he was concerned with mathematical sentences that are either true or false but "indeterminate" in the sense of being unprovable.

$\mathcal{L}_{\mathsf{FDE}}$. Specifically, $\mathcal{L}_{\mathsf{K}_3}$ "ignores" or fails to recognize the value b in $\mathcal{L}_{\mathsf{FDE}}$. The details are as follows.

SYNTAX

The syntax is S_{cpl}. As before, we shall take $\supset$ and $\equiv$ to be defined connectives.

SEMANTICS

An $\mathcal{L}_{\mathsf{K}_3}$-model $\mathcal{M}$ is a structure $\langle \mathcal{V}, \mathcal{D}, \mathbb{C}, \nu \rangle$, where $\mathcal{V} = \{1, 0, \mathsf{n}\}$, $\mathcal{D} = \{1\}$, and $\mathbb{C}$ and ν are as before.

Admissible Valuations

Admissible $\mathcal{L}_{\mathsf{K}_3}$-valuations are precisely those $\mathcal{L}_{\mathsf{FDE}}$-valuations such that

$$\nu(A) \neq \mathsf{b}\text{ , for any } A \in \mathcal{S}.$$

As above, $\mathcal{L}_{\mathsf{K}_3}$ is just the language one gets from $\mathcal{L}_{\mathsf{FDE}}$ by "ignoring" b. Hence, admissible $\mathcal{L}_{\mathsf{K}_3}$-valuations are a proper subset of admissible $\mathcal{L}_{\mathsf{FDE}}$-valuations: the ones that ignore b. We can use the same operator diagrams, with the b rows and columns deleted.

As is easy to see, $\mathcal{L}_{\mathsf{K}_3}$ is a proper extension of $\mathcal{L}_{\mathsf{FDE}}$. That $\mathcal{L}_{\mathsf{K}_3}$ is an extension of $\mathcal{L}_{\mathsf{FDE}}$ follows from the fact that every $\mathcal{L}_{\mathsf{K}_3}$-model is an $\mathcal{L}_{\mathsf{FDE}}$-model; that it is a *proper* extension follows from the fact that, for example, $A, {\sim}A \Vdash_{\mathsf{K}_3} B$ but $A, {\sim}A \nVdash_{\mathsf{FDE}} B$. (Proof is left as exercise.)

TABLEAUX

Not surprisingly, a tableaux procedure for K3 arises directly out of FDE. By adding only the following (closing off) rule to FDE one thereby gains a strongly sound and complete procedure with respect to $\mathcal{L}_{\mathsf{K}_3}$-consequence (and, derivatively, logical truth): If $\langle A, \oplus \rangle$ and $\langle {\sim}A, \oplus \rangle$ occur on a branch, the branch *closes off*. (Why does this rule apply to K3-tableaux but not FDE?)

NOTABLE FEATURES AND $\mathcal{L}_{\text{Ł}_3}$

Like $\mathcal{L}_{\mathsf{FDE}}$, $\mathcal{L}_{\mathsf{K}_3}$ is devoid of logical truths, and precisely for the same reason: both recognize the possibility in which every sentence may be Gappy. Accordingly, Excluded Middle fails: $\nVdash_{\mathsf{K}_3} A \vee {\sim}A$.

For the same reason, *material identity* fails: $\nVdash_{\mathsf{K}_3} A \supset A$. Where $A \supset A$ is read as a conditional, this failure is initially puzzling. After all, if A is true, then (surely!) A is true. That said, one must recall that the hook is only a conditional by courtesy; it is a disguised disjunction, namely, ${\sim}A \vee A$. Accordingly, the failure of material identity is just the failure of Excluded Middle, for which some motivation (viz., the liar) was given.

The language $\mathcal{L}_{Ł_3}$

One might think that in light of the foregoing $\mathcal{L}_{K_3}$ does not have a genuine conditional, and so one might want to add a conditional to the language. In effect,[6] this is what happens with the language $\mathcal{L}_{Ł_3}$, formulated by Łukasiewicz [68]. ('$\mathcal{L}_{Ł_3}$' may be pronounced: *L sub Wook three*.)

$\mathcal{L}_{Ł_3}$ is precisely the same as $\mathcal{L}_{K_3}$ except that C in $S_{Ł_3}$ (and, given our current convention, $\mathbb{C} \in \mathcal{M}$) contains the additional primitive connective (operator) $\rightarrow$. Admissible $\mathcal{L}_{Ł_3}$-valuations agree with admissible $\mathcal{L}_{K_3}$-valuations on the common connectives; and with respect to $\rightarrow$ every admissible $\mathcal{L}_{Ł_3}$-valuation is such that v "accords with" the diagram:

$\rightarrow$	1	n	0
1	1	n	0
n	1	1	n
0	1	1	1

Whether this makes for a "genuine conditional" is up for debate; however, what is clear is that *identity* holds for $\rightarrow$, as one may check by defining $\Vdash_{Ł_3}$ in the usual way and examining the diagram above. To be sure, $A \vee {\sim}A$ still fails (and, hence, material identity); however, $\mathcal{L}_{Ł_3}$ is not devoid of logical truths, given that $A \rightarrow A$ is designated on all admissible valuations.

8.3 Truth Value Gluts

What does the Liar teach us? According to the first answer we learned that some (meaningful, declarative) sentences are gappy, notably l. There are a few reasons to be dissatisfied with the first answer. Perhaps the biggest problem is a *revenge problem*. Suppose, as above, that we admit three values—True, False, and Neither. Presumably, we still want to respect the *Exhaustion Principle*, according to which *every sentence is true or not true*. But, then, the original problem re-emerges in *strengthened* form:

The first displayed sentence in §8.3 is not true.

Let 'L' name the first displayed sentence in §8.3. It would seem that if L is true then it is not true. If L is not true, then it is true—since it truly says that it is not true. By the Exhaustion Principle, L is true or L is not true, and hence L is *both* true and not true. Contradiction again.

The "revenge problem" for the first (gappy) answer connects designated values with assertability. Specifically, one naturally thinks of *un*designated sentences as those that are never properly assertable, while designated sentences are properly assertable.[7] Given this, the gappy response based on

[6] though this is not historically or even chronologically accurate

[7] This is not to say that designated values are understood in terms of assertability; they may be understood as ways of being true, which connects to assertability via the principle: True sentences (on any way of being true) are assertable.

$\mathcal{L}_{K_3}$ seems to be problematic. After all, L appears to be the same sort of sentence as l, and so one expects that any satisfactory response to the latter must also apply to the former. But, then, what value should L receive on the (given) gappy approach? Answer: that L is neither true nor false; it is gappy (receives the value n). But one would think that if a sentence is neither true nor false, then it is not true, in which case L is not true, given that L is neither true nor false. The trouble is that none of this holds up in $\mathcal{L}_{K_3}$. After all, the sentence 'L is not true' is undesignated on this approach; hence, to assert that L is not true is to assert an undesignated sentence, and that seems awkward (at best).

The revenge problem is this: The proponent of the (given) gappy answer, modelled via $\mathcal{L}_{K_3}$, cannot properly assert her answer! What the gappy theorist *wants* to say is that L is not true; but saying *that* is to assert an undesignated sentence. Accordingly, the gappy solution is one of silence: Whereof one cannot speak, one should be silent.

The so-called *glut* theorist thinks that we *can* speak; she proposes not truth value gaps but, rather, *truth value gluts*. A sentence which is both true and false is said to be *glutty*. Whereas gappy sentences are underdetermined with respect to truth and falsity, glutty sentences are overdetermined: both values apply. L is one such sentence. With this lesson in mind, the "problematic" contradiction is *accepted*, in the sense that it is designated.

On this approach we have "discovered" only one non-classical category into which our (meaningful, declarative) sentences fall: the *glut* at the intersection of Truth and Falsity. Accordingly, we are once again led only to a three-valued semantics: Truth, Falsity, and Both (aka, Glutty).

As with the first answer, pressing questions emerge: How are the three values distributed among compound sentences? Like the first answer, we shall take a "classical" stance in order to complete this second response.

THE LANGUAGE $\mathcal{L}_{LP}$

This second answer to the Liar motivates a language standardly called '$\mathcal{L}_{LP}$' (with 'LP' mnemonic for 'Logic of Paradox').[8] The language, just as its gappy counterpart, arises by fiddling with $\mathcal{L}_{FDE}$. Specifically, $\mathcal{L}_{LP}$ "ignores" or fails to recognize the value n in $\mathcal{L}_{FDE}$. The details are as follows.

SYNTAX

The syntax is S_{cpl}. As before, we shall take $\supset$ and $\equiv$ to be defined connectives.

[8] As before, the language is frequently called 'LP' but we shall reserve this name for the given tableaux system. The language was advanced by Graham Priest [76].

SEMANTICS

An $\mathcal{L}_{\mathsf{LP}}$-model, $\mathcal{M}$, is a structure, $\langle \mathcal{V}, \mathcal{D}, \mathbb{C}, \nu \rangle$, where $\mathcal{V} = \{1, \mathsf{b}, 0\}$, $\mathcal{D} = \{1, \mathsf{b}\}$, and $\mathbb{C}$ and ν are as before.

Note that b is designated due to its informal motivation, where '$\nu(A) = \mathsf{b}$' is read as 'A is both true and false'. The idea is that any way of being true, including the glutty way, ought to be designated.

Admissible Valuations

Admissible $\mathcal{L}_{\mathsf{LP}}$-valuations are precisely those $\mathcal{L}_{\mathsf{FDE}}$-valuations such that

$$\nu(A) \neq \mathsf{n}\ , \text{ for any } A \in \mathcal{S}.$$

As above, $\mathcal{L}_{\mathsf{LP}}$ is just the language one gets from $\mathcal{L}_{\mathsf{FDE}}$ by "ignoring" n. Hence, admissible $\mathcal{L}_{\mathsf{K}_3}$-valuations are a proper subset of admissible $\mathcal{L}_{\mathsf{FDE}}$-valuations: the ones that ignore n.

As with $\mathcal{L}_{\mathsf{K}_3}$, $\mathcal{L}_{\mathsf{LP}}$ is a proper extension of $\mathcal{L}_{\mathsf{FDE}}$. That $\mathcal{L}_{\mathsf{LP}}$ is an extension of $\mathcal{L}_{\mathsf{FDE}}$ follows from the fact that every $\mathcal{L}_{\mathsf{LP}}$-model is an $\mathcal{L}_{\mathsf{FDE}}$-model; that it is a *proper* extension follows from the fact that, *nota bene*, $\Vdash_{\mathsf{LP}} A \vee {\sim}A$ but, as above, $\nVdash_{\mathsf{FDE}} A \vee {\sim}A$. (Proof is left as exercise.)

Therefore we now have logical truths in this language. It is easy to see (looking at the operator diagrams and recalling the similar facts above) that $\mathcal{L}_{\mathsf{LP}}$ has an admissible valuation which assigns b to all sentences. Hence, this language has no unsatisfiable sets. Yet, the language has valid arguments, for it is no longer the case that 'A therefore B' is valid exactly if $\{A, {\sim}B\}$ is unsatisfiable. For example, 'A, therefore A' is valid although $\{A, {\sim}A\}$ is satisfiable!

TABLEAUX

Not surprisingly, a tableaux procedure for LP arises directly out of FDE. Indeed, by adding only the following (closing off) rule to FDE one thereby gains a sound and complete procedure with respect to $\mathcal{L}_{\mathsf{LP}}$-consequence (and, derivatively, logical truth): If $\langle A, \ominus \rangle$ and $\langle {\sim}A, \ominus \rangle$ occur on a branch, the branch *closes*. (Why is this rule not applicable in K_3?)

NOTABLE FEATURES AND $\mathcal{L}_{\mathsf{RM}_3}$

A notable feature of $\mathcal{L}_{\mathsf{LP}}$ is that every logical truth of $\mathcal{L}_{\mathsf{CPL}}$ is a logical truth of $\mathcal{L}_{\mathsf{LP}}$.[9] In particular: $\Vdash_{\mathsf{LP}} {\sim}(A \wedge {\sim}A)$, which is to say that the Law of Non-Contradiction is valid in $\mathcal{L}_{\mathsf{LP}}$! Yet, as we know, a contradiction (a sentence of the form $A \wedge {\sim}A$) may be satisfiable in $\mathcal{L}_{\mathsf{LP}}$.

While the glutty response seems to afford a viable and, in many ways, natural reply to the Liar, one might be dissatisfied with the "conditional" (viz., the hook) in $\mathcal{L}_{\mathsf{LP}}$. Unlike $\mathcal{L}_{\mathsf{K}_3}$, material identity holds in $\mathcal{L}_{\mathsf{LP}}$. (Proof: exercise.) The trouble, however, is that material modus ponens fails: $A, A \supset$

[9] Proof is left as exercise.

$B \nVdash_{LP} B$. (Just let $v(A) = b$ and $v(B) = 0$.) That said, the previous warning applies: the hook is only a conditional by courtesy; it is a disguised disjunction, namely, $\sim A \vee B$. Indeed, for this very reason "material modus ponens" is simply ***disjunctive syllogism***, which likewise fails: $A, \sim A \vee B \nVdash_{LP} B$. While the failure of disjunctive syllogism is initially alarming, the glutty theorist has an explanation at hand: Presumably, disjunctive syllogism was christened a "law" while ignoring sentences such as the Liar, which, after all, are easy sorts of sentence to overlook.

The language $\mathcal{L}_{RM_3}$

Disjunctive syllogism (material modus ponens) aside, the issue of a detachable conditional (i.e., one for which modus ponens holds) remains. As with $\mathcal{L}_{K_3}$, one might want to introduce a genuine, or at least detachable, conditional. This, in effect, is what happens with the language $\mathcal{L}_{RM_3}$.[10]

$\mathcal{L}_{RM_3}$ is precisely the same as $\mathcal{L}_{LP}$ except that $\mathcal{C}$ in S_{RM_3} (and, given our current convention, $\mathbb{C} \in \mathcal{M}$) contains the primitive connective (operator) $\rightarrow$. In turn, admissible $\mathcal{L}_{RM_3}$-valuations agree with admissible $\mathcal{L}_{LP}$-valuations on the common connectives; and with respect to $\rightarrow$ every admissible $\mathcal{L}_{RM_3}$-valuation is such that v "accords with" the diagram:

$\rightarrow$	1	b	0
1	1	0	0
b	1	b	0
0	1	1	1

Whether $\mathcal{L}_{RM_3}$ provides a "genuine conditional" is debatable; however, it is clear that its conditional is at least detachable, as may be checked by defining $\Vdash_{RM_3}$ in the usual way and examining the diagram above.

8.4 MEANINGLESS?

What does the Liar teach us? A common thought is that l and L are simply meaningless; they are declarative sentences but none the less meaningless. Of course, there are different ways in which a (declarative) sentence might properly be called 'meaningless'. Perhaps the best example involves so-called *category mistakes*, as in 'The square of two smiles when it looks in the mirror' or the more familiar 'Colorless green ideas sleep furiously'. The trouble is that neither l nor L seems to involve a category mistake. So, in what sense are they meaningless? Various answers have been given but the most common (though arguably least sophisticated) thought is that *self-reference* or *circularity* is the problem. In order to avoid ad hocery, this sort

[10] The name stems from the corresponding logical system, which is traditionally called 'RM_3', a logic within a family of n-valued relevance logics based on the system 'R-mingle'. (The 'R' stems from a name of one of the earliest relevance logics, developed by Anderson and Belnap, who also discuss R-mingle). We return to some basics of relevance logic in Part IV.

of response usually calls for an all-out ban on circular sentences, assigning each to the category of *meaningless*.

This response faces numerous problems, including, perhaps, the revenge problem discussed above. For present purposes we note only that the whiff of meaninglessness motivates a third response to the liar. According to this response, the lesson is similar to the first answer: The Liar teaches us that there are gappy (because meaningless) declarative sentences. The difference between this response and the first (strong Kleene) response arises at the level of compound sentences.

Unlike the first response, the current approach takes a "non-classical" stance. The motivation, here, is the idea of an *infectious* meaninglessness, one that spreads throughout any compound. The idea is nicely captured by a Chinese proverb: *A single jot of rat's dung spoils the soup*. In other words, if A is meaningless then any conjunction is likewise meaningless if A figures as one of its conjuncts; the same goes for all other connectives—the rat's dung spoils the entire soup.

THE LANGUAGE $\mathcal{L}_{B_3}$

This "meaningless" response to the Liar motivates the language $\mathcal{L}_{B_3}$.[11] The syntax remains S_{cpl}. In a sense, $\mathcal{L}_{B_3}$ emerges by fiddling with $\mathcal{L}_{FDE}$, but the fiddling is more drastic. While $\mathcal{L}_{B_3}$, like $\mathcal{L}_{K_3}$, ignores b in $\mathcal{L}_{FDE}$, it also deviates with respect to admissible $\mathcal{L}_{FDE}$-valuations.

SEMANTICS

An $\mathcal{L}_{B_3}$-model, $\mathcal{M}$, is a structure, $\langle \mathcal{V}, \mathcal{D}, \mathbb{C}, v \rangle$, where (keeping in mind the looseness with respect to $\mathbb{C}$)

$$\begin{aligned} \mathcal{V} &= \{1, n, 0\} \\ \mathcal{D} &= \{1\} \\ \mathbb{C} &= \{\wedge, \vee, \sim\} \\ v &: \mathcal{S} \longrightarrow \mathcal{V} \end{aligned}$$

'$v(A) = n$' may be read 'A is meaningless', where, needless to say, meaninglessness is not a way of being true (not designated).

Admissible Valuations

Admissible $\mathcal{L}_{B_3}$-valuations are $\mathcal{L}_{B_3}$-valuations that "accord with" the following diagrams:

[11]This language was originally proposed by the Russian logician, D. Bochvar [13]. Kleene [56] proposed a similar language, often called *Weak Kleene*. Bochvar actually proposed a slightly more complex language than what we give here; he defined both *internal* and *external* connectives, each defined by different matrices. For present purposes, we stick only to the so-called internal matrices, which are the same as Kleene's weak matrices.

$\sim$	
1	0
n	n
0	1

$\wedge$	1	n	0
1	1	n	0
n	n	n	n
0	0	n	0

$\vee$	1	n	0
1	1	n	1
n	n	n	n
0	1	n	0

So, with respect to "purely classical input", input only from $\{1, 0\}$, every admissible $\mathcal{L}_{B_3}$-valuation yields a purely classical output;[12] however, even a jot of rat's dung spoils the soup. Accordingly, we see again that there are no logical truths; it is possible for all sentences to receive the value n.

We observe that $\mathcal{L}_{B_3}$ is not an extension of $\mathcal{L}_{FDE}$ given that, for example, *Addition* holds in the latter but not the former; that is, $A \Vdash_{FDE} A \vee B$ but $A \nVdash_{B_3} A \vee B$. Moreover, $\mathcal{L}_{FDE}$ is not an extension of $\mathcal{L}_{B_3}$ given that, for example, *Explosion* holds in the latter but not the former; that is, $A, \sim A \Vdash_{B_3} B$ but $A, \sim A \nVdash_{FDE} B$. We leave definitions and corresponding proofs as exercise.

PROOF THEORY

A tableau procedure may be constructed for $\mathcal{L}_{B_3}$ but we will leave that to the interested reader. (Note: Value markers will be essential.)

EXERCISES 8.4.1

1 Let A be any statement, and $\langle A \rangle$ a name of statement, A. Some philosophers have held that a minimal condition on truth is that for any statement, A, the following holds:

$$\langle A \rangle \text{ is true if and only if } A.$$

That is often called the *T-schema*. Now, suppose that some statements are said to be neither true nor false. What effect, if any, does this have on the given condition on truth? What conditions should be imposed on *falsity*? How should the given 'if and only if' be understood (under what conditions will it be understood to be true, false)?

2 The first displayed sentence in §8.3 is not true. Is that true? false? what?

3 Consider the following argument against the thesis that some statements of the form A *and not*-A could be true (as well as being false).

1. Assume that A *and not*-A is true.
2. Then A is true. [from (1)]
3. Then A *or* B is true. [from (2)]
4. *not*-A is true. [from (1)]

[12] Proof is left as exercise

5. Therefore, B is true. [from (3) and (4)]

The upshot is (allegedly) that if A *and not*-A is true, then *every* statement is true. (Recall that B is arbitrary.) The question is: Is this a good reason for rejecting the thesis that some statements of the form A *and not*-A are true—even granting that, as seems fairly clear, we (rationally) ought to reject that *every* statement is true?

4 *Curry's paradox*, so called after Haskell Curry [24], involves a sentence which says of itself only that *if* it is true then every sentence is true. (E.g., 'If this conditional is true, then everything is true'.) So, a Curry sentence is a conditional the antecedent of which attributes truth to the entire conditional and the consequent is some (obviously) false sentence. In $\mathcal{L}_{LP}$ the only "conditional" is a material conditional, and so any Curry sentence in that language is equivalent to a version of the Liar—a so-called *disjunctive* version, like 'This sentence is not true *or* every sentence is true'. Accordingly, the second answer to the liar treats Curry sentences in like manner: they are true and false. The situation is different in $\mathcal{L}_{RM_3}$. Give an argument showing that if Curry sentences are true in $\mathcal{L}_{RM_3}$, then so too are all sentences.

5 The argument that l (similarly L) is both true and false uses Modus Ponens. Accordingly, the given argument for treating the liar sentences as gluts seems to be undermined if one adopts $\mathcal{L}_{LP}$. But is this so? Can you find argument forms that are valid in $\mathcal{L}_{LP}$ that afford an argument for the conclusion that l is both true and false?

6 Consider the infinite series

K_1) For all $i \geq 2$, (K_i) is not true.

K_2) For all $i \geq 3$, (K_i) is not true.

K_3) For all $i \geq 4$, (K_i) is not true.

⋮ ⋮

This is Yablo's paradox [108, 109], which exchanges self-reference (or, more generally, circularity) for infinity. What bearing does this have on the third ("meaningless") response to the liar?

7 As we mentioned, Bochvar defined "external connectives" in addition to the "internal" ones of $\mathcal{L}_{B_3}$. Define the unary operator $\top$ thus:

A	TA
1	1
n	0
0	0

The external connectives (which we'll indicate with subscripted 'e' for external) are defined thus, for any admissible valuation ν of the (expanded) language:

$$\begin{aligned}\nu({\sim_e}A) &= \nu({\sim}TA)\\ \nu(A \wedge_e B) &= \nu(TA \wedge TB)\\ \nu(A \vee_e B) &= \nu(TA \vee TB)\end{aligned}$$

Discuss what effect, if any, these external connectives have with respect to the "revenge problem".

FURTHER READING

In addition to the references in the text Alasdair Urquhart's [98] provides a more advanced discussion of the material here. Barwise and Etchemendy [5], Belnap and Gupta [41], McGee [71], Priest [77], and Simmons [89] provide further discussion of the Liar, as do the earlier volumes by Martin [69, 70].

Unlike FDE, LP is not a relevance logic; however, it (like FDE) is a so-called paraconsistent logic. (A paraconsistent language is one in which an arbitrary sentence and its negation do *not* imply every sentence.) Woods [107] gives a recent discussion of paraconsistent logics and their relation to paradoxes and the "abstract sciences".

For discussion of Yablo's paradox see [6] and references therein.

One of themselves, even a prophet of their own, said,
The Cretans are always liars, evil beasts, slow bellies.
This witness is true.
– St. Paul, *Epistle to Titus*

Chapter 9
Heaps, Supertruth, and the Continuum

In §8 we looked at a few languages that admit truth value gaps; in each case, familiar "laws of logic", such as Excluded Middle, fail. In this chapter we briefly discuss a technique—namely, supervaluations—which accommodates gaps and preserves the "laws" of classical logic. As in §8 we motivate the given approach via paradox: in this case, the so-called *sorites* paradox (from the Greek 'soros' for *heap*). With the sorites at hand we also mention a generalization of Łukasiewicz's language $\mathcal{L}_{Ł_3}$, namely the language $\mathcal{L}_{Ł_\aleph}$ (pronounced 'El-sub-aleph'), which we briefly present in §9.3.[1]

9.1 The Sorites Paradox

The sorites paradox is a so-called *little-by-litte* paradox that can arise from some sort of indeterminacy involved in the application of various expressions.[2] Consider, for example, the following argument, taken from the Megarian logician Eubulides of Miletus.[3]

> 1 grain of wheat does not make a heap.
>
> If 1 grain of wheat does not make a heap, then 2 grains of wheat do not make a heap.
>
> If 2 grains of wheat do not make a heap, then 3 grains of wheat do not make a heap.

---

[1] 'ℵ' is the first letter of the Hebrew alphabet, selected by Cantor to denote one "size" of infinity, in this case the continuum.

[2] Exactly what sort of indeterminacy is highly controversial. Needless to say, we shall step lightly around such controversy.

[3] Eubulides apparently had a great eye for paradox, given that he is generally credited not only with the sorites but also with both the Liar and the so-called *Hooded Man*, which in common parlance is a puzzle about opacity. (You know your father but you do not know the hooded man before you; however, your father *is* the hooded man before you.)

If 3 grains of wheat do not make a heap, then 4 grains of wheat do not make a heap.

⋮

If 99,999 grains of wheat does not make a heap, then 100,000 grains of wheat do not make a heap.

Therefore, 100,000 grains of wheat do not make a heap.

Classical logic deems this argument to be valid. What is troubling is that each of the premises seems to be true; however, the conclusion seems to be false.

The paradox, of course, does not depend only on the predicate 'is a heap (of wheat)'. If that were the case, the paradox would be less troubling than it appears. What makes the paradox apparently very troubling is that it arises for *most* predicates (and many singular terms) in natural language. In particular, a sorites paradox arises for any predicate that is tolerant with respect to "small" changes.[4] The given tolerance is reflected in the fact that, for many predicates, if the predicate applies to x then it still applies to x despite a "small" change in x. So, if Agnes is a child at t, then Agnes is a child at $t + n$, where n is some "small" unit. But, then, eventually Agnes is a child at $t + k$, where k is some "big" unit (e.g., forty years). Virtually every predicate of natural language reflects the given tolerance, and this is what makes the sorites particularly troubling.

The problem is not merely a case of counter-intuition; genuine inconsistency arises. Consider, for example, the "reverse" sorites argument concerning 'is a heap (of wheat)'.

100,000 grains of wheat makes a heap.

If 100,000 grains of wheat makes a heap, then 99,999 grains of wheat makes a heap.

If 99,999 grains of wheat makes a heap, then 99,998 grains of wheat makes a heap.

If 99,998 grains of wheat makes a heap, then 99,997 grains of wheat makes a heap.

⋮

[4] Alas, 'small' is itself a paradigm example, even with respect to numbers: If n is a small number, then the successor of n is a small number. 1 is a small number. Hence, via numerous applications of Modus Ponens, k is a small number—where k is the *biggest natural number* you choose to pick!

If 2 grains of wheat makes a heap, then 1 grain of wheat makes a heap.

Therefore, 1 grain of wheat makes a heap.

Classical logic deems the argument valid and the premises seem to be true. The trouble, however, is that the conclusion seems to be false. But, now, putting the two arguments together, we have it that 1 grain of wheat makes a heap *and* does not make a heap. Contradiction.[5]

Responses

The sorites paradox is at the center of much contemporary work in philosophical logic and philosophy of language, and many responses to the paradox have been given.[6] For example, so-called *epistemicists* [92, 106] bite the bullet, as it were, clinging to classical logic and maintaining that sorites arguments are valid but unsound. On this view sorites arguments are unsound because there is in fact a sharp (but perhaps unknowable) boundary between being a heap and not being a heap. A fortiori, a single grain of wheat *does* make the difference between a heap of wheat and a collection of grains that is not a heap, although we will never know which number of grains marks the boundary.

Another bullet-biting response [97, 104] proposes an arbitrary decision: Either accept the original argument as sound or accept its corresponding "reverse" version. Once the decision is made, accept that no (or, in "reverse", every) number of grains makes a heap.

Against the foregoing views are approaches that posit *gaps* and those that posit *degrees of truth* (in some sense). We will briefly concentrate on these approaches; however, we shall mostly concentrate on the logical tools involved in (some versions of) such approaches, rather than worry about the detailed responses to the sorites. Accordingly, we turn first to an approach which invokes *supervaluations*. After discussing supervaluations in a general setting, we briefly sketch a supervaluational response to the sorites.

9.2 Gaps and Supervaluations

Suppose that, for whatever reason, you think that some statements are gappy, and that A is one such sentence. Questions:

---

[5]One might say that just as the Liar sentence is true and false, so too is the given sentence about wheat. This is certainly an option, but it is not a happy one: Given the ubiquity of vagueness, one would (by parity of reasoning) be led to the conclusion that virtually *every* sentence is both true and false. This is hard to believe, to say the least; and it is a far cry from holding that mere Liar-like sentences are true and false, where such sentences carry no observational consequences—unlike most vague sentences. Accordingly, we shall briefly discuss a few other, more standard responses to the sorites, leaving the "ubiquitous contradictions" proposal to the side.

[6]References for reading on the sorites are given in the further reading section, page 144. For present purposes, we merely note a few well-known responses.

1. Is the disjunction of A and its negation true?

2. Is the conjunction of A and its negation false?

The answer to both (1) and (2) is 'No' if the languages in §8 model your gaps. Some philosophers have disliked this answer. The thought is that logical truth, validity, and the like is a matter of *form*, as opposed to content. The thought is that, for example, even if A is gappy the disjunction of A and its negation is logically true, due to its form, just as the conjunction of A and its negation is logically false, in virtue of its form. Indeed, the idea is that classical logic captures all (and only) the right logical forms (at least with respect to the propositional level). The trouble is that $\mathcal{L}_{\mathsf{CPL}}$ fails to recognize gaps. The task, then, is to accommodate gaps while none the less preserving $\Vdash_{\mathsf{CPL}}$, the consequence relation of $\mathcal{L}_{\mathsf{CPL}}$.

Why might one say that all sentences of the form $A \vee {\sim}A$ are true if, in some cases, A is gappy? The "intuition" seems to be this: that *if* p were given a classical truth value, then $p \vee {\sim}p$ *would be* true. In other words, p might be gappy as things stand; however, if p *were* to have a truth value (either True or False) then $p \vee {\sim}p$ would be true, provided that we retain a properly classical understanding of negation and disjunction. Similarly for other classically valid forms: Any such form is one for which *classical input* yields *classical output*. The trouble, of course, is that gaps are not classical input. The task, once again, is to accommodate gaps while retaining the going "intuition" about classically validity.

What to do? One natural idea is to fiddle with $\mathcal{L}_{\mathsf{FDE}}$ along the lines of §8. But how? If the proposed fiddling proceeds along previous lines—for example, by fiddling with the matrices—an immediate difficulty looms. For example, suppose that, according to one's fiddling, if p has the value n then $p \vee {\sim}p$ has the value t. The question is: How does one avoid the unwelcome consequence that, where q also has value n, the sentence, $p \vee {\sim}q$, has the value t?[7] No straightforward solution suggests itself, at least if we limit our fiddling to the style of §8.

What, then, can be done? What we want is a language in which $p \vee {\sim}p$, in addition to every other classical logical truth, is true even if p takes the value n. More generally, we want a gappy language in which its underlying consequence relation, $\Vdash$, lines up perfectly with $\Vdash_{\mathsf{CPL}}$, in the sense that $\mathcal{X} \Vdash A$ iff $\mathcal{X} \Vdash_{\mathsf{CPL}} A$. Fiddling with $\mathcal{L}_{\mathsf{FDE}}$-valuations will not do the trick; however, "superimposing" a sort of valuation on certain extensions of $\mathcal{L}_{\mathsf{FDE}}$ will do the trick. Such superimposing gives rise to supervaluations, which are described below.

[7] We say that this is unwelcome; what we mean is that the guiding "intuition" (arising, for example, from Aristotle's treatment of future contingents) does not welcome the given result.

SUPERVALUATIONAL LANGUAGES

The driving "intuition", as above, is that *if* p were to receive a classical truth value, then $p \vee \sim p$ would be true, and similarly for any other classically valid form. We formalize this idea in terms of so-called *supervaluations*. The details are as follows.

Semantics

We begin with an arbitrary language $\mathcal{L}$ with syntax S_{cpl} (with usual defined connectives) and a set $\mathbb{V}$ of admissible valuations, which assign values to sentences from a set that includes some designated elements and some non-designated ones. We define:

DEFINITION 9.1 (SUPERVALUATIONS) An assignment σ to some or all sentences of $\mathcal{L}$ is a *supervaluation* of $\mathcal{L}$ just in case there is a set $\mathbb{V}_\sigma$ of admissible valuations of $\mathcal{L}$ such that σ assigns value x to A iff all elements of $\mathbb{V}_\sigma$ assign x to A, and σ is undefined at A if there is no such value.

DEFINITION 9.2 (SUPERVALUATIONAL LANGUAGE) Let $\mathcal{L}$ be a language. Then $\mathcal{L}^S$ is the language which is just like $\mathcal{L}$ except that its admissible valuations are the supervaluations of $\mathcal{L}$, which satisfy a sentence of $\mathcal{L}^S$ iff they assign it one of the designated elements of $\mathcal{L}$.

Note that we are liberalizing the notion of valuation here; we are allowing among them functions that are not defined for the entire set of sentences ("partial functions").[8] We have three categories:

» Truths: sentences assigned a designated element;

» Falsehoods (or anti-truths, if you like): sentences assigned one of the original non-designated elements;

» Truth-value Gaps: Neither Truths nor Falsehoods.

An important fact about supervaluational languages is recorded in

THEOREM 9.1 *If* $\mathcal{X} \Vdash A$ *in* $\mathcal{L}^S$ *then* $\mathcal{X} \Vdash A$ *in* $\mathcal{L}$.

PROOF THM 9.1 First of all the set $\mathbb{V}_\sigma$ is allowed to contain only a single member v, in which case $\sigma = v$. Therefore all admissible valuations of $\mathcal{L}$ are admissible valuations of $\mathcal{L}^S$, and hence the latter is an extension of $\mathcal{L}$, in which case all arguments valid in $\mathcal{L}^S$ are also valid in $\mathcal{L}$. QED

[8] We could easily go back to the old more conservative notion by extending the partial function to assign value 17, say, to each sentence for which it was originally undefined (requiring only that 17 be a new value, not in the range of the admissible valuations of $\mathcal{L}$). This would require only minor changes in phrasing in what follows.

Does the converse of Theorem 9.1 also hold? Not necessarily. Suppose that the language $\mathcal{L}$ is three-valued with $\mathcal{V} = \{1, b, 0\}$ and $\mathcal{D} = \{1, b\}$. (As before, $\mathcal{D}$ comprises designated elements of $\mathcal{V}$.) Imagine now that B $\Vdash$ A in $\mathcal{L}$. Let a B-truth-assignment be any valuation that assigns 1 to B. Suppose that some B-truth-assignments assign 1 to A while others assign b to A, so that all such assignments designate A. Now let $\mathbb{V}_\sigma$ comprise all admissible valuations that assign 1 to B. Clearly the corresponding supervaluation (there is just one) assigns nothing at all to A; it satisfies premise B but not conclusion A. So there we would have an argument valid in a language $\mathcal{L}$ but not in the associated (supervaluational) language $\mathcal{L}^S$.

While the converse of Theorem 9.1 does not hold, a related fact emerges:

THEOREM 9.2 *If $\mathcal{L}$ has only one designated element, then $\mathcal{X} \Vdash$ A in $\mathcal{L}^S$ if $\mathcal{X} \Vdash$ A in $\mathcal{L}$.*

PROOF THM 9.2 Suppose that an argument from $\mathcal{X}$ to A is valid in $\mathcal{L}$. In that case, if supervaluation σ satisfies all sentences in $\mathcal{X}$, it assigns the same designated element (call it 'x') to each such sentence (each element of $\mathcal{X}$), in which case all members of $\mathbb{V}_\sigma$ do likewise. Hence, all elements of $\mathbb{V}_\sigma$, being admissible valuations of $\mathcal{L}$, must assign x to A, and therefore σ does too. QED

We note that the canvassed languages in which satisfaction is defined in terms of a single designated element fall under both Theorems 9.1 and 9.2. If, for example, $\mathcal{L}$ is $\mathcal{L}_{CPL}$ or $\mathcal{L}_{K_3}$ then the corresponding language $\mathcal{L}^S$ will have the same valid sentences and arguments as $\mathcal{L}$.

The Language $\mathcal{L}^{\star}_{K_3}$

Before returning to the sorites we pause to note a further connection between supervaluations, $\mathcal{L}_{CPL}$, and $\mathcal{L}_{K_3}$. In particular, the language $\mathcal{L}_{CPL}$ can in a certain sense be transformed into the language $\mathcal{L}_{K_3}$ and the result may respect some of the linguistic intuitions for which the latter was designed, without quite as much damage to our classical logic.

Suppose that we think of the third value n of $\mathcal{L}_{K_3}$ as just being a sort of gap waiting to be filled. Then we can define:

DEFINITION 9.3 (COMPLETIONS) An admissible $\mathcal{L}_{CPL}$-valuation ν is a *completion* of admissible $\mathcal{L}_{K_3}$-valuation κ exactly if ν assigns 1 to all sentences to which κ assigns 1 and ν assigns 0 to all sentences to which κ assigns 0.

DEFINITION 9.4 (COUNTERPARTS) A supervaluation σ of $\mathcal{L}_{CPL}$ is an $\mathcal{L}_{K_3}$-*counterpart* just in case there is an admissible valuation ν of $\mathcal{L}_{K_3}$ such that for any sentence A, $\sigma(A)$ is the value that all completions of ν assigns to A, and undefined if there is no such value.

DEFINITION 9.5 ($\mathcal{L}^{\star}_{K_3}$) The language $\mathcal{L}^{\star}_{K_3}$ is the language just like $\mathcal{L}_{CPL}$ except that its admissible valuations are the $\mathcal{L}_{K_3}$-counterparts, and such a valuation satisfies A iff it assigns 1 to A.

Evidently, an admissible $\mathcal{L}^{\star}_{K_3}$-valuation yields gaps, at the very least for the atomic sentences to which the corresponding valuation in $\mathcal{L}_{K_3}$ assigns the "gappy" value n. That said, there are certainly logical truths in $\mathcal{L}^{\star}_{K_3}$. To this end we mention a few notable theorems.

THEOREM 9.3 *$\mathcal{X} \Vdash A$ in $\mathcal{L}^{\star}_{K_3}$ if $\mathcal{X} \Vdash_{CPL} A$.*

PROOF THM 9.3 To prove Theorem 9.3 it suffices to have a look at the proof of Theorem 9.2, where the argument did not depend on all supervaluations of $\mathcal{L}_{CPL}$ being admissible and, so, works just as well here. QED

What about the converse of Theorem 9.3? Suppose we have a classical two-valued valuation ν which provides a counterexample to the claim that $\mathcal{X} \Vdash_{CPL} A$. In this case ν will engender a counterexample to the claim that $\mathcal{X} \Vdash A$ in $\mathcal{L}^{\star}_{K_3}$ if we can prove the following:

LEMMA 9.1 *There is an admissible $\mathcal{L}_{K_3}$-valuation κ such that ν is a completion of κ and all completions of κ satisfy $\mathcal{X}$.*

That Lemma 9.1 holds is easy enough to see: $\mathcal{L}_{K_3}$ happens to be an extension of $\mathcal{L}_{CPL}$ in that all those two-valued valuations are among its admissible valuations. ($\mathcal{L}_{K_3}$ has such non-classical beasts as the valuation that assigns n to all sentences, which is why no sentence is valid in this language; but it also has valuations that assign n to no sentence at all, and those are classical.) So κ can just be ν itself. Therefore:

THEOREM 9.4 *$\mathcal{X} \Vdash A$ in $\mathcal{L}^{\star}_{K_3}$ only if $\mathcal{X} \Vdash_{CPL} A$.*

A Note on Tableaux

Given Theorems 9.3 and 9.4 we need not search far for a suitable tableaux system for $\mathcal{L}^{\star}_{K_3}$. After all, we already have CPL (see §4) which, given Theorems 9.3 and 9.4 and the adequacy of $\vdash_{CPL}$ with respect to $\Vdash_{CPL}$, yields that CPL-tableaux are sufficient to test supervalidity.

SUPERVALUATIONS AND THE SORITES

One response to the sorites is that the argument is valid but has a gappy premise(s). By invoking supervaluations one may accommodate such gaps while none the less retaining the classical consequence relation, as discussed in §9.2. But supervaluations can do more than merely preserve classical consequence in the face of gaps; they can also serve as a metaphor, of sorts, that suits a particular conception of language. By way of illustration consider the familiar exchange between Humpty Dumpty and Alice in Lewis Carroll's *Through The Looking Glass*:

"... There's glory for you!" [said Humpty]

"I don't know what you mean by 'glory'," Alice said.

Humpty Dumpty smiled contemptuously. "Of course you don't—till I tell you. I meant ' there's a nice knock-down argument for you! ' "

"But 'glory' doesn't mean 'a nice knock-down argument'," Alice objected.

"When *I* use a word," Humpty Dumpty said, in a rather scornful tone, "it means just what I choose it to mean—neither more nor less."

"The question is," said Alice, "whether you *can* make words mean so many different things."

"The question is," said Humpty Dumpty, "which is to be master—that's all."

Humpty Dumpty's position is far too crude. Still, there may be some features of language to which Humpty's "master" declarations apply.

Consider the predicate 'is a child'. On one hand, English is *settled* with respect to many uses of 'is a child'. The predicate truly applies to any human under the age of five; it falsely applies to any human over the age of fifty. With respect to these cases, the predicate is *settled*, and neither Humpty nor anyone else is masterful enough to change the situation. On the other hand, there are many cases where the language is apparently *un*settled: Is a sixteen year old human a child? In the absence of some sort of *arbitrary decision* (e.g., a legal decision or the like), there seems to be no answer to this question, as the language seems to be entirely unsettled on the matter.

Another example: Specify the exact time at which Aristotle became a person! Without some arbitrary decision, there seems to be no way to so specify. The trouble is that the language is unsettled with respect to the predicate 'is a person'. There are *some* sentences of the form 'Aristotle is a person at t' that are true; there are *some* false sentences of that form; however, in between the true and false sentences there seem to be gaps—reflecting the unsettled (or indeterminate) nature of the language. These indeterminate cases are the ones wherein Humpty's view sits well, at least on the going conception of language.

According to the foregoing picture, sentences fall into three categories: True, False, and Unsettled. The idea, then, is along Humpty's line: We (language users) are at liberty to settle the Unsettled cases as we wish; the only constraint is that our decisions cannot force changes on the settled cases. Aside from this constraint, we are masters when dealing with the Unsettled cases, where, after all, the decisions concern not the objects themselves but, rather, how we choose to speak about such objects.

A Response to the Sorites

So much for Humpty. The question is: What role do supervaluations play in all this? Supervaluations afford not only a suitable semantic framework;

they also serve as a metaphor. The picture is one in which the language is settled with respect to various cases but unsettled in others.

Let us say that when (by arbitrary decision) we settle some of the otherwise unsettled cases, we *precisify* the language. The idea, then, is that among the many ways of precisifying the language some options are "admissible" while others are not admissible. With this in mind, the metaphor behind supervaluations is clear: We can think of *completions* as *admissible precisifications* of the language. Of course, the "admissible precisifications" are precisely those "completions" of the language that accord with the *settled* cases. Accordingly, such precisifications will preserve not only the currently settled *contingent* truths and falsehoods; they will likewise preserve all "previous" logical truths, given the nature of supervaluations.

Now the picture sharpens: On the current conception we adopt a supervaluational stance with respect to indeterminate (vague) language. Specifically, a sentence is true iff it is true on all admissible precisifications; it is false iff it is false on all admissible precisifications; otherwise, it is gappy. Given the results of §9.2, we preserve classical consequence while none the less admitting gaps.

Responding to the sorites argument is now clear: such arguments are valid but at least one of the (conditional) premises is untrue—in fact, gappy. To be sure, the precise point at which one goes from a true (conditional) premise to a gappy (conditional) premise is not known; however, so long as there is a gappy premise, the otherwise troubling conclusion is averted.

9.3 SLIDING DOWN THE CONTINUUM

A common objection to the foregoing supervaluational response is that it draws an "unintuitive boundary" around its three categories: True, False, and Gappy. The may be "higher-order vagueness". The criticism applies equally well to any classical, two-valued response; indeed, it applies to any n-valued response, where $n \in \mathbb{N}$. The criticism rests on the "intuition" that, for example, going from n millimeters to $n - 1$ millimeters cannot take you from being tall to being not tall. Of course, on the supervaluational approach, that b is not tall does not imply that 'b is tall' is *false*. None the less, the criticism is that "intuitively" there is no "sharp boundary" between being tall and not being tall: If 100 men are lined up from tallest to shortest, and each man differs in height by only one millimeter (or less, if need be), it seems that there is no settled boundary marking the n such that n millimeters is tall but $n - 1$ is not tall.

The basic problem, according to the going criticism, is that going from (say) an adult to a child is not a *discrete* process; rather, it is a *continuous* process. In some important sense, being a child (or heap, or person) is a *fading* process; one moves from being a child to an adult very, very gradually. It is precisely this gradual, indeed continuous, phenomenon that the supervaluational and other finitely-valued approaches neglect.

According to the foregoing response, then, what we learn from the sorites is that truth itself is continuous, in some sense. Given the gradual process involved in going from *a child* to *an adult*, it is natural to think that 'Agnes is a child' itself gradually fades from truth to falsity. What we need to recognize, according to the going response, is not a discretely ordered set of semantic values; rather, we need to recognize a *continuum* of such values. In doing so, we will be able to recognize the problem with sorites arguments while none the less respecting the continuous phenomena that they represent.

Łukasiewicz's Language $\mathcal{L}_{Ł_{\aleph}}$

The foregoing picture motivates various infinitely-valued languages.[9] We will just present Łukasiewicz's continuum-valued language, $\mathcal{L}_{Ł_{\aleph}}$. Infinitely-valued responses to the sorites frequently involve semantics that differ from $\mathcal{L}_{Ł_{\aleph}}$, especially with respect to the conditional; however, such differences are easy to understand once the basics of $\mathcal{L}_{Ł_{\aleph}}$ are in hand.[10]

The driving "intuition", as above, is that the semantic value of sentences may gradually fade from truth to falsity. This is naturally modelled by taking $\mathcal{V}$, in the usual many-valued structures, to comprise continuum-many elements. So, a natural approach is to let $\mathcal{V}$ comprise all real numbers between 0 and 1, which may be recorded thus: $\mathcal{V} = [0, 1]$. The idea (on the current approach) is that 1 corresponds to Truth, 0 to Falsity; any of the (infinitely many) other values corresponds to a value which is *more or less true (false)*, depending on where the value lies in the continuum. (So, e.g., .9 represents a value closer to truth than the value represented by .8, and so on.) The details run as follows.

Syntax

The syntax is the usual S_{cpl}, with the usual defined connectives, but expanded with the extra primitive (conditional) $\rightarrow$. The sentences are defined inductively in the usual way.

---

[9] Sometimes, the given languages and corresponding logics are called 'fuzzy languages' (logics); however, this term is probably best reserved for languages underwritten by a semantics that invokes so-called *fuzzy sets*, which we will not discuss. (We do provide references for the interested interested reader. See page 144.)

[10] We should note that Łukasiewicz and Tarski [68] proposed the given language merely as a generalization of Łukasiewicz's 3-valued semantics, and not with an eye on the sorites. That said, Łukasiewicz did think that the infinitely-valued language had philosophical significance, mostly in terms of "degrees of possibility".

Semantics
Models are structures of the usual many-valued sort.[11] Specifically, $\mathcal{M}_{Ł_{\aleph}} = \langle \mathcal{V}, \mathcal{D}, \mathbb{C}, \nu \rangle$, where

$$\begin{aligned} \mathcal{V} &= [0,1] \\ \mathcal{D} &= \{1\} \\ \mathbb{C} &= \{\odot_{\sim}, \odot_{\vee}, \odot_{\wedge}, \odot_{\rightarrow}\} \\ \nu &: \mathcal{S} \longrightarrow \mathcal{V} \end{aligned}$$

The elements of $\mathbb{C}$ are specified as follows. Let m and n be any elements of $\mathcal{V}$.[12] Let $\triangle(m,n)$ be the *maximum* of m and n, and let $\bigtriangledown(m,n)$ be the *minimum* of m and n. Then the operators corresponding to $\sim$, $\vee$, and $\wedge$ are these:

$$\begin{aligned} \odot_{\sim}(m) &= 1 - m \\ \odot_{\vee}(m,n) &= \triangle(m,n) \\ \odot_{\wedge}(m,n) &= \bigtriangledown(m,n) \end{aligned}$$

The operator corresponding to $\rightarrow$ is this:

$$\odot_{\rightarrow}(m,n) = \begin{cases} 1 & \text{if } m \leqslant n \\ 1-(m-n) & \text{otherwise.} \end{cases}$$

The intuitive motivation behind these functions is fairly straightforward. Consider negation. As Agnes grows, the truth value of 'Agnes is short' gradually goes down while the truth value of 'Agnes is not short' gradually goes up. The relation between the two is modeled by $\odot_{\sim}$, so that the value of $\sim A$ is a direct function of the value of A. Conjunctions and disjunctions are equally straightforward. A conjunction is only as valuable as its "worst" conjunct, as it were. The idea is that a conjunction has approached truth precisely to the degree that its worst conjunct has approached truth. Hence, $\nu(A \wedge B)$ is "as true as" its least conjunct, that is, the minimum of $\nu(A)$ and $\nu(B)$. Disjunctions, in turn, are simply the dual case of conjunctions: a disjunction has approached truth precisely to the degree that its "best" disjunct has approached truth.[13]

[11] For purposes of this section we will break from our convention of ambiguity; instead, we will explicitly denote elements of $\mathbb{C}$ as $\odot_{\varphi}$, where $\odot$ is some given operator corresponding to the connective φ in $\mathcal{C}$.

[12] Recall, as above, that $\nu(A)$ is an element of $\mathcal{V}$, which is a real number between 0 and 1, and so (for heuristic purposes) you can think of the following functions "acting on" $\nu(A)$, for each $A \in \mathcal{S}$.

[13] For those familiar with probability, we give a brief warning: Do not conflate *degrees of truth* and probabilities! There are similarities, to be sure; however, they are not the same. (Proof: exercise.)

What about $\rightarrow$? The idea, as with many conditionals, is that $A \rightarrow B$ "reduces" in truth value if it goes from "more truth" to "less truth". In the classical case, the conditional "goes down" in truth value precisely if A is true but B false. In the current case, one has (infinitely) more values between truth and falsity; so, the extent to which $A \rightarrow B$ "reduces" in truth value is exactly the difference between 1 (truth) and the slide from A to B: $v(A \rightarrow B) = 1 - (v(A) - v(B))$, at least when $v(A) > v(B)$. For example, if A and B are 'Agnes is a girl' and 'Agnes is a child', and these have values 0.6 and 0.4, then $A \rightarrow B$ has value 0.8. Of course, as per the classical case, if $v(A)$ is "less true" or "equally as true as" $v(B)$, then one *cannot* slide downwards, and so $A \rightarrow B$ is simply true.[14]

Notable Features

There are various notable features of $\mathcal{L}_{Ł_{\aleph}}$ but we mention only two with an eye on the sorites. We leave other features for exercises.

FACT 9.1 $A, A \rightarrow B \Vdash_{Ł_{\aleph}} B$

PROOF FACT 9.1 Suppose not. Then $v(A) = (A \rightarrow B) = 1$ and $v(B) < 1$, for some admissible v. As v is admissible and $v(A \rightarrow B) = 1$, we have it that $v(A) \leqslant v(B)$. (See the definition of $\odot_{\rightarrow}$.) But, then, $v(A) \neq 1$. Contradiction. QED

The other feature concerns what we will call an *untruth index*. Specifically, we say that $1 - v(A)$ is the "index" (or measure) of A's untruth: the "distance" of A from Truth.

FACT 9.2 $(1 - v(B)) \leqslant [(1 - v(A)) + (1 - v(A \rightarrow B))]$

PROOF FACT 9.2 Either $v(A) \leqslant v(B)$ or $v(A) > v(B)$. In the former case, $v(A \rightarrow B) = 1$, in which case $(1 - v(A)) + (1 - v(A \rightarrow B))$ is $1 - v(A)$, and hence $1 - v(B) \leqslant 1 - v(A)$. In the latter case, $v(A) - v(B) = i$, where $0 < i \leqslant 1$. But, then, $(1 - v(A))$ plus $1 - (1 - i)$ is $(1 - v(A)) + i$, which is just $v(B)$. QED

The upshot of Fact 9.2 is that an application of Modus Ponens never takes one further from truth than the sum of the "distance" from truth of each premise. The upshot of Fact 9.1 is that any application of Modus Ponens is valid in $\mathcal{L}_{Ł_{\aleph}}$.

---

[14]We are not endorsing this view of conditionals, of course; we are simply recording one motivation for the given semantics.

A Degree Response to the Sorites

The corresponding response to the sorites is now plain: Typical sorites arguments are *valid* but not sound. The reason they are valid is that (repeated applications of) Modus Ponens is valid in the given language. That such arguments are not sound follows from the fact that the conditionals themselves are not true. To see this, let $h_{100,000}$ be '$100,000$ grains makes a heap' and, in general, h_i is 'i grains make(s) a heap'. For simplicity, consider a valuation such that $v(h_i) = \frac{i}{100,000}$, so that $v(h_{100,000}) = 1$, $v(h_{99,999}) = .99999$, ..., and $v(h_0) = 0$. Then the first premise of our sorites argument, namely $h_{100,000}$, is true; however, each of the other premises is untrue, though only the conclusion is false. Each conditional, $h_i \rightarrow h_{i-1}$, has the same value, namely $1 - (v(h_i) - v(h_{i-1}))$, which is .99999, which is not 1 and, hence, not Truth. Moreover, each application of Modus Ponens, while valid, yields a conclusion that gradually approaches, and at h_0 reaches, 0. To be sure, *were* all the premises true (value one), then the soritical argument would be sound; but as they're not, it's not.

Of course, given "degrees of truth" it may be reasonable to distinguish between validity and acceptable inference. Likewise, it may be reasonable to distinguish between truth and rational acceptability. One might, for example, think that .99999 is close enough to truth to be acceptable. In this case, most of the soritical premises are not strictly speaking true, but the conditionals themselves are none the less acceptable. This is a reasonable position. What is important to note is that *in this case* repeated applications of Modus Ponens will not preserve "acceptability". In other words, if one takes an *acceptable inference*, as opposed to a valid inference, to be one such that the conclusion is at least as true as the least valuable premise, then "long chains" of otherwise acceptable applications of Modus Ponens will not be acceptable. After all, as one slides down the soritical premises each individual application of Modus Ponens is itself acceptable (so understood); however, at each such application one slides closer and closer to falsity, eventually reaching 0 at the conclusion h_0. (We leave a precise formulation and corresponding proof of this point as exercise.)

While the continuum-valued response has some nice features, we close by noting a common *Tu Quoque*. As we noted, one of the main criticisms of the supervaluational approach is that it bucks intuition, requiring an unintuitive "cut-off point" between heaps and non-heaps—that a single grain of wheat makes the difference between a heap and non-heap. The main charge, in the end, is that there just seems to be no such point at which one goes from a heap to non-heap, a child to adult, and so on. On the basis of this charge the continuum is invoked in an effort to recognize the "continuous nature of truth" (as it were). But, now, the *Tu quoque* is plain: The continuum-valued approach is committed to a "sharp point" at which

Agnes ceases to be one hundred percent short (a child, rich, and so on)! Hence, if the original charge is supposed to undermine the supervaluational (or any other finitely-valued) approach, it also undermines the continuum-valued approach. Adding values, even continuum many of them, will not remove *that* problem—if, in the end, it is a problem at all.

EXERCISES 9.3.1

1 Complete all exercises listed in the text.

2 Does a supervaluation have a base?

3 How, if at all, might supervaluations be used as a response to the Simple Liar, where a simple Liar sentence says of itself only that it is false? (What about the strengthened Liar?)

4 Show that probabilities (classically understood) and degrees of truth (as per $\mathcal{L}_{Ł_{\aleph}}$) do not work the same. (Hint: Consider conjunctions.)

5 Show that arguments valid in $\mathcal{L}_{Ł_{\aleph}}$ are valid in $\mathcal{L}_{Ł_3}$ (see page 122 for $\mathcal{L}_{Ł_3}$).

6 Show the following with respect to $\mathcal{L}_{Ł_{\aleph}}$, or provide a counterexample.

1. $\Vdash_{Ł_{\aleph}} A \rightarrow (B \rightarrow A)$
2. $\Vdash_{Ł_{\aleph}} {\sim}{\sim}A \rightarrow A$
3. ${\sim}A \rightarrow {\sim}B \Vdash_{Ł_{\aleph}} A \rightarrow B$
4. $A \rightarrow B \Vdash_{Ł_{\aleph}} (A \wedge C) \rightarrow B$
5. $\Vdash_{Ł_{\aleph}} (A \rightarrow B) \vee (B \rightarrow A)$
6. $A \rightarrow B \Vdash_{Ł_{\aleph}} {\sim}B \rightarrow {\sim}A$
7. $\Vdash_{Ł_{\aleph}} A \vee {\sim}A$
8. $\Vdash_{Ł_{\aleph}} {\sim}(A \wedge {\sim}A)$
9. $A \rightarrow B \Vdash_{Ł_{\aleph}} {\sim}A \vee B$
10. $A \rightarrow B \Vdash_{Ł_{\aleph}} {\sim}(A \wedge {\sim}B)$
11. $A \rightarrow B, B \rightarrow C \Vdash_{Ł_{\aleph}} A \rightarrow C$

FURTHER READING

In addition to the works cited above two very useful collections on the sorites (and vagueness, generally), each equipped with many references, are Keefe and Smith's [55] and Graff and Williamson's [40]. Williamson [106] provides a useful overview of various responses to the sorites, and also formulates and defends a so-called epistemicist position. Another recent collection that touches on both the sorites and Liar-like paradox is Beall's [7].

For the supervaluation approach to the Liar paradox, including the Strengthened Liar and further variations, see van Fraassen's [99, 100] and, for application to the sorites, see Fine's [34]. Achille Varzi [102] and Hyde [52] discuss so-called *subvaluations* and corresponding paraconsistent responses to the sorites.

More advanced discussion of Łukasiewicz's continuum-valued language is given by Urquhart [98].

Without philosophy thoughts are, as it were, cloudy and indistinct:
its task is to make them clear and to give them sharp boundaries.
– Ludwig Wittgenstein, *Tractatus Logico-Philosophicus*

Part IV

Metatheory

Chapter 10
Further Tools

Metalogical investigation, to which we soon turn, requires a variety of tools beyond those furnished in §2. Our aim in this chapter is to provide the requisite tools.

10.1 Functions: Composition, Preservation

Two more topics concerning functions will be useful: *composing* and *preserving*. We treat each topic in turn.

Functions can be *composed* (sometimes called *compounding*). Recall the following examples of functions from §2: $f(x) = \frac{0}{x}$, $g(x) = \sqrt{x}$, and $h(x) = x^2$. We can now construct the composite functions

$$fg : fg(x) = f(g(x)) = f(\sqrt{x}) = \frac{0}{\sqrt{x}}$$

$$gh : gh(x) = g(h(x)) = g(x^2) = \sqrt{x^2} = x.$$

So, if q and s are functions, then qs is a function (a composite of q and s); and by repeating the process, qsq and $qsqss$, and so on, are all functions. So goes *composition*.

Functions can *preserve* properties of their arguments. Example: squares are always positive. So, if we take a positive number as argument and square it we shall get a postive number "in return". Hence, the squaring function *preserves* the property of being *positive*. Similarly, multiplication by 3 is a function that preserves the property of being an odd integer. (Try it!)

The notion of preserving is so important that we shall define it precisely:

Definition 10.1 Function f of degree n *preserves* property P exactly if the following is the case:

» for any $x_1, \ldots, x_n$ and y, if $f(x_1, \ldots, x_n) = y$ and $x_1, \ldots, x_n$ all have property P, then y has property P too.

To illustrate these concepts we note that a valid argument form is in effect a truth-preserving function; it transforms given premises into a conclusion which is true if those premises are true. Recall the following function on sets of sentences of a given language $\mathcal{L}$ from Exercises 3.6.1:

$$Cn(\mathcal{X}) = \{A : \mathcal{X} \Vdash A\}$$

(suppressing the reference to $\mathcal{L}$ in our notation here). Since the values of this function, as well as its arguments, are sets of sentences, we can compose it with itself:

$$Cn\,(Cn(\mathcal{X})) = \{A : Cn(\mathcal{X}) \Vdash A\}$$

But it is easy to see (prove as Exercise!) that the result of this composition is just the function itself:

$$Cn\,(Cn(\mathcal{X})) = Cn(\mathcal{X})$$

which, in turn, is one good way of stating the transitivity of implication in a given language.

What does the function *Cn* preserve? If all the members of $\mathcal{X}$ are true, then so are all the members of $Cn(\mathcal{X})$. So, *Cn* preserves truth: it preserves the property of being satisfied by any given valuation, and so it also preserves the property of satisfiability.

To end with a slightly different sort of example, consider one of the normal modal languages, and the function which, when applied to any sentence A of that language, has value $\Box$A. That function does not preserve truth—but it does preserve validity. Does it preserve satisfiability? Does it preserve satisfiability within any given model? (The question is: if A is true in some world in a given model, does it follow that $\Box$A is true in some world in that model?)

10.2 INFINITY

A set has a size: the number of members it has (also called its *cardinality* or sometimes *power*). This size may be finite (in which case it is one of the natural numbers $0, 1, 2, 3, \ldots$) or infinite, and we introduce here a few basic concepts related to infinity.

A function f with domain $\mathcal{X}$ and range $\mathcal{Y}$ is *one-to-one* iff $f(x) = f(y)$ implies that $x = y$; and it is *onto* iff for every element y of $\mathcal{Y}$ there is an element x of $\mathcal{X}$ such that $f(x) = y$.

Two sets are *equipollent* (intuitively: they have the same size) iff there exists a one-to-one mapping of one onto the other. (Why is this a symmetric relationship?) Set $\mathcal{X}$ is *larger* than $\mathcal{X}'$ (and $\mathcal{X}'$ *smaller* than $\mathcal{X}$) just in case they are not equipollent but $\mathcal{X}'$ is equipollent to a subset of $\mathcal{X}$.

Let $\mathbb{N}$ be the set of natural numbers. The size of $\mathbb{N}$, of course, is greater than any natural number; so $\mathbb{N}$ is infinite; its cardinality is the *smallest infinite size*. That there are larger infinite sizes than the size of $\mathbb{N}$ may be surprising but the idea is fairly straightforward, at least given the "method of measurement", namely, one-to-one mappings.

Any set equipollent to $\mathbb{N}$ is called *denumerable* (or *countable*); larger sets are called *non-denumerable* (or *uncountable*). $\mathbb{R}$, the set of real numbers, is non-denumerable. Any set equipollent to $\mathbb{R}$ is said to have *the power (or cardinality) of the continuum*.

Aside from $\mathbb{R}$, what sets have the power of the continuum? A familiar example is $\wp(\mathbb{N})$, the powerset of $\mathbb{N}$. In short: There are more sets of natural numbers than there are natural numbers. That this is so follows from a general fact on which Cantor's paradise (as Hilbert called it) is based: $\wp(\mathcal{X})$ is larger than $\mathcal{X}$, for any set $\mathcal{X}$ whatsoever. This, *nota bene*, also applies to $\wp(\mathcal{X})$, $\wp(\wp(\mathcal{X}))$, $\wp(\wp(\wp(\mathcal{X})))$, and so on. The core of the proof runs thus: Suppose (for reductio) that f maps the members of $\mathcal{X}$ one-to-one onto $\wp(\mathcal{X})$. Let $\mathcal{Y}$ be $\{x \in \mathcal{X} : x \notin f(x)\}$. Since $\mathcal{Y}$ is a subset of $\mathcal{X}$, there must (by supposition) be a member y of $\mathcal{X}$ such that $\mathcal{Y} = f(y)$. Question: Is y a member of $\mathcal{Y}$ or is it not? Both alternatives lead to a contradiction. (Make sure that you see this!) This argument was due to Cantor, and its form of reasoning is called *Cantor's method of diagonal proof*.

We are dealing with infinite structures in our study of logic, but they are mostly denumerable. An example is furnished by our "tableaux" constructions for various logics; these are examples of what are more generally called *trees* (in mathematics, not ordinary life). While each step in the construction is finitary, the given trees may grow infinitely long branches. In this context *trees* are understood thus:

DEFINITION 10.2 (TREE) A tree is a triple $\mathcal{T} = \langle \mathcal{N}, \mathcal{R}, r \rangle$ where $\mathcal{N}$ is a non-empty set (the nodes), $\mathcal{R}$ is a binary relation on $\mathcal{N}$, and r is a function that assigns each member of $\mathcal{N}$ a natural number (its rank) such that:

1. there is a unique node with rank 0 (the origin of the tree)

2. the nodes of rank $k > 0$ are exactly those nodes that bear $\mathcal{R}$ to nodes of rank $k - 1$, and not to nodes of any other rank.

We say that a tree has the *finite branching property* exactly if for every natural number k there are at most finitely many nodes with rank k.

As an illustration imagine a *binary* tree with origin O. After each node there are precisely two nodes that bear $\mathcal{R}$ to it. Thus O has rank 0, and then there are 2 nodes of rank 1, and 4 nodes of rank 2, and 8 nodes of rank 3, and so forth. How many nodes are there altogether? The answer is $1+2+4+8+\ldots$, which is just the size of $\mathbb{N}$, countable infinity. The set of nodes is therefore denumerable. But how many branches are there? The set of branches is non-denumerable. We won't prove the non-denumerability of the branches but, by way of closing our discussion of infinity, we will prove a result that we rely on when making use of trees in our study of logic:

LEMMA 10.1 (KÖNIG'S LEMMA) *If a tree with the finite branching property has infinitely many nodes then it has an infinite branch.*

PROOF LEM 10.1 Let $\mathcal{T} = \langle \mathcal{N}, \mathcal{R}, r \rangle$ be a tree with the finite branching property but infinitely many nodes. For each node x define $\mathcal{T}(x)$ to be the set of nodes that lie on branches passing through x. Now let $\mathcal{N}^\star$ be $\{x \in \mathcal{N} : \mathcal{T}(x) \text{ is infinite}\}$. Clearly the origin of $\mathcal{T}$ belongs to $\mathcal{N}^\star$, and if x bears $\mathcal{R}$ to y in $\mathcal{N}^\star$ then y belongs to $\mathcal{N}^\star$ too. So we have here a new tree, $\mathcal{T}^\star$, which is a subtree of $\mathcal{T}$.

Consider now any node of $\mathcal{T}^\star$, call it 'x'. Could x be an endpoint of some branch of $\mathcal{T}$? No, for then $\mathcal{T}(x)$ would just include the members of that branch, which have ranks 0, ... up to the rank of x, in which case $\mathcal{T}(x)$ would be finite. Could x never the less be an endpoint of some branch of $\mathcal{T}^\star$? In that case x would have infinitely many branches continuing through it—since $\mathcal{T}(x)$ is infinite—but its "descendants" of the next rank would not. So there would be infinitely many nodes of $\mathcal{T}$ that all bear $\mathcal{R}$ to x. This contradicts the supposition that $\mathcal{T}$ has the finite branching property. Hence, nodes of $\mathcal{T}^\star$ are not endpoints of branches in $\mathcal{T}^\star$: the branches in $\mathcal{T}^\star$ never end. But, of course, any branch of $\mathcal{T}^\star$ must be part of a branch of $\mathcal{T}$, and so $\mathcal{T}$ has branches that never end. QED

10.3 INDUCTIVE SETS AND INDUCTION

In §2 we discussed *inductively defined sets*, and we have since seen many such sets in preceding chapters. When a set has been introduced by an inductive definition, as we briefly mentioned in §2, the proof procedure of *mathematical induction* is applicable. The general pattern of a proof by induction is as follows:

» Every basis element (i.e., element described in the basis clause) has property P.

» Every mode of generation preserves property P.

» Therefore, every element has property P.

In the case of the set of sentences the foregoing pattern would take the following more specific form:

» Every atomic sentence has property P.

» If $A_1, \ldots, A_n$ have property P, so does $\varphi(A_1, \ldots, A_n)$, for each connective φ of degree n, for each n.

» Therefore, all sentences have property P.

Sometimes the above pattern is called *natural* (sometimes *weak*) induction, to distinguish it from a variant, namely *strong* induction:

» For any sentence A, if all sentences of length less than A have property P, then A has property P.

» Therefore, every sentence has property P.

This may look a bit puzzling at first. What has happened to the basis clause? The answer is that if A is an atomic sentence then there are no sentences of length less than A. Therefore, the hypothesis that something or other is true for all sentence of length less than A is, in this case, "vacuously true", and so of no help.

The pattern of strong induction can also be generalised to any set for which the members can be given numerical degrees, where the degrees are natural numbers:

DEFINITION 10.3 (GENERAL STRONG INDUCTION) Let each member of $\mathcal{X}$ have associated with it a natural number, its "degree". If the following holds:

» for all x in $\mathcal{X}$: if all elements of $\mathcal{X}$ of degree less than the degree of x have property P then x has property P

then all members of $\mathcal{X}$ have property P.[1]

In the case of sentences the obvious degree to assign is the *length* (number of symbols contained); but sometimes it can be number of connectives contained, or number of distinct atomic sentences contained. Whichever feature, F, is selected for the degree (be it length, number of connectives, or etc.) we say that our inductive proof is an *induction on* F. In the case of *length*, then, one does an induction on the length of sentences.

By way of illustration consider a sentential syntax:

» PRINCIPLE OF INDUCTION: Let $\langle \mathcal{A}, \mathcal{C}, \mathcal{S} \rangle$ be a sentential syntax, and $\mathcal{J}$ a set. If $\mathcal{J}$ has the following properties:

  » all atomic sentences are in $\mathcal{J}$

  » if φ is in $\mathcal{C}$ and $A_1, \ldots, A_n$ are in $\mathcal{J}$, then $\varphi(A_1, \ldots, A_n)$ is also in $\mathcal{J}$

[1] Note that $\mathcal{X}$ need not be infinite. Note also that *rank in a tree* is a good example of such a "degree" assignment.

then all of $\mathcal{S}$ is part of $\mathcal{J}$, that is, $\mathcal{S} \subseteq \mathcal{J}$.

Suppose we want to show that each sentence of S_{cpl} has in it exactly as many lefthand parentheses as righthand parentheses. If A is a sentence of S_{cpl}, let $l(A)$ be the number of lefthand parentheses in A, and let $r(A)$ be the number of righthand parentheses in A.

We prove the given assertion by translating it thus: let $\mathcal{J}$ be the set of sentences A of S_{cpl} which are such that $l(A) = r(A)$. Then we note:

- If A is atomic, then there are no parentheses in A, by definition of S_{cpl}. So, if A is atomic, then $l(A) = 0 = r(A)$. Hence, all atomic sentences are in $\mathcal{J}$.
- With respect to the complex sentences we note:
  - The number of parentheses in ~A are exactly the same as in A, in which case, if A is in $\mathcal{J}$ then ~A is too; and
  - if $B = (A \wedge C)$ then $l(B) = 1 + l(A) + l(C)$ and $r(B) = r(A) + r(C) + 1$. These numbers are equal if $l(A) = r(A)$ and $l(C) = r(C)$. But this is indeed so if A and C are in $\mathcal{J}$. Therefore, if A and C are in $\mathcal{J}$, so is $(A \wedge C)$.
  - Similarly if B is $(A \vee C)$, $(A \supset C)$, or $(A \equiv C)$.

By the Principle of Induction we have now proved that all sentences of S_{cpl} are in $\mathcal{J}$, that is, have as many lefthand parentheses as righthand parentheses.

10.4 Enumeration of Sentences

The sentences of a sentential syntax form an inductively defined set, as we saw at the very outset. In the course of various proofs to come we will need to think of this set as systematically ordered in such a fashion that we can always meaningfully write:

- the first sentence such that...[2]

This will be easiest to guarantee if in fact all the sentences are ordered so that we can speak of the first sentence of the language, the second sentence,... and so forth, going through all the natural numbers. When that is possible we say that we have an *enumeration* of the set.

Any denumerable set has an enumeration. We could stop with this observation. But one will have a better grasp of the proofs if one thinks in terms of a quite specific sort of enumeration which is generally called the *alphabetical ordering* of the expressions of the language.

[2] If that is possible the set is called *well-ordered*.

It is rather complicated to enumerate the set of sentences if its specification starts with an infinite set of atomic sentences. From any subset of these, infinitely many more sentences are generated. How, then, shall we get them all into a simple numerically ordered row? It can be done, but there is a simpler way. If we want to have infinitely many atomic sentences let us produce them from just two symbols—for example, the letter p and $'$, the single quote (or prime symbol)—as an inductively defined set:

» p is an atomic sentence

» if A is an atomic sentence, so is A'

» nothing is an atomic sentence except by virtue of the above.

This helps because now our entire syntax is built up from a finite vocabulary of *primitive expressions*: the letter p, the single quote, the two parentheses, and the connectives. Let n be the number of primitive expressions.

Given that the set of all expressions of the language (which are just the finite sequences of vocabulary items, including of course the sentences) is generated in this way, we can define the so-called *alphabetical ordering* which is quite similar to the ordering used for dictionaries and telephone books.

To begin, we must arbitrarily order the primitive expressions. This corresponds to the traditional ordering of the letters in our alphabet, which has no particular principle governing it (except respect for past practice). Then we enumerate the expressions of the language as follows:

» First come the expressions of length 1: these are the primitive expressions, in the order decided upon. Let us designate them accordingly as $e_1, e_2, \ldots, e_n$.

» Secondly come the expressions of length 2. There are n^2 of these. Where $\prec$ is our *comes before* relation, these expressions are ordered by the rule: $e_i e_j \prec e_k e_m$ iff either $i < k$, or else $i = k$ and $j < m$.

You can see that this is the rule whereby in a dictionary 'on' comes before 'so' but also before 'or', though not before 'in'.

» Thirdly come the expressions of length 3. There are n^3 of these. They are ordered by the rule: $e_i e_j e_k \prec e_m e_n e_p$ iff either $i < m$, or else $i = m$ and $j < n$, or else $i = m$ and $j = n$ and $k < p$.

And so on. The result is a complete enumeration. We can state the rule also in inductive form (as it were) as follows:

» The primitive expressions have the stipulated order.

» If E is an expression of length less than E' then $E \prec E'$.

» If E, E' are any expressions of the same length and e, e' are primitive expressions, then $Ee \prec E'e'$ iff $E \prec E'$ or else $E = E'$ *and* $e \prec e'$.

As a simple example take the case of a small alphabet selected from our usual English one, containing just the first and second letters $\mathtt{a}$ and $\mathtt{b}$, so that the expressions are precisely all the finite strings of $\mathtt{a}$s and $\mathtt{b}$s. The enumeration of these expressions would then go like this:

$$\mathtt{a}, \mathtt{b}, \mathtt{aa}, \mathtt{ab}, \mathtt{ba}, \mathtt{bb}, \mathtt{aaa}, \mathtt{aab}, \mathtt{aba}, \mathtt{abb}, \mathtt{baa}, \mathtt{bab}, \mathtt{bba}, \mathtt{bbb}, \ldots$$

and those explicitly displayed here would be the 1st through 14th expressions in the language. (They include all the expressions of length less than 4, so their total number must of course be 2 plus 2^2 plus 2^3, which is 14 as it should be.)

10.5 VALUATION LEMMA

The most important principle concerning valuations is that if a valuation has a base then it is entirely determined by the values it gives to the atomic sentences. This principle we tend to take for granted and rely on implicitly; but we can demonstrate it by once again using the method of induction. We can make the point equivalently by proving that if valuations with the same base agree on the values of the atomic sentences then they agree on all sentences.

LEMMA 10.2 (VALUATION LEMMA) *Let* v *and* v' *be valuations of sentential syntax* $\mathtt{Synt}$, *which have a base in common. If* A *is a sentence of* $\mathtt{Synt}$, *and* $v(p) = v'(p)$ *for every atomic sentence* p *in* A, *then* $v(A) = v'(A)$.

PROOF LEM 10.2 This is proved by the Principle of Induction. Let $\mathtt{Synt} = \langle \mathcal{A}, \mathcal{C}, \mathcal{S} \rangle$ and v and v' both have base $\mathcal{B} = \langle \mathcal{V}, \mathbb{C}, \odot \rangle$. Furthermore, let the atomic sentences in A be $p_1, \ldots, p_n$. We don't apply the Principle of Induction directly to $\mathtt{Synt}$. Instead we consider a smaller syntax $\mathtt{Synt}^\star = \langle \{p_1, \ldots, p_n\}, \mathcal{C}, \mathcal{S}_{\mathtt{Synt}^\star} \rangle$ where $\mathcal{S}_{\mathtt{Synt}^\star}$ (the set of sentences) is specified inductively as follows:

» $p_1, \ldots, p_n$ are in $\mathcal{S}_{\mathtt{Synt}^\star}$

» if φ is an m-ary connective in $\mathcal{C}$, and $A_1, \ldots, A_m$ are in $\mathcal{S}_{\mathtt{Synt}^\star}$, then so is $\varphi(A_1, \ldots, A_m)$

» nothing is in $\mathcal{S}_{\mathtt{Synt}^\star}$ except by virtue of (a) and (b).

$\mathtt{v}$ and $\mathtt{v}'$ are automatically valuations of $\mathtt{Synt}^{\star}$ as well, with the same base $\mathcal{B}$.

Now, let $\mathcal{J}$ be the set of all sentences in $\mathcal{S}_{\mathtt{Synt}^{\star}}$ on which $\mathtt{v}$ and $\mathtt{v}'$ agree. We need to prove that all of $\mathcal{S}_{\mathtt{Synt}^{\star}}$ is part of $\mathcal{J}$.

» All atomic sentences of $\mathcal{S}_{\mathtt{Synt}^{\star}}$ are in $\mathcal{J}$, since $\mathtt{v}$ and $\mathtt{v}'$ agree on $\mathtt{p}_1, \ldots, \mathtt{p}_n$;

» If $\mathtt{A} = \varphi(\mathtt{A}_1, \ldots, \mathtt{A}_n)$ then $\mathtt{v}(\mathtt{A}) = \odot_{\varphi}(\mathtt{v}(\mathtt{A}_1), \ldots, \mathtt{v}(\mathtt{A}_n))$ and $\mathtt{v}'(\mathtt{A}) = \odot_{\varphi}(\mathtt{v}'(\mathtt{A}_1), \ldots, \mathtt{v}'(\mathtt{A}_n))$ because $\mathcal{B}$ is a base for $\mathtt{v}$ and $\mathtt{v}'$. So, if $\mathtt{A}_1, \ldots, \mathtt{A}_n$ are in $\mathcal{J}$, then

$$\mathtt{v}(\mathtt{A}_1) = \mathtt{v}'(\mathtt{A}_1), \ldots, \mathtt{v}(\mathtt{A}_n) = \mathtt{v}'(\mathtt{A}_n)$$

and therefore $\mathtt{v}(\mathtt{A}) = \mathtt{v}'(\mathtt{A})$. So then $\mathtt{A}$ is also in $\mathcal{J}$.

The required conclusion now follows by the Principle of Induction applied to $\mathcal{S}_{\mathtt{Synt}^{\star}}$. Clearly, $\mathtt{A}$ is in $\mathcal{S}_{\mathtt{Synt}^{\star}}$ and, hence, $\mathtt{v}$ and $\mathtt{v}'$ agree on $\mathtt{A}$. But this conclusion follows for any sentence $\mathtt{A}$ at all; therefore, $\mathtt{v}$ and $\mathtt{v}'$ agree on all sentences in $\mathtt{Synt}^{\star}$. QED

EXERCISES 10.5.1

1 Suppose that $\mathtt{f}$ is of degree 1 and $\mathtt{h}$ of degree 2 (see §2.3). What could be meant by the composite functions $\mathtt{fh}$ and $\mathtt{hf}$? Given an example for each.

2 Show that if $\mathtt{f}$ maps $\mathcal{X}$ into $\mathcal{Y}$ and $\mathtt{g}$ maps $\mathcal{Y}$ into $\mathcal{Z}$, then $\mathtt{gf}$ maps $\mathcal{X}$ into $\mathcal{Z}$.

3 Define *branch of a tree*.

4 Prove that the set of rational numbers is denumerable. (Hint: think of all the rational fractions displayed in a table that starts with the infinite rows:

$$\frac{0}{1}, \frac{0}{2}, \frac{0}{3}, \ldots$$
$$\frac{1}{1}, \frac{1}{2}, \frac{1}{3}, \ldots$$

and so forth, and see if you can match the entries with the natural numbers.)

5 Let $\mathcal{L}$ be some (formal) language. Let $\mathtt{f}$ be a function which takes $\mathcal{L}$-sentences into $\mathcal{L}$-sentences, and such that for any such sentence, $\mathtt{A}$ implies $\mathtt{f}(\mathtt{A})$. Question: What properties does $\mathtt{f}$ preserve?

6 With respect to syntax S, v_1, and v_2, discussed in exercise 3 of Exercises 3.6.1 (page 33), use the Principle of Induction to prove that

1. Every sentence A of S is s.t. if A is not p then $v_1(A) = 0$;
2. Every sentence A of S is s.t. if it contains more than three symbols, then $v_2(A) = 0$.

FURTHER READING

Further reading on these topics may be found in many places. For some of the purely mathematical ideas, see Bloch's [11]. For both the mathematical ideas and their application to logic and semantics see van Fraassen's [101] and Boolos, Burge and Jeffrey's [14].

Le Corbusier was the sort of relentlessly rational intellectual
that only France loves wholeheartedly,
the logician who flies higher and higher in ever-decreasing circles
until, with one last, utterly inevitable induction,
he disappears up his own fundamental aperture
and emerges in the fourth dimension as a needle-thin umber bird.
– Tom Wolfe, *From Bauhaus to Our House*

Chapter 11
Logical Systems and Completeness

We proceed now to the study of logics in a higher key, so to speak. Metalogic is the abstract study of languages and logics with precise methods of proof for the comparison of languages and the adequacy (soundness and completeness) of logics for their corresponding languages. As we engage with issues pertaining to all languages and logics in general, we cover most (but not all) of the languages and logics discussed in previous chapters.

11.1 Logical Systems

A logical system is formulated for a particular syntax (perhaps the syntax of a specific language under study) and we focus here on sentential syntax. Recall from §3.2 that a sentential syntax comprises the set of sentences of a given language, which has an inductive definition:

» All atomic sentences (a set specified independently) are sentences;

» if φ is an n-ary connective and $A_1, A_2, \ldots, A_n$ are sentences then $\varphi(A_1, A_2, \ldots, A_n)$ is a sentence;

» nothing is a sentence except by virtue of the above.

To specify a logical system we must similarly provide inductive definitions of its set of theorems and of its consequence relation $\vdash$. It may be possible to simply do the latter, while defining the theorems as consequences of the empty set. But sometimes it is more convenient to just define the set of theorems directly and define $\vdash$ from that. For example, in CPL we know that $A \vdash B$ just in case $\vdash {\sim}A \vee B$, and we can use that fact to define the consequence relation there.

Axiomatic and Simple Derivation Systems

We shall call a logical system *axiomatic* if it provides an inductive definition of its set of theorems in the following way:

- the basis elements are a set of sentences called its axioms;
- the generating clauses are its *theorem derivation rules*; each generates a new theorem from a finite set of axioms or theorems;
- the inductive definition takes the form:
  - all axioms are theorems;
  - if a sentence follows from theorems by means of a theorem derivation rule then it is a theorem;
  - nothing is a theorem except in virtue of the above.

The above inductive definition can be phrased alternatively as follows:

- A *proof* of B is a finite list of sentences $A_1, A_2, \ldots, A_n$ each member of which is either an axiom or follows from preceding members by a theorem derivation rule, and whose last member is B. A sentence is a *theorem* if and only if it has a proof.[1]

What could be a *theorem derivation rule*? Some can just be rules that correspond to simple valid arguments, such as that A follows from $A \vee A$. But some are not. Both in quantificational logic and in modal logic we know of such examples:

Universal Generalization:	If Fy is a theorem then so is $\forall x Fx$.
Necessitation:	If A is a theorem then so is $\Box A$.

In neither case is there a valid argument from the first to the second sentence, though the latter is logically true if the former is.

In some cases there are no rules needed that create theorems from theorems except for the very simple rules that echo valid arguments. That is in fact the case with our most familiar system CPL, which can be formulated as what we shall here call a *simple derivation system*. Such a system has its consequence relation specified inductively by listing a set of derivation rules. Now the most straightforward way of specifying the consequence relation of such a system is as follows:

- A *derivation of* A *from* $\mathcal{X}$ is a finite sequence of sentences each of which is either a member of $\mathcal{X}$ or follows from preceding members by means of a derivation rule, and whose last member is A; $\mathcal{X} \vdash A$ if and only if there is a derivation of A from $\mathcal{X}$

[1] It is essential that a proof is finite. To see why, imagine that we allow infinitely long proofs and have the rule that A follows from $A \vee A$. Then for any sentence A, such as 'God exists', one could offer the "proof":

$$\ldots, A \vee A \vee A \vee A, A \vee A \vee A, A \vee A, A$$

which has no beginning (it is infinitely long), uses no axioms, but has each member follow from the preceding by means of that rule.

In the next section we will show such a simple formulation of CPL directly, in connection with our discussion of its tableaux system.

We note that there are limitations on both the sorts of systems that we have now discussed. The axiomatic systems yield a logical consequence relation only if all consequences are faithfully reflected in the theorems (in the way, for example, that in CPL the relationship $A \vdash B$ exists precisely if $\vdash {\sim}A \vee B$) while simple derivation systems are inadequate if there is need for rules like Universal Generalization or Necessitation. While axiomatic logical systems used to be the form of choice, it is for this reason (and also because they were typically not very user friendly) that the preference shifted to a more inclusive type of logical system that tackles the consequence relation directly.

CONTOURS OF NATURAL DEDUCTION SYSTEMS

We'll use the name *natural deduction system* in a general way for logical systems that provide an inductive definition of their consequence relation in the following way:

» the basis elements are a set of basic deductions of form

$$\mathcal{X} \vdash A$$

(these include axioms of the above sort, in the form $\vdash A$, the special case of $\mathcal{X}$ being the empty set of premises)

» meta-derivation rules of the form

$$\text{if } \mathcal{X}, A_i \vdash B_i \text{ (where } i = 1, \ldots, n \in \mathbb{N}\text{), then } \mathcal{X}, A \vdash B$$

(these include theorem derivation rules of the above sort, of form

$$\text{if } \vdash B_1, \text{ and } \vdash B_2, \ldots, \text{ and } \vdash B_n \text{ then } \vdash B$$

the special case of empty sets of premises).

Given the aim of cataloguing implication in a (sentential) language we can tell quite a bit beforehand about the logic. To begin, the logical consequence relationship must have the same general characteristics as implication in a language, including especially the following

If A is a member of $\mathcal{X}$ then $\mathcal{X} \Vdash A$.

If $\mathcal{X} \Vdash A$ then $\mathcal{X}, B \Vdash A$

If, for every $A \in \mathcal{Y}$, $\mathcal{X} \Vdash A$ and $\mathcal{Y} \Vdash B$, then $\mathcal{X} \Vdash B$.

In addition to these characteristics, the logical consequence relationship must clearly reflect the properties of the various connectives and the corresponding truth conditions for complex sentences. Accordingly, we expect the following general form for natural deduction systems formulated for sentential syntaxes:

» STRUCTURAL RULES

Prime: If A is in $\mathcal{X}$ then $\mathcal{X} \vdash$ A.

Weak:[2] If $\mathcal{X} \vdash$ A then $\mathcal{X}$, B $\vdash$ A.

Trans: If, for every A in $\mathcal{Y}$, $\mathcal{X} \vdash$ A and $\mathcal{Y} \vdash$ B, then $\mathcal{X} \vdash$ B.

» CONNECTIVE RULES: These are special rules each of which reflects some logical relationship due to the properties of one or more connectives.

In general, the latter will be especially user-friendly if they simply introduce or eliminate one connective at a time. In the structural rules above (and in what follows) what appears to the left of the turnstiles are sets of sentences; *we shall not need to have these sets ordered in any way*. In §11.2 we illustrate all these ideas with the simple case of CPL.

EXERCISES 11.1.1

1 Prove from the inductive definition of the set of theorems, in an axiomatic system, that a sentence is a theorem if and only if it has a proof.

2 Show that the rule Weak is redundant, given Prime and Trans.

11.2 TABLEAUX FOR CPL RECONCEIVED

None of the sorts of logical system that we just canvassed looks at first blush like a tableaux system, although the latter has been so far throughout our standard for logical calculation. And it must surely be admitted that the tableaux provide a syntactic, mechanical, humanly user-friendly way of finding out whether a given sentence or argument is valid in the given language! But in fact tableaux systems are just special forms that we can connect with the above types; we'll illustrate this now for the especially simple case of CPL.

To begin let us devise a simple derivation system for CPL, which we'll call 'CPL(Der)'. For simplicity we will take it that all the connectives are defined in the usual way from just two of them, $\sim$ and $\wedge$, the negation and conjunction connectives; all sentences are now assumed to have these two as the only connectives in them. The rules will be:

[2]This is standardly called 'Weakening' and the next is standardly called 'Transitivity'.

DN) *derive* $D \wedge A \wedge C$ *from* $D \wedge {\sim}{\sim}A \wedge C$.
NK) *derive* $(D \wedge {\sim}A \wedge C) \vee (D \wedge {\sim}B \wedge C)$ *from* $D \wedge {\sim}(A \wedge B) \wedge C$.

In these rules the sentences D and C may be absent. For example, (DN) allows the inference of ~~A from A.

Notice that (DN) and (NK) decrease the complexity of the sentences on which they operate in a certain way: pretty soon neither will be applicable any more. Thus their application will produce from any given sentence a finite list of sentences, with the last member one to which they are not applicable. We shall call a derivation so produced, until neither rule is applicable any more, a *standard derivation*. We shall call a standard derivation *closed* precisely if its last member is a disjunction (of one or more sentences) and such that in each disjunct we see both E and ~E for some sentence E. We now specify the logical consequence relation as follows:

> $A_1, \ldots, A_n \vdash B$ in CPL(Der) iff some standard derivation from $A_1 \wedge \ldots \wedge A_n \wedge {\sim}B$ is closed.

Do you see that we have here simply a different way of making up a tableau? Instead of drawing branches that split we make up a disjunction of the parts they split into; those parts are then regarded as conjunctions of all the preceding formulas that have not been boxed.

THEOREM 11.1 (ARGUMENT SOUNDNESS) *If* $A_1, \ldots, A_n \vdash B$ *in* CPL(Der) *then* $A_1, \ldots, A_n \Vdash B$ *in* $\mathcal{L}_{CPL}$.

To prove this we note that if $A_1, \ldots, A_n \vdash B$ then by definition (in our present set up) there exists a closed standard derivation from $A_1 \wedge \ldots \wedge A_n \wedge {\sim}B$. Therefore, it will suffice to show that the members of a closed standard derivation are one and all unsatisfiable. (Why is that sufficient in the present case?)

It is clear first of all that the last member of a closed standard derivation is unsatisfiable in $\mathcal{L}_{CPL}$, since each disjunct is unsatisfiable there. So to finish the proof we need to show that if any member is unsatisfiable, and has a preceding member, then that preceding member is also unsatisfiable. (Exercise: put this argument into precise inductive form.) But that follows from the following:

LEMMA 11.1 *All members of a standard derivation are semantically equivalent (they imply each other in* $\mathcal{L}_{CPL}$*).*

The proof is straightforward (and omitted here).

THEOREM 11.2 (ARGUMENT COMPLETENESS) *If* $A_1, \ldots, A_n \Vdash B$ *in* $\mathcal{L}_{CPL}$, *then* $A_1, \ldots, A_n \vdash B$.

This is best proved by contraposition. Suppose that the premises do not logically imply B, that is, that a standard derivation from $A_1 \wedge \ldots \wedge A_n \wedge \sim B$ has in its last member a contradiction-free disjunct. We propose to prove that in that case all members of the derivation are satisfiable. (Again, why does that suffice in the present case?)

On the given supposition the last member of the derivation has a disjunct, call it C, which does not have E and ~E in it for any sentence E. But we know more: neither (DN) nor (NK) is applicable to the last member of the derivation, in which case C contains neither double negations nor negated conjunctions. In other words, C is a conjunction of only atomic sentences and negations of atomic sentences. Accordingly we begin to construct a valuation as follows:

> For any atomic sentence A,
>
> $$v(A) = \begin{cases} 1 & \text{if A is a conjunct in C} \\ 0 & \text{otherwise.} \end{cases}$$
>
> The values assigned by v to other sentences of the syntax are determined by the conditions on admissible $\mathcal{L}_{CPL}$-valuations.

This valuation clearly satisfies C, since it satisfies every conjunct in C. But, then, it satisfies the last member of the derivation, which has C as a disjunct. Now we can appeal once again to Lemma 4 (page 163): all members of the derivation are equivalent and hence they are all satisfiable in $\mathcal{L}_{CPL}$.

NATURAL DEDUCTION SYSTEM FOR CPL

Tableaux systems are very mechanical and do not attempt to duplicate natural patterns of reasoning. In that respect natural deduction systems are superior, since they often suffice to formulate arguments that occur naturally in discourse. Accordingly, we'll here present a natural deduction formulation CPL(NAT) of CPL as well, which can in turn be used as the basis for extensions of CPL such as the normal modal logics.

In what follows scripted upper case letters from the end of the alphabet ('$\mathcal{X}$', '$\mathcal{Y}$' and so on) will be used to stand only for sets of sentences. Also, it will be convenient to pick out one sentence as the standard *absurdity* (an "explosive" sentence), the one from which all else follows. For purposes of CPL we will select $p \wedge \sim p$ for our "absurdity", where p is the first atomic sentence; and we will call it $\perp$.

Note that in the following formulation an expression like '$\mathcal{X}, A, B$' denotes $\mathcal{X} \cup \{A, B\}$, so that the order in which it is written does not matter; so, for example, $\mathcal{X}, A, B$ is the same as $\mathcal{X}, B, A$.

» STRUCTURAL RULES

» Prime: If A is in $\mathcal{X}$ then $\mathcal{X} \vdash$ A.

» Weak: If $\mathcal{X} \vdash$ A then $\mathcal{X}, \mathcal{Y} \vdash$ A.

» Trans: If $\mathcal{X} \vdash A_1, \ldots, \mathcal{X} \vdash A_n$ and $A_1, \ldots, A_n \vdash B$, then $\mathcal{X} \vdash$ B.

» CONNECTIVE RULES

» $\perp$ Intro: $A, {\sim}A \vdash \perp$

» $\perp$ Elim: $\perp \vdash A$

» Excl: If $\mathcal{X}$, B $\vdash$ A and $\mathcal{X}$, ~B $\vdash$ A then $\mathcal{X} \vdash$ A.

» DNeg: $A \vdash {\sim\sim}A$.

» $\wedge$ Intro: $A, B \vdash (A \wedge B)$

» $\wedge$ Neg: $A, {\sim}B \vdash {\sim}(A \wedge B)$
$\quad {\sim}A, B \vdash {\sim}(A \wedge B)$
$\quad {\sim}A, {\sim}B \vdash {\sim}(A \wedge B)$

When we say that CPL(NAT) and CPL(Der) are two formulations of the logic CPL we clearly imply that their logical consequence relations are all the same. Is that really true? One way to go about proving as much is to see how the rules of one relate to those of the other. We call derivation rules and metarules *admissible* for a logical system if adding them would not change the logical consequence relation. One claim to be inspected here is therefore that the rules of CPL(Der) are admissible for CPL(NAT), and that the metarules of CPL(NAT) are admissible for CPL(Der). We will list some exercises that go a ways toward proving this claim.

Of course there is another way to check the relationship: namely, by proving argument soundness and completeness with respect to $\mathcal{L}_{\text{CPL}}$ directly for CPL(NAT) as well. And we should confess here that CPL(NAT) too is constructed specifically to allow for a certain kind of perspicuous completeness proof, which generalizes easily to other logics. This we will take up in §11.6.

Some Sample Deductions in CPL(NAT)

The system CPL(NAT) is very minimal, and at first sight it may not seem at all adequate. To dispel that impression to some extent, we'll here provide some sample deductions, and require some others in the exercises.

T1. If $\mathcal{X}, \sim A \vdash A$ then $\mathcal{X} \vdash A$.

PROOF:

1. $\mathcal{X}, \sim A \vdash A$	(Given)
2. $\mathcal{X}, A \vdash A$	(Prime)
3. $\mathcal{X} \vdash A$	(1), (2), (Excl)

T2. If $\mathcal{X}, \sim A \vdash \bot$ then $\mathcal{X} \vdash A$.

PROOF:

1. $\mathcal{X}, \sim A \vdash \bot$	(Given)
2. $\bot \vdash A$	($\bot$ Elim)
3. $\mathcal{X}, \sim A \vdash A$	(1), (2), (Trans)
4. $\mathcal{X}, A \vdash A$	(Prime)
5. $\mathcal{X} \vdash A$	(3), (4), (Excl)

T3. If $\mathcal{X} \vdash A$ and $\mathcal{X} \vdash \sim A$ then $\mathcal{X} \vdash \bot$.

PROOF:

1. $\mathcal{X} \vdash A$	(Given)
2. $\mathcal{X} \vdash \sim A$	(Given)
3. $A, \sim A \vdash \bot$	($\bot$ Intro)
4. $\mathcal{X} \vdash \bot$	(1)–(3), (Trans)

T4. $A \wedge B, \sim A \vdash A$.

PROOF:

1. $B, \sim A \vdash \sim(A \wedge B)$	($\wedge$ Neg)
2. $(A \wedge B), B, \sim A \vdash \sim(A \wedge B)$	(1), (Weak)
3. $(A \wedge B), B, \sim A \vdash (A \wedge B)$	(Prime)
4. $(A \wedge B), B, \sim A \vdash \bot$	*Invoke T3*
5. $\bot \vdash A$	($\bot$ Elim)
6. $(A \wedge B), B, \sim A \vdash A$	(4), (5), (Tran)
7. $(A \wedge B), \sim B, \sim A \vdash A$	*by a proof similar to (1)–(6)*
8. $(A \wedge B), \sim A \vdash A$	(6), (7), (Excl)

T5. $A \wedge B \vdash A$.

PROOF:

1. $(A \wedge B), \sim A \vdash A$	*Invoke T4*
2. $(A \wedge B), A \vdash A$	(Prime)
3. $(A \wedge B) \vdash A$	(1), (2), (Excl)

EXERCISES 11.2.1

1 Prove the following in CPL(NAT). Note that the disjunction (similarly material implication) connective needs first to be eliminated by means of its standard definition in terms of the other two connectives.

T6. $(A \wedge B) \vdash B$.
T7. $A, \sim(A \wedge B) \vdash \sim B$.
T8. $\sim\sim A \vdash A$.
T9. $D \wedge \sim\sim A \wedge C \vdash (D \wedge A \wedge C)$.
T10. $A \vdash A \vee B$.
T11. If $A \vdash C$ and $B \vdash C$ then $(A \vee B) \vdash C$.
T12. $\sim(A \wedge B) \wedge C \vdash (\sim A \wedge C) \vee (\sim B \wedge C)$.
T13. $\mathcal{X}, A \vdash B$ iff $\mathcal{X} \vdash (A \supset B)$.

OPTION: You may prove some of (T6)–(T13) after doing the next exercise, using your results from that exercise.

2 We have assumed the other connectives to be defined from the two we have, so that no special Connective Rules were needed for them. Devise such rules for disjunction, the material conditional, and material equivalence, with those definitions as guide, and prove their admissibility.

3 Prove that CPL(NAT) is argument sound for $\mathcal{L}_{CPL}$.

11.3 MANY-VALUED LANGUAGES AND LOGICS

In earlier chapters we have encountered a number of many-valued languages. An inquiry into their relationships will introduce new techniques that will also be useful in the study of other languages and logics.

A many-valued language is characterized by the fact that all its admissible valuations have the same base, and that the same elements are designated. Thus a three-valued language has a base that has three elements, and so forth. We can imagine (and in connection with the sorites puzzle, saw) also an infinitely-valued language whose base therefore had infinitely many elements. In this section we shall focus on finitely-valued languages.

The language $\mathcal{L}_{CPL}$ is two-valued, and the base for each of its valuations is in effect what in other contexts is called B_2, the 2-element Boolean algebra.[3] An *algebra* is a set with some operations on it; in this case we have

$$\mathfrak{B}_2 = \langle\{1,0\},\{\sim^2,\wedge^2,\vee^2\}\rangle$$

[3] Although we will use the term 'Boolean algebra' in a general way we will not stop here to define it; for our purposes it will suffice to give some examples only.

where those operations are definable by means of the simple equations:

$$\begin{aligned} \sim^2(x) &= 1 - x \\ \wedge^2(x, y) &= x \cdot y \\ \vee^2(x, y) &= (x + y) - (x \cdot y) \end{aligned}$$

$\mathfrak{B}_2$ becomes a *base* for the admissible valuations of $\mathcal{L}_{\mathsf{CPL}}$ if we add the function $\odot$ that assigns the operations $\sim^2$, $\wedge^2$, $\vee^2$ to the connectives $\sim$, $\wedge$, $\vee$, respectively, in the obvious way. In keeping with our earlier terminology we will call the result, namely

$$\langle \{1, 0\}, \{\sim^2, \wedge^2, \vee^2\}, \odot \rangle$$

an $\mathcal{L}_{\mathsf{CPL}}$ *structure*. (There is only one $\mathcal{L}_{\mathsf{CPL}}$ structure!)

ADMISSIBLE VALUATIONS AND MATRICES

To know what the admissible valuations are and what they do we cannot stop with the given base; in order to specify which sentences are satisfied by a valuation, we must also say which elements are designated. The result of adding this ingredient yields a *matrix*. As before, we shall enter this ingredient, the set of designated elements, as second item, to form the $\mathcal{L}_{\mathsf{CPL}}$ *matrix*:

$$\langle \{1, 0\}, \{1\}, \{\sim^2, \wedge^2, \vee^2\}, \odot \rangle$$

In general, then, a *matrix* is a quadruple, whose elements are, in order, the set of *values*, the set of *designated values*, the *operations*, and the *interpretation function* that assigns one operation each to the connectives of the *associated syntax*. (That syntax, of course, is always the sentential syntax whose set of connectives is the range of the interpretation function; hence, it is determined if the matrix is given.) We shall call the triple that results from deleting the second element the matrix's *associated base*, and the couple that results from additionally deleting the last element the matrix's *associated algebra*.

DEFINITION 11.1 Let $\mathfrak{M}$ be a matrix. $\mathcal{L}$ is the $\mathfrak{M}$*-language* (the *many-valued language whose matrix is* $\mathfrak{M}$, the language for which matrix $\mathfrak{M}$ is *adequate*) just in case all admissible valuations of $\mathcal{L}$ have as base the associated base of $\mathfrak{M}$ and satisfy a sentence of $\mathcal{L}$ iff they assign that sentence a designated element of $\mathfrak{M}$.

If $\mathcal{L}$ is the $\mathfrak{M}$-language, we also say that $\mathfrak{M}$ is the $\mathcal{L}$*-matrix*. If $\mathfrak{M}$ has n values then we can call the $\mathfrak{M}$-language an n*-valued language*. We can adapt other similar terms in obvious ways, and say for example that sentences or arguments are *valid in the matrix* just if they are valid in the many-valued language whose matrix it is.

A Variety of Matrices

Now we are ready to look at the variety of matrices that yield various kinds of many-valued languages and to relate these to each other.

There are Boolean algebras with more than 2 elements, and they provide simple examples of many-valued languages that are easily related to $\mathcal{L}_{\mathsf{CPL}}$. For example, with respect to $\wedge$ the 4-element Boolean algebra $\mathfrak{B}_4$ is like the matrix we discussed for the language $\mathcal{L}_{\mathsf{FDE}}$; the difference concerns $\sim$. In $\mathcal{L}_{\mathsf{FDE}}$ negation is a fixed point at b and n; in $\mathfrak{B}_4$ negation has no fixed points. (See §7.3 for terminology.) We will call the elements of $\mathfrak{B}_4$ by familiar names: $1, \mathsf{b}, \mathsf{n}, 0$.

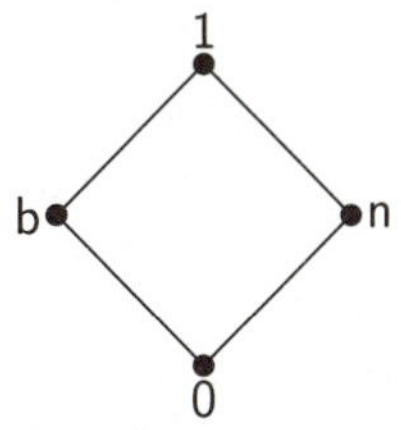

Figure II.1: $\mathfrak{B}_4 = \langle\{1, \mathsf{b}, \mathsf{n}, 0\}, \{\sim^4, \wedge^4, \vee^4\}\rangle$

Just as 1 and 0 are each other's negation, so to speak, so are b and n, while conjunction is again glb and disjunction lub (see §7.3).[4]

It is easy enough to see how we get a base for valuations of our classical sentential syntax here, using the obvious matching of operators to connectives. But to define a matrix we must make a choice: which elements are to be designated? Let us consider both the obvious choices, of either designating 1 alone or designating both 1 and one of the two new values.

Definition II.2 The *liberal* $\mathfrak{B}_4$ matrix is the matrix

$$\mathfrak{B}_4(\mathtt{lib}) = \langle\{1, \mathsf{b}, \mathsf{n}, 0\}, \{1, \mathsf{b}\}, \{\sim^4, \wedge^4, \vee^4\}, \odot\rangle$$

with associated algebra $\mathfrak{B}_4$, with elements 1 and b designated, and where $\odot$ (the interpretation function) matches $\sim^4, \wedge^4, \vee^4$ to $\sim, \wedge, \vee$, respectively, in the classical sentential syntax.

Definition II.3 The *conservative* $\mathfrak{B}_4$ matrix is the matrix

$$\mathfrak{B}_4(\mathtt{con}) = \langle\{1, \mathsf{b}, \mathsf{n}, 0\}, \{1\}, \{\sim^4, \wedge^4, \vee^4\}, \odot\rangle$$

with associated algebra $\mathfrak{B}_4$, with only element 1 designated, and where $\odot$ matches $\sim^4, \wedge^4, \vee^4$ to $\sim, \wedge, \vee$, respectively, in the classical sentential syntax.

---

[4] The same may be said with respect to $\mathfrak{B}_2$, diagramed by drawing a vertical line from node 1 (at the top) down to 0 (at the bottom).

At this point one should suspect that the logics of the corresponding matrix languages will not be very different from CPL. The question is: How can one *confirm* this suspicion?

THEOREM 11.3 CPL *is statement and argument complete for both the* $\mathfrak{B}_4(\mathtt{lib})$ *and* $\mathfrak{B}_4(\mathtt{con})$.

The upshot of Theorem 11.3 is that the arguments and sentences valid in either the liberal or conservative $\mathfrak{B}_4$ matrices are all valid in $\mathcal{L}_{\mathsf{CPL}}$ (and hence, as we know, provable in CPL). The *proof* is fairly obvious: All admissible valuations of $\mathcal{L}_{\mathsf{CPL}}$ are also admissible valuations for those matrices. In our earlier terminology, $\mathcal{L}_{\mathsf{CPL}}$ is an *extension* of both those languages; the assignment of values in the 2-element Boolean algebra is automatically a legitimate assignment of the same values in the 4-element Boolean algebra. Supposing, then, that we have a classical counterexample to the argument from premise-set $\mathcal{X}$ to conclusion A, that will also be at once a counterexample to the given argument in the two new languages.

Note what is relied on in this argument: not only are the operations the same when restricted to 1 and 0, but element 1 is designated in both cases and element 0 is undesignated in both cases. So the valuation in question which assigned designated values to all premises and an undesignated value to the conclusion in the 2-valued matrix still does so in both of the other matrices.

THEOREM 11.4 CPL *is statement and argument sound for the liberal* $\mathfrak{B}_4$ *language.*

The upshot of Theorem 11.4 is that the arguments and sentences invalid in the liberal $\mathfrak{B}_4$ matrix are all invalid in $\mathcal{L}_{\mathsf{CPL}}$ (and therefore not provable in CPL). We cannot prove this in the same way, since the 4-valued matrix allows for valuations that assign the non-classical values b and n to sentences. None the less, a counterexample to an argument in $\mathfrak{B}_4(\mathtt{lib})$ can be turned into a two-valued counterexample: simply replace b and n by 1 and 0, respectively! That this may be done is established by the following lemma.

LEMMA 11.2 *Let* h *be the function from* $\{1, \mathsf{b}, \mathsf{n}, 0\}$ *to* $\{1, 0\}$ *defined thus:*

$$\begin{aligned} h(1) &= 1 \\ h(0) &= 0 \\ h(\mathsf{b}) &= 1 \\ h(\mathsf{n}) &= 0 \end{aligned}$$

If v *is an admissible valuation for* $\mathfrak{B}_4(\mathtt{lib})$ *then the function*

$$hv(A) = h(v(A))$$

is an admissible valuation for the $\mathcal{L}_{\mathsf{CPL}}$*-matrix. The valuation* hv *assigns designated (respectively, undesignated) elements to the same sentences as* v *does.*

The proof of the second part is by inspection; but the first part must be proved by checking carefully the conditions under which hv is a valuation with the correct base. We leave this as an exercise.[5]

We would also like to prove the same thing for $\mathfrak{B}_4(\mathrm{con})$:

THEOREM 11.5 CPL *is statement and argument sound for the conservative* $\mathfrak{B}_4$ *language.*

But now there is a problem with using only h: since b is not designated, h now maps an undesignated value into a designated one. Fortunately, the problem is resolved by using both h and a similar function g, which acts oppositely on values b and n.

LEMMA 11.3 *Let* h *and* g *be functions from* $\{1, \mathsf{b}, \mathsf{n}, 0\}$ *to* $\{1, 0\}$ *defined:*

$$h(1) = 1 \qquad g(1) = 1$$
$$h(0) = 0 \qquad g(0) = 0$$
$$h(\mathsf{b}) = 1 \qquad g(\mathsf{b}) = 0$$
$$h(\mathsf{n}) = 0 \qquad g(\mathsf{n}) = 1$$

If v *is an admissible valuation for* $\mathfrak{B}_4(\mathrm{con})$ *then the functions defined (for all sentences* A*) by*

$$hv(A) = h(v(A))$$
$$gv(A) = g(v(A))$$

are admissible valuations for the $\mathcal{L}_{\mathrm{CPL}}$*-matrix. The valuations* hv *and* gv *assign designated elements to the same sentences to which* v *assigns a designated value.*

The proof of the second part of Lemma 11.3 is by inspection. In the first part the claim about hv has the same proof as in Lemma 11.2; the proof for gv, of course, is entirely similar, mutatis mutandis.

By way of completing the proof of Theorem 11.5, suppose that v is a counterexample to the argument from premise-set $\mathcal{X}$ to conclusion A in matrix $\mathfrak{B}_4(\mathrm{con})$. Then v assigns 1 to all members of $\mathcal{X}$ and assigns either b or n or 0 to A. It is clear then that either hv or gv will provide the counterexample for the two-valued case; they assign 1 to all the premises and at least one of the two will assign 0 to the conclusion.

[5]The function h is a *homomorphism* from the 4-valued Boolean algebra into the 2-valued Boolean algebra. That means that the operators in the two algebras are "respected" by h, in the sense easily illustrated with one of them:

$$h(x \wedge^4 y) = h(x) \wedge^2 h(y)$$

That is the clue to the proof of Lemma 11.2, put in mathematical terminology.

We have now seen that at least three different languages all have the same logic, namely CPL. Other matrices of course yield languages with different logics. You will recall the three valued matrix that was constructed on the basis of the proverb that a single jot of rat's dung spoils the soup. That was Bochvar's matrix; it is easy to see that all the admissible valuations for the $\mathcal{L}_{\mathsf{CPL}}$ matrix are also admissible valuations for Bochvar's matrix. Accordingly, $\mathcal{L}_{\mathsf{CPL}}$ is an extension of that language, and the arguments and sentences valid in Bochvar's matrix must all be classically valid. But we cannot use the tricks of our two lemmas above in this case, since there is no element in the Boolean algebra that is its own negation.[6] The situation is similar in the case of FDE (first degree entailment) and that of LP (the Logic of Paradox). When it comes to 1 and 0 we see no difference between the Boolean matrix and the four corners of truth. But two of those corners behave very non-classically: $\mathsf{b} = {\sim}\mathsf{b}$ and $\mathsf{n} = {\sim}\mathsf{n}$. So all we can conclude from this comparison is that nothing can be valid in FDE or in LP that is not also valid in CPL; to at least that extent they do not escape the confines of classical logic.

EXERCISES 11.3.1

1 To define the operators of the 4-element Boolean algebra we can use precisely the same equations as for the 2-element algebra, provided we define the arithmetic operations "modulo 1" for all four values. Thus the product operation must be defined there by (for all x):

$$(1 \cdot x) = (x \cdot 1) = (x \cdot x) = x$$

$$(0 \cdot x) = (x \cdot 0) = 0$$

$$(\mathsf{b} \cdot \mathsf{n}) = (\mathsf{n} \cdot \mathsf{b}) = 0$$

Give the similar definitions for $-$ and $+$.

2 Complete the proof of Lemma 11.2.

11.4 EXPRESSIVE AND FUNCTIONAL COMPLETENESS

There may not be a complete logic for a given language! One possible obstacle is poverty of the language itself, in that not everything one would want to express in the language can actually be expressed in it. Such poverty may not be an accidental feature. One example of essential *expressive incompleteness* is Alfred Tarski's famous proof [95] that a language cannot contain its own truth predicate, that is, that there can be no way to name all the sentences, and then have a predicate that correctly applies to such a name

[6] That is to say, there does not exist any homomorphism from the associated algebra of Bochvar's matrix to a Boolean algebra.

if and only if the named sentence is true.[7] But in some cases the poverty is remediable, and that is the sort of case we will investigate here.

Recall the three-valued language $\mathcal{L}_{Ł_3}$ constructed by Łukasiewicz, which had the following matrix:

1. The operations $\sim, \vee, \wedge$, and $\rightarrow$ act exactly like the classical ones (i.e. as on a Boolean matrix) when acting on the values 1 and 0

2. There is a third value n such that $\sim(\mathsf{n}) = \mathsf{n}$.

3. The operations $\vee, \wedge$ act as "maximum" and "minimum" if we think of 1 as highest and 0 as lowest element, with n in between. (This extends principle (1).)

4. The conditional $\rightarrow$ can be defined by:

   (a) if x is lower than or equal to y then $(x \rightarrow y) = 1$

   (b) if x is higher than y then $(x \rightarrow y) = (\sim x \vee y)$

5. The equivalence $\leftrightarrow$ can be defined by:

$$(x \leftrightarrow y) = (x \rightarrow y) \wedge (y \rightarrow x)$$

Note that $x \leftrightarrow y$ has value 1 iff $x = y$; it has value 0 iff x and y are distinct *and* neither x nor y is n; $x \leftrightarrow y$ has value n iff x and y are distinct *and* one of them is n. Excluded Middle still fails (and, hence, material identity); however, this language is not devoid of logical truths, given that $A \rightarrow A$ is designated on all admissible valuations.

For present purposes the question is: How rich is Łukasiewicz's 3-valued language in its expressive resources? Another Polish logician, Słupecki (pronounced roughly 'Swuppeski'), pointed out that the operator π defined by the equation:

$$\pi x = \mathsf{n}\,, \quad \text{for all values } x$$

cannot be defined from the operators listed by Łukasiewicz. What is the reason for this, and what does this claim of poverty amount to precisely?

To make it precise we must first retreat again from our user-friendly but sloppy practice of using the same symbol for a connective and for the corresponding operator in the matrix. Thus we should return to distinguishing the connective (for example) $\wedge$ from the corresponding operator $\odot_{\wedge}$. The question, then, is what, *if any*, connective—let's use the symbol '‡'—we could define in Łukasiewicz's language such that $\odot_{‡}$ is the operator π.

---

[7] Raymond Smullyan [91] provides a fairly user-friendly introduction to Tarski's given proof, as well as its connection to Gödel's famous incompleteness theorem.

The answer, of course, is that there is no such connective. Can you see why? All the connectives we have are such that if the parts they connect fail to have value n, then the resultant does not have value n either. That is a characteristic which distinguishes them from π. Let us make this reasoning precise.

DEFINITION 11.4 Sentence A *expresses the* n*-ary operator* φ in language $\mathcal{L}$ if and only if A contains exactly n distinct atomic sentences $A_1, \ldots, A_n$ of $\mathcal{L}$ and $v(A) = \varphi(v(A_1), \ldots, v(A_n))$ for all admissible valuations v of $\mathcal{L}$.

THEOREM 11.6 *No sentence of* $\mathcal{L}_{Ł_3}$ *expresses Słupecki's operator* π.

LEMMA 11.4 *For all admissible valuations* v *of* $\mathcal{L}_{Ł_3}$ *and all sentences* A *of* $\mathcal{L}_{Ł_3}$*, if* v *assigns either* 0 *or* 1 *to all atomic sentences in* A *then* v *assigns either* 0 *or* 1 *to* A.

This is proved by induction (Exercise). It is clear that π can therefore not be expressed by any sentence of this language, since all admissible valuations would have to give value n to $\ddagger A$, even if they gave 1 to A.

In this discussion of what can be expressed in a language we have restricted ourselves to sentential connectives and the functions (operators) which correspond to them. For this sort of case it is usual to employ the term 'functional' rather than 'expressive'. We have proved the functional incompleteness of $\mathcal{L}_{Ł_3}$.

Słupecki proved something more. He proved that if π is added to $\mathcal{L}_{Ł_3}$, thereby forming $\mathcal{L}^{\pi}_{Ł_3}$, the result is functionally complete. The proof draws on some very nice features common to many languages. If a language is functionally complete then it will have the given features, so that in some sense the method of proof is general. We consider a given many-valued language which has an adequate matrix.

» FEATURE I. The matrix is finite; and for each value x in the matrix the *constant operator* Π_x defined

$$\Pi_x(y) = x\,, \quad \text{for all } y$$

is expressed by a sentence of the language.

» FEATURE II. The matrix has a ("highest") designated value 1 and a ("lowest") non-designated value 0 . For each value x in the matrix the *parametric operator* Δ_x defined

$$\Delta_x(y) = \begin{cases} 1 & \text{if } y = x \\ 0 & \text{if } y \neq x \end{cases}$$

is expressed by a sentence of the language.

» FEATURE III. There is a sentence of the language that expresses an *associative meet operator* $\wedge$ such that for all values x

$$(x \wedge 1) = (1 \wedge x) = x$$
$$(x \wedge 0) = (0 \wedge x) = 0$$

» FEATURE IV. There is a sentence of the language that expresses an *associative join operator* $\curlyvee$ such that for all values x

$$(x \curlyvee 0) = (0 \curlyvee x) = x$$
$$(x \curlyvee 1) = (1 \curlyvee x) = 1$$

It will once again be convenient to use the same symbol for connective and operator—just as long as we stay personally aware of the distinction. So, for example, we will write '$\Delta_x(A)$' for a sentence which expresses the parametric operator for value x, with the sentence A replacing whatever atomic sentence was used.

You will have recognized Słupecki's π as the constant operator for the value n, and that the last two features describe the familiar conjunction and disjunction in the many-valued languages we have inspected. What else? Can you provide sentences in $\mathcal{L}_{cpl}$ and also in $\mathcal{L}_{Ł_3}$ that express the other constant and parametric operators? (Exercises.)

Before turning to the general claim that these four features suffice for functional completeness, let us do a very simple example. How could we proceed to define just any connective at all in the case of our familiar classical propositional language? Consider the connective θ such that $(A\theta B)$ receives value 1 iff A and B receive distinct values. To begin we can make up a truthtable:[8]

A	B	$A\theta B$
1	1	0
1	0	1
0	1	1
0	0	0

In trying to find a sentence definable in terms of our usual connectives that will act as $A\theta B$ is supposed to act, we can reason as follows:

[8]Of course, the corresponding operator diagram, namely

$\odot_\theta$	1	0
1	0	1
0	1	0

may likewise be used but for present purposes the truthtable is more illuminating.

If A and B have value 1 then the right value is 0, and if A and B have respectively values 1 and 0 then the right value is 1, and if....

There is certainly a sentence that is guaranteed to get value 0 in the first row:

$$A \wedge B \wedge (A \wedge \sim A).$$

Note that the last conjunct is precisely a sentence that expresses the constant operator for the value 0, while the first and second conjuncts correspond to the entries for A and B in the first row. (What value does this sentence get in the other rows?) We can make up similar sentences that are guaranteed to get the right value in each row, and are peculiarly connected with just that row, in the way we did for the first one:

Row	Sentence
1	$A \wedge B \wedge (A \wedge \sim A)$
2	$A \wedge \sim B \wedge (A \vee \sim A)$
3	$\sim A \wedge B \wedge (A \vee \sim A)$
4	$\sim A \wedge \sim B \wedge (A \wedge \sim A)$

Each sentence receives 0 in the rows by which it was not inspired. So, by forming the disjunction of the given sentences we get a long sentence that receives precisely the value we want in each row;[9] specifically, $A\theta B$ can be defined as

$$[A\wedge B\wedge(A\wedge\sim A)]\vee[A\wedge\sim B\wedge(A\vee\sim A)]\vee[\sim A\wedge B\wedge(A\vee\sim A)]\vee[\sim A\wedge\sim B\wedge(A\wedge\sim A)]$$

It's not elegant, but it suffices.[10]

Turning now to the general case, let us be given some n-ary operator φ, and see how we can design a sentence that will express it. The operator diagram will have a large number of rows, each listing a possible assignment of values to n distinct atomic sentences. Let these atomic sentences be $A_1, \ldots, A_n$ and let us consider the kth row in which these receive, respectively, the values $x(k,1), \ldots, x(k,n)$. To describe this situation we use the sentence:

$$ROW(k) \quad = \quad \Delta_{x(k,1)}A_1 \wedge \ldots \wedge \Delta_{x(k,n)}A_n$$

This sentence will have value 1 in row k, and value 0 in every other row. (Can you see why?) Now consider what φ is meant to do here. The corresponding connective applied to $A_1, \ldots, A_n$ is meant to produce a sentence with value:

$$val(k) \quad = \quad \varphi\,(x(k,1), \ldots, x(k,n))$$

[9] Indeed, it's so long that we reduce the font size to fit it within the margins!

[10] What shorter sentence can you find to do the job?

So let us choose the constant operator for value val(k), which is expressed by the sentence $\Pi_{\text{val}(k)}(A_1)$, and conjoin that to ROW(k), yielding the sentence $\text{ROW}(k)^+$, which is

$$\text{ROW}(k) \wedge \Pi_{\text{val}(k)}(A_1)$$

Properties of conjunction guarantee that this sentence, namely $\text{ROW}(k)^+$, will receive value val(k) in row k, and will receive 0 in every other row. (Make sure that you see this!)

Finally, let us disjoin all the "plus"-sentences to form

$$\text{ROW}(1)^+ \vee \ldots \vee \text{ROW}(m)^+$$

where m is the number of all rows. The resulting disjunction will receive value val(i) in row i for each number i from 1 to m. That is exactly what we wanted: it is a sentence that expresses the given operator φ.

Exercises 11.4.1

1 If the sentence $(\ldots P \ldots)$ expresses the unary operator φ and P' is any other atomic sentence then $(\ldots P' \ldots)$ also expresses φ. (Prove by induction for a matrix language.) Prove also (is this really different?) that if A is any other sentence then $v(\ldots A \ldots) = \varphi(v(A))$, for any admissible valuation v.

2 Prove that in $\mathcal{L}_{Ł_3}$ the remaining connectives can be defined in terms of $\sim$ and $\rightarrow$.

3 Replacing neutral value n by the number $\frac{1}{2}$, write equations that precisely define the action of the operators corresponding to those connectives in $\mathcal{L}_{Ł_3}$.

4 Consider the parametric operators for $\mathcal{L}_{cpl}$, $\mathcal{L}_{Ł_3}$, and Bochvar's "rat's dung" 3-valued language, and in particular how they may be expressible in those languages. Is Bochvar's language functionally complete? If not, what could you add to make it so?

5 Our general functional completeness proof was given somewhat informally in terms of rows in truth tables. Rewrite the argument purely (and more formally) in terms of admissible valuations.

11.5 A General Completeness Proof Method

Early in this chapter we examined logical systems of various sorts, the most general being the natural deduction systems. In this section we introduce a method for proving strong completeness for such a system, with respect to a given language, which will be suitable for a very large variety of logics. In fact, the only substantive requirement will be that there is an explosive sentence—an absurdity, in the classical sense of implying all sentences.

We assume a given sentential syntax, S, letting LS be a logical system for S. Let $\vdash$, the logical consequence relation in LS, be such that the Structural Rules (page 162) hold—they are either part of or admissible in LS. We will also assume that this logic is *finitary*: if $\mathcal{X} \vdash A$ then $\mathcal{X}$ has a finite subset $\mathcal{Y}$ such that $\mathcal{Y} \vdash A$.

Let $\mathcal{X}$ be some set of sentences in S, in which case the following definitions apply:

DEFINITION 11.5 $\mathcal{X}$ is *closed under deduction* in LS iff for every sentence A, if $\mathcal{X} \vdash A$ then A is in $\mathcal{X}$.

DEFINITION 11.6 $\mathcal{X}$ is a *theory* (of LS, an LS-theory) iff $\mathcal{X}$ is closed under deduction in LS.

DEFINITION 11.7 $\mathcal{X}$ is *inconsistent* (with respect to LS) iff all sentences are logical consequences of $\mathcal{X}$ in LS. A set is *consistent* iff it is not inconsistent.

DEFINITION 11.8 $\mathcal{X}$ is a *maximal consistent set* of LS (briefly, a *maxi-set* of LS, an LS maxi-set) iff $\mathcal{X}$ is consistent and such that if B is not in $\mathcal{X}$ then $\mathcal{X}, B \vdash A$, for every sentence A.[11]

DEFINITION 11.9 The sentence $\bot$ is an *absurd sentence* (of LS iff $\{\bot\}$ is inconsistent (i.e. ... iff $\bot \vdash A$, for all sentences A).

We note that a set $\mathcal{X}$ is inconsistent if and only $\mathcal{X} \vdash \bot$. (Why is that so?) The definition we adopt here for inconsistency is appropriate because we do not assume that the language has anything like classical negation.

SOME PRELIMINARY THEOREMS

In what follows we will suppress explicit reference to LS, as long as we are only discussing one logical system at a time. We now prove a few preliminary theorems on the road to our "completeness template", which is covered in the next subsection.

THEOREM 11.7 *Every maxi-set is a theory.*

PROOF THM 11.7 Suppose that $\mathcal{X}$ is a maxi-set and that $\mathcal{X} \vdash A$. If A is not in $\mathcal{X}$ then by supposition $\mathcal{X}, A \vdash B$ for every sentence B. By Trans and Prime it follows that $\mathcal{X} \vdash B$ for every sentence B, but that contradicts what is given, namely, that $\mathcal{X}$ is consistent. Therefore, A is in $\mathcal{X}$. We conclude that $\mathcal{X}$ is closed under deduction in LS.

[11]That is, $\mathcal{X}$ is in LS-maxi-set iff $\mathcal{X}$ is consistent and the addition of any new sentence to $\mathcal{X}$ produces a set that is inconsistent with respect to LS.

Theorem 11.8 (Extension Theorem) *If* LS *has an absurd sentence then every set $\mathcal{X}$ which is consistent wrt* LS *is part of a maxi-set of* LS.

This is the engine behind strong completeness proofs for logical systems. We prove the theorem by providing a recipe for constructing the target maxi-set $\mathcal{X}^\star$ by extending the given consistent set $\mathcal{X}$.

Recipe for Target Maxi-set: Let $\mathcal{X}$ be a set consistent wrt LS. Let $A_1, A_2, \ldots$ be all the sentences of S, in alphabetic order.[12] We define the series $\mathcal{Z}$ of sets $\mathcal{X}_1, \mathcal{X}_2, \ldots$ as follows, for all $k \in \mathbb{N}$:

$$\mathcal{X}_{k+1} = \begin{cases} \mathcal{X} & \text{if } k = 0 \\ \mathcal{X}_k \cup \{A_k\} & \text{if } k > 0 \text{ and } \mathcal{X}_k \cup \{A_k\} \text{ is consistent} \\ \mathcal{X}_k & \text{otherwise.} \end{cases}$$

The recipe, then, is just this: If A_1 can consistently be added to $\mathcal{X}$ (i.e. if $\mathcal{X} \cup \{A_1\}$ is consistent), then add it, thereby forming $\mathcal{X}_2$, our second element in the series; otherwise, leave it out and just let $\mathcal{X}_2$ be our original consistent $\mathcal{X}$. In turn, if A_2 can consistently be added to $\mathcal{X}_2$, then add it (thereby forming $\mathcal{X}_3$); otherwise, leave it out and just let $\mathcal{X}_3$ be $\mathcal{X}_2$. And so on, for all subsequent stages.

With series $\mathcal{Z}$ in hand we proceed to define $\mathcal{X}^\star$, our target maxi-set, to be the set of all sentences $A_i \in S$ such that A_i is in $\mathcal{X}_k$, for some $k \in \mathbb{N}$. In other words, we define $\mathcal{X}^\star$ to be the generalized union of $\mathcal{Z}$:

$$\mathcal{X}^\star = \bigcup \mathcal{Z} = \mathcal{X}_1 \cup \mathcal{X}_2 \cup \ldots$$

Lemma 11.5 *Each set $\mathcal{X}_j$ is consistent.*

The proof of Lemma 11.5 is by induction. We leave it as exercise.

Lemma 11.6 *$\mathcal{X}^\star$ is a maxi-set.*

Proof Lem 11.6 We must first prove that $\mathcal{X}^\star$ is consistent. Suppose to the contrary that $\mathcal{X}^\star \vdash \bot$. Then $\mathcal{X}^\star$ has a finite subset, namely

$$\mathcal{Y} = \{A_{k_1}, A_{k_2}, \ldots, A_{k_n}\}$$

which has $\bot$ as a consequence. Each sentence in $\mathcal{Y}$ was either in $\mathcal{X}$ already or added at the stage corresponding to its index; so if j is the largest of these indices then all of them belong to $\mathcal{X}_j$. But, then, by Trans it follows that $\mathcal{X}_j$ has $\bot$ as a consequence as well, and is therefore inconsistent, which is impossible.

[12] See §10.4 for the discussion of enumeration.

With consistency established we must now prove that $\mathcal{X}^\star$ is maximal in the relevant sense. Suppose that A_m is not in $\mathcal{X}^\star$ although $\mathcal{X}^\star \vdash \mathsf{A}_\mathsf{m}$, in which case A_m was not added at stage $\mathsf{m}+1$. Given the recipe, A_m was not added at stage $\mathsf{m}+1$ only if $\mathcal{X}_\mathsf{m}, \mathsf{A}_\mathsf{m} \vdash \bot$, which by Weak implies that $\mathcal{X}^\star, \mathsf{A}_\mathsf{m} \vdash \bot$. Hence, by Tran, $\mathcal{X}^\star \vdash \bot$. But we already have it that $\mathcal{X}^\star \nvdash \bot$, and so the supposition is impossible. QED

GENERAL COMPLETENESS TEMPLATE

We can now proceed to the general form for a strong completeness proof for such a logic as LS.

THEOREM 11.9 (COMPLETENESS TEMPLATE) LS *is strongly complete for language $\mathcal{L}$ if* LS *pertains to the syntax of $\mathcal{L}$ and the following two conditions hold:*

1. *(Separation) If it is not the case that $\mathcal{X} \vdash \mathsf{A}$ in* LS *then there is a maxi-set of* LS *which contains all of $\mathcal{X}$ but not* A.
2. *(Value-coding) If $\mathcal{X}$ is a maxi-set of* LS *then there is an admissible valuation v of $\mathcal{L}$ such that v satisfies* A *iff* A *is in $\mathcal{X}$, for all sentences* A *of $\mathcal{L}$.*

The proof is easy (and is here left as exercise); it is clear that all the work in applying the template go into establishing the Separation and Value-coding conditions for the specific logic and language in question.

Strong Completeness of CPL(NAT)

By way of illustrating the template we apply it to the case of CPL(NAT) and $\mathcal{L}_{\mathsf{CPL}}$.

THEOREM 11.10 *The natural deduction system* CPL(NAT) *is strongly complete for the language $\mathcal{L}_{\mathsf{CPL}}$.*

In view of Theorem 11.9, this theorem will follow from the lemmas that we now prove for this logic and language. For the absurd sentence $\bot$ we choose $(\mathsf{p} \wedge {\sim}\mathsf{p})$, where p is the first atomic sentence of the syntax.

LEMMA 11.7 *If it is not the case that $\mathcal{X} \vdash \mathsf{A}$ in* CPL(NAT) *then there is a maxi-set of* CPL(NAT) *which contains all of $\mathcal{X}$ and* ~A.

PROOF LEM 11.7 We know from the Extension Theorem that there is a maxi-set of CPL(NAT) which contains all of $\mathcal{X}$ and also ~A if $\mathcal{X} \cup \{{\sim}\mathsf{A}\}$ is consistent.[13] To show such consistency, assume the Lemma's antecedent and suppose (for reductio) that $\mathcal{X}, {\sim}\mathsf{A}$ is not consistent. Then $\mathcal{X}, {\sim}\mathsf{A} \vdash \bot$ and, by (T2),[14] $\mathcal{X} \vdash \mathsf{A}$, contrary to our assumption. Hence, there is a maxi-set that contains all of $\mathcal{X}$ and ~A. QED

[13] As in earlier sections we will frequently denote $\mathcal{X} \cup \{{\sim}\mathsf{A}\}$ by '$\mathcal{X}, {\sim}\mathsf{A}$'.

[14] see exercises, page 167

LEMMA 11.8 (SEPARATION) *If it is not the case that* $\mathcal{X} \vdash A$ *in* CPL(NAT) *then there is a maxi-set of* CPL(NAT) *which contains all of* $\mathcal{X}$ *but not* A.

PROOF LEM 11.8 Simply continue the proof of Lemma 11.7: Because that maxi-set contains $\sim A$ it cannot also contain A, since by definition every maxi-set is consistent. [Recall Rule ($\perp$ Intro)]. QED

LEMMA 11.9 *If* $\mathcal{Y}$ *is a maxi-set of* CPL(NAT) *then for all sentences* A, B

1. $\sim A$ *is in* $\mathcal{Y}$ *if and only if* A *is not in* $\mathcal{Y}$
2. $(A \wedge B)$ *is in* $\mathcal{Y}$ *if and only if* A *and* B *are both in* $\mathcal{Y}$

PROOF LEM 11.9 Concerning (1) it is clear that A and $\sim A$ cannot both be in $\mathcal{Y}$ since maxi-sets are consistent. But if A is not in $\mathcal{Y}$, then since maxi-sets are theories, closed under deduction, it follows that it is not the case that $\mathcal{Y} \vdash A$. Hence, by Lemma 9 there is a maxi-set, call it '$\mathcal{Q}$', which contains all of $\mathcal{Y}$ and $\sim A$. Since adding new elements to $\mathcal{Y}$ would make it inconsistent, it follows that $\mathcal{Y}$ itself is $\mathcal{Q}$.

Concerning (2), suppose first that $\mathcal{Y}$ is a maxi-set that contains $(A \wedge B)$. By (T4)[15] and Weak, $\mathcal{Y} \vdash A$ and $\mathcal{Y} \vdash B$. Being a maxi-set $\mathcal{Y}$ is a theory and, hence, contains all its own consequences, including these two. On the other hand, suppose that A and B are both in $\mathcal{Y}$. By rules ($\wedge$ Intro) and Weak, it follows that $\mathcal{Y} \vdash (A \wedge B)$ and, so, as before, $(A \wedge B)$ must be in $\mathcal{Y}$. QED

LEMMA 11.10 (VALUE-CODING) *If* $\mathcal{X}$ *be a maxi-set of* CPL(NAT), *then there is an admissible valuation* v *of* $\mathcal{L}_{CPL}$ *such that* v *satisfies* A *iff* A *is in* $\mathcal{X}$, *for all sentences* A *of* $\mathcal{L}_{CPL}$.

PROOF LEM 11.10 This follows immediately from Lemma 11.9 if we define the function v to be the assigment such that, for all sentences A of the language,

$$v(A) = \begin{cases} 1 & \text{if A is in } \mathcal{X} \\ 0 & \text{otherwise.} \end{cases}$$

After all, the admissibility conditions for valuations of $\mathcal{L}_{CPL}$ are simply that every sentence be assigned one of these values and that

$$v(\sim A) = 1 \text{ iff } v(A) = 0, \quad \text{and } v(A \wedge B) = 1 \text{ iff } v(A) = 1 = v(B).$$

QED

[15] See exercises, page 167

So goes the completeness proof. The reader may reasonably suspect that the system CPL(NAT) was formulated in the way we did precisely with this sort of completeness argument in mind! That its construction followed a specific recipe towards the given goal will become very clear in the next section.

EXERCISES 11.5.1

1 Prove that $\vdash$ in CPL(NAT) is finitary.

2 In Exercises 11.2.1 the Connective Rules were extended to disjunction, material implication, and material equivalence. Extend Lemma 11.9 to those connectives, using the rules you devised.

11.6 COMPLETENESS IN MANY-VALUED LOGIC

Let $\mathcal{L}$ be a matrix language with adequate matrix $\langle \mathcal{V}, \mathcal{D}, \mathbb{C}, \odot \rangle$. Question: Can we construct a logical system that is sound and complete with respect to $\mathcal{L}$? Recall that we listed some nice features such a language can have which are necessary and sufficient for functional completeness. Somewhat similar but less onerous conditions are sufficient to allow us to construct such a logic:[16]

DEFINITION 11.10 An operator Δ on a matrix is *quasi-parametric* iff there is a value x such that $\Delta(y)$ is designated just in case $y = x$ (in which case Δ is said to be associated with this value).

» FEATURE A. The matrix is finite and has at least one designated and one undesignated element.

» FEATURE B. The language has an absurd sentence $\perp$ which is assigned an undesignated element by all admissible valuations.

» FEATURE C. For each value x in $\mathcal{V}$ there is an associated quasi-parametric operator Δ_x expressed by some sentence A of $\mathcal{L}$ (which we will write as: $\Delta_x(A)$).

Our aim to show that if $\mathcal{L}$ has features (A)–(C) then one can construct a sound and complete logical system LS for $\mathcal{L}$. In particular, the general method for completeness proofs given in the preceding section can be utilized.

[16] Whether it is also possible under other conditions we leave aside; J. Pollock [73] provides a more extensive exploration.

PRELIMINARIES

The logic LS will be a natural deduction system; so, it has the Structural Rules (page 162) common to all such logics, and such rules are sound for all languages. In addition, LS has three groups of rules that pertain to its special connectives and the absurd sentence $\bot$. We cover the groups in turn.

RULE GROUP I:

1. $\bot \vdash A$
2. If $x \neq y$ then $\Delta_x(A), \Delta_y(A) \vdash \bot$
3. If x is designated then $\Delta_x(A) \vdash A$
4. If x is not designated then $\Delta_x(A), A \vdash \bot$

This group generalizes the Principle of Non-Contradiction: a sentence cannot have more than one value; to assert a sentence is to imply that it has a designated value and conversely; and from the absurd everything follows. Note that, as usual, a set is inconsistent with respect to LS if and only if the absurd sentence is derivable from it; this fact we will use implicitly throughout.

RULE GROUP II:

1. Let $u, \ldots, z$ be all the elements of the matrix. Then:

$$\text{If } \mathcal{X}, \Delta_u(B) \vdash A \text{ and } \ldots \text{ and } \mathcal{X}, \Delta_z(B) \vdash A \text{ then } \mathcal{X} \vdash A.$$

This group generalizes the Principle of the Excluded Middle (and the rule Excl of our system CPL(NAT)): the sentence B must have one of the possible values in the matrix.

RULE GROUP III:

1. Let φ^m be a connective in $\mathcal{L}$. Let $r, \ldots, z$ be m values (not necessarily all distinct). Let w be the value $\odot_{\varphi^m}(r, \ldots, z)$. Then:

$$\Delta_r(A_1), \ldots, \Delta_z(A_m) \vdash \Delta_w(\varphi^m(A_1, \ldots, A_m)).$$

Group III, you might recognize, reproduces the rows in operator diagrams, in a way that is quite reminiscent of how that was done in the proof of functional completeness.

Before turning to the target results we note that, of course, in CPL there are only two quasi-parametric operators each of which can be expressed very simply:

$$\Delta_1(P) = P \quad \text{and} \quad \Delta_0(P) = {\sim}P.$$

As an exercise write out the above system for just this case and compare with CPL(NAT): Is there any difference?

SOUNDNESS AND COMPLETENESS

The soundness of the above system for $\mathcal{L}$ is proved straightforwardly, constantly applying the idea that $\Delta_x(A)$ is designated if and only if A has value x, for any sentence A.

For the completeness proof we utilize our proof template (page 180), which is applicable given the presence of absurd sentence $\bot$. So, as with any application of the template, we must prove the following two lemmas:

LEMMA 11.11 (SEPARATION) *If it is not the case that $\mathcal{X} \vdash A$ in* LS *then there is a maxi-set of* LS *which contains all of $\mathcal{X}$ but not* A.

PROOF LEM 11.11 Suppose that it is not the case that $\mathcal{X} \vdash A$ in LS. Then there is an undesignated value x such that it is not the case that $\mathcal{X}, \Delta_x(A) \vdash \bot$, as otherwise we would have it that $\mathcal{X}, \Delta_y(A) \vdash A$ for all values y. (Which Rules are we invoking here?) But, then, by Rule Group II, it would follow that $\mathcal{X} \vdash A$, contrary to supposition. Thus $\mathcal{X} \cup \{\Delta_x(A)\}$ is consistent and, hence, is part of a maxi-set of LS. But in view of rule (4) of Rule Group I, the given maxi-set cannot contain A since x is non-designated. Hence, there is a maxi-set of LS which contains all of $\mathcal{X}$ but not A. QED

LEMMA 11.12 (VALUE-CODING) *If $\mathcal{X}$ is a maxi-set of* LS *then there is an admissible valuation v of $\mathcal{L}$ such that v satisfies* A *iff* A *is in $\mathcal{X}$, for all sentences* A *of $\mathcal{L}$.*

PROOF LEM 11.12 Let $\mathcal{X}$ be a maxi-set of LS. Define the valuation v as follows:

$$v(A) = x \quad \text{iff} \quad \Delta_x(A) \text{ is in } \mathcal{X}$$

We first need to establish that v is a well-defined function which assigns a unique value to all sentences of $\mathcal{L}$. In turn, we must show that v is an admissible valuation. Finally, we must show that v satisfies all and only the sentences in $\mathcal{X}$. We take each task in turn.

Well-defined function? Given rules (1) and (2) of Rule Group I and the consistency of $\mathcal{X}$, there can be *at most* one value x such that $\Delta_x(A)$ is in $\mathcal{X}$. Moreover, there must be *at least* one such value. Suppose otherwise. Then, for some value y, at least one of the sets formed by adding $\Delta_y(A)$ to $\mathcal{X}$ must be consistent; if it were not so then, given Rule Group II, $\mathcal{X}$ would not be consistent, in which case $\mathcal{X}$ would not be a maxi-set, contrary to supposition. But if $\Delta_y(A)$ is not in $\mathcal{X}$ and can consistently be added then $\mathcal{X}$ is not a maxi-set, again contrary to supposition.

Is v admissible? Yes, as Rule Group III guarantees that v satisfies the required condition for a matrix language, namely that

$$v(\varphi^m(A_1, \ldots, A_m)) = \odot_{\varphi^m}(v(A_1), \ldots, v(A_m)).$$

Does v satisfy all and only the sentences in $\mathcal{X}$? v satisfies A iff $\Delta_x(A)$ is in $\mathcal{X}$, for some designated value x, in which case A is also in $\mathcal{X}$. Moreover, A cannot belong to $\mathcal{X}$ unless $\Delta_x(A)$ is in $\mathcal{X}$ for some designated value x, as otherwise $\Delta_y(A)$ would be in $\mathcal{X}$ for some non-designated value y (see above), which, on pain of inconsistency (by Rule Group I), would preclude A from being in $\mathcal{X}$. QED

Hence, both our lemmas are established, and by the Completeness Template Theorem our completeness claim for LS with respect to $\mathcal{L}$ now follows.

EXERCISES II.6.1

1 Construct a sound and complete logical system for $\mathcal{L}_{Ł_3}$ with Słupecki's connective added.

FURTHER READING

Curry's [25] is an invaluable source for many of the topics in this (and the next) chapter.

Logic, like whiskey,
loses its beneficial effect
when taken in too large quantities.
– Lord Dunsany

Chapter 12
Meta-Theorems for Non-Classical Logics

We are now ready to use our new meta-logical resources for a new look beyond many-valued logic at the other logics we have been studying. But before turning specifically to modal, intuitionistic, and relevance logics, as well as the logic of conditionals, we want to show clearly how all these logics fit into a single theoretical framework.

12.1 Unification

There are two aspects to this unified view of our subject. The first is the general concept of a language and its logic. This applies far beyond the scope of this book, to almost all topics studied in philosophical logic. The second pertains specifically to the logics studied here, to show in what sense they all belong to a single family with a single form of semantic analysis.

To begin then, we have the general concept of a language with its syntax and its admissible valuations, together with the concept of satisfaction. In terms of these notions alone, given that the syntax specifies a set of sentences, we can define the logical relations of validity and satisfiability. The task of logic is then to catalogue those relations systematically by certain criteria relating to our human and technological limitations. That task is performed by devising logical systems of the various sorts that we have introduced. Some desiderata may not be met, or be possible to meet: we'd like to find a decision procedure for validity, for example, but in the case of some languages validity is not decidable. Then we settle for lesser forms of success.

Here we are studying only languages with a sentential syntax, in which every admissible valuation will at the very least derive from a valuation that has a base (in the sense that we shall explain below).

But is this point useful to us? Certainly, and we shall exploit it when we can. The very first benefit we derive from this kinship is that the general completeness proof template we have introduced will apply not only the many-valued logics above but to most of the other logics as well. When it only applies in part (as will be the case for intuitionistic logic) there will be an easy and fairly obvious adjustment so as to make it fit there as well. In addition, we shall draw on this kinship among the languages to help us to raise specific questions and suggest specific conjectures, for example concerning the extent to which infinite structures can be ignored when cataloguing the relations of validity and satisfiability.

To help us move easily back and forth between the different languages and logics it will be useful here to show how many-valued languages and modal languages are related on a formal or abstract level. First of all we'll show explicitly how an admissible valuation of a modal language provides (in effect) a matrix for that language. Then we will show conversely how a matrix in general can be viewed as deriving from some possible world model. Thus the two sorts of languages are intimately related from a formal, abstract point of view, even if their intuitive sense and motivation remains quite different.

To begin then let us take the normal modal language $\mathcal{L}_K$, and consider one of its admissible valuations. Recall that for this to be an admissible valuation it must be $v(w_0, A)$ for a model $\mathcal{M} = \langle \mathcal{W}, \mathcal{R}, v \rangle$ of that language and a world w_0 in $\mathcal{W}$. We can phrase this to ourselves by saying that for this admissible valuation, the model depicts a set of possible worlds among which w_0 is the actual world. That model must satisfy the following description:

» An $\mathcal{L}_K$-model is a triple $\mathcal{M} = \langle \mathcal{W}, \mathcal{R}, v \rangle$ such that $\mathcal{W}$ is non-empty, $\mathcal{R} \subseteq \mathcal{W} \times \mathcal{W}$, and v is a map from $\mathcal{W} \times \mathcal{S}$ (worlds and sentences) to $\{1, 0\}$ such that

  » $v(w, {\sim}A) = 1$ iff $v(w, A) = 0$

  » $v(w, A \wedge B) = 1$ iff $v(w, A) = v(w, B) = 1$

  » $v(w, \Box A) = 1$ iff $v(w', A) = 1$ for all w' s.t. $w\mathcal{R}w'$

But there is a different way of looking at this. You will recall (from exercises 5 and 6 of Exercises 5.3.1, page 59) that the admissible valuation v has a base supplied by this model. That base, as we shall now explicitly point out, enlarges into a matrix for our valuation.

According to Def 3.2, we have it that

» a *base* for valuation v of sentential syntax $S = \langle \mathcal{A}, \mathcal{C}, \mathcal{S} \rangle$ consists of a set $\mathcal{V}$ of elements and a set $\mathbb{C}$ of operators on those elements, and a rule associating one operation $\odot_\varphi$ in $\mathbb{C}$ with each connective φ in $\mathcal{C}$, in such a way that

  » $v(A) \in \mathcal{V}$, for each sentence A of $\mathcal{S}$

» for all sentences $A_1, \ldots, A_n$ and each n-ary connective φ in $\mathcal{C}$:
$\nu(\varphi(A_1, \ldots, A_n)) = \odot_\varphi(\nu(A_1), \ldots, \nu(A_n))$

The question is: How does this relate to our model and admissible valuation for language $\mathcal{L}_K$? The answer cannot be immediately obvious. A look at the defined function ν_w quickly reveals that in general it cannot have a base. The only values it can assign are 1 and 0, but if the sentences A and B are assigned the same truth value 1 by ν_w it does not follow at all that the sentences $\Box$A and $\Box$B are assigned the same value! Nevertheless we can display a valuation with a base, and define satisfaction in such a way for it that it satisfies a sentence precisely and only if ν_w assigns 1 to that sentence. How is that possible?

As in Exercises 5.3.1 (5 and 6), the function ν (in effect) assigns to each sentence A a set of worlds: *the proposition expressed by that sentence*, namely $\nu_{\mathcal{M}}(A) = \{w : \nu(w, A) = 1\}$. Also there is for each world w the set of worlds "accessible" from w, namely $\mathcal{R}(w) = \{w' : w\mathcal{R}w'\}$. The connectives, in turn, correspond to operations on the sets of worlds (on the "propositions") as follows:

Table 12.1: *Connectives and Corresponding Operators*

$\nu_{\mathcal{M}}({\sim}A) = \mathcal{W} - \nu_{\mathcal{M}}(A)$	$\odot_{\sim}(\mathcal{X}) = \mathcal{W} - \mathcal{X}$
$\nu_{\mathcal{M}}(A \wedge B) = \nu_{\mathcal{M}}(A) \cap \nu_{\mathcal{M}}(B)$	$\odot_{\wedge}(\mathcal{X}, \mathcal{Y}) = \mathcal{X} \cap \mathcal{Y}$
$\nu_{\mathcal{M}}(A \vee B) = \nu_{\mathcal{M}}(A) \cup \nu_{\mathcal{M}}(B)$	$\odot_{\vee}(\mathcal{X}, \mathcal{Y}) = \mathcal{X} \cup \mathcal{Y}$
$\nu_{\mathcal{M}}(\Box A) = \{w : \mathcal{R}(w) \subseteq \nu_{\mathcal{M}}(A)\}$	$\odot_{\Box}(\mathcal{X}) = \{u : \mathcal{R}(u) \subseteq \mathcal{X}\}$

With this redefined notion of the function $\nu_{\mathcal{M}}$ we can reconstruct the *admissible* valuation ν as follows:

» $\nu_{\mathcal{M}}$ *satisfies* A iff w_0 is a member of $\nu_{\mathcal{M}}(A)$.

But now we can also rephrase this to ourselves as:

» the *designated propositions* are precisely those that contain w_0

and we have in effect made the transition to describing our admissible valuation that derives from a modal model as equally deriving from a matrix.

To sum up, let us define a "little" many-valued language which appears in the modal semantics as follows:

» If $\mathcal{M} = \langle \mathcal{W}, \mathcal{R}, \nu \rangle$ is an $\mathcal{L}_K$-model and $w_0 \in \mathcal{W}$, then $\mathcal{L}_K(\mathcal{M}, w_0)$ is the many-valued language with matrix $\mathfrak{M}(w_0) = \langle \mathcal{V}, \mathcal{D}, \mathbb{C}, \odot \rangle$, where:

  » $\mathcal{V} = \wp(\mathcal{W})$

  » $\mathcal{D} = \{\mathcal{X} \in \mathcal{V} : w_0 \in \mathcal{X}\}$

  » $\mathbb{C}$ and $\odot$ are as specified in Table 12.1.

One can now see that v, regarded as a function that assigns sets of worlds to sentences, is precisely the admissible valuation for this new "little" language which gives to a sentence a designated value if and only if that sentence is satisfied by our original admissible valuation v_{w_0} of $\mathcal{L}_\mathsf{K}$.

Despite the "translation" above, modal languages are not simply many-valued languages because there is not just one base for all modal valuations (of a given language). Moreover, for each base there are many matrices, which, in effect, emerge by taking as designated elements all the sets of worlds that contain a given world w—for any choice of w that you like. Accordingly, modal languages are in effect languages in which the admissible valuations belong to a large family of matrices rather than just one. You might say: a modal language is the "disjunction" of all those "little" many-valued languages that correspond to its admissible valuations in the foregoing fashion.[1]

Going the Other Way

It is also possible to make this transition between languages in the opposite direction. As an example we'll take the "liberal" four-valued Boolean matrix studied in §11.

Boolean algebra $\mathfrak{B}_4$, as depicted in Figure 11.1 (page 169), has elements 1, b, n, and 0, where b and n act pretty much like 1 and 0 do. Moreover, when we form a matrix from this algebra the "liberal" decision is to have both 1 and b designated, where, as in §11 (again, page 169), 1 and 0 are each other's negation, as are b and n, while conjunction is again glb and disjunction lub. This *liberal* $\mathfrak{B}_4$-matrix is defined by Def 11.2, according to which

» the *liberal* $\mathfrak{B}_4$ matrix is the matrix

$$\mathfrak{B}_4(\mathrm{lib}) = \langle\{1,\mathsf{b},\mathsf{n},0\},\{1,\mathsf{b}\},\{\sim^4,\wedge^4,\vee^4\},\odot\rangle$$

with associated algebra $\mathfrak{B}_4$, with elements 1 and b designated, and where $\odot$ (the interpretation function) matches $\sim^4,\wedge^4,\vee^4$ to $\sim,\wedge,\vee$, respectively, in the classical sentential syntax.

Suppose, now, that model $\mathcal{M} = \langle\mathcal{W},\mathcal{R},\mathsf{v}\rangle$ contains just two worlds, w_1 and w_2. In that case there are just four propositions, which we can name suggestively, and four operations:

Table 12.2: *Propositions and Operators*

$1 = \mathcal{W} = \{w_1, w_2\}$	$\odot_\sim(\mathcal{X}) = \mathcal{W} - \mathcal{X}$
$\mathsf{b} = \{w_1\}$	$\odot_\wedge(\mathcal{X},\mathcal{Y}) = \mathcal{X} \cap \mathcal{Y}$
$\mathsf{n} = \{w_2\}$	$\odot_\vee(\mathcal{X},\mathcal{Y}) = \mathcal{X} \cup \mathcal{Y}$
$0 = \emptyset$	$\odot_\Box(\mathcal{X}) = \{u : \mathcal{R}(u) \subseteq \mathcal{X}\}$

[1] Semantics of modal logic before Kripke had this format, with such examples as the Henle matrices for S5.

Concentrating for a moment on the first operation, we see at once that $\mathsf{b} = \odot_{\sim}(\mathsf{n})$ and $\mathsf{n} = \odot_{\sim}(\mathsf{b})$. That looks—or should look—very familiar! Only a few more moments suffice to check that the operator diagrams are precisely the same as for the four-element Boolean algebra that we studied in §11. But here we have a Boolean algebra with an additional operator, the one corresponding to necessity. If we ignore that, and take the world w_1 as our "actual world" (so that $\mathsf{1}$ and b are the "designated propositions") we will in effect have precisely our matrix $\mathfrak{B}_4(\mathtt{lib})$.

SUMMARY

So to sum it all up, we can think of those truth-values of many-valued languages, both the familiar ones and the strange ones, as propositions—even represent them in general by means of sets of worlds, in possible world models.[2] And conversely we can think of the possible world models as elaborate ways of providing matrices with values that represent characters going beyond the mere division into *True* and *False*.

EXERCISES 12.1.1

1 In §5.4 we discussed the limiting case that relation $\mathcal{R}$ is *universal*: every world bears it to every other world. The given language was $\mathcal{L}_{\mathsf{UA}}$ and the logic S5. Show that in its models the necessity operator on propositions turns the set of all worlds into itself and turns every other proposition into the empty set. Using this fact revisit the exercises for that language and see whether they are made easier in retrospect.

12.2 THE STANDARD NORMAL MODAL LOGICS

We will work with a minimal syntax, omitting all but three connectives: $\sim$, $\wedge$, and $\Box$. We will refer to this simply as *the modal (sentential) syntax*, sometimes using '$\mathsf{S_m}$'.

We have encountered six normal modal logics corresponding to the six languages $\mathcal{L}_{\mathsf{K}}$, $\mathcal{L}_{\mathsf{K}}^{\mathsf{ser}}$, $\mathcal{L}_{\mathsf{K}}^{\mathsf{r}}$, $\mathcal{L}_{\mathsf{K}}^{\mathsf{rs}}$, $\mathcal{L}_{\mathsf{K}}^{\mathsf{rt}}$, and $\mathcal{L}_{\mathsf{K}}^{\mathsf{rst}}$. As noted along the way, those normal modal logics have standard names, namely K, D, T, B, S4, and S5. (All but B were introduced in §5.5, with B discussed in Exercises 5.4.2 (5).) We can summarize the given languages as follows.

STANDARD NORMAL MODAL LANGUAGES

For index $\mathsf{j} = \mathsf{K}, \mathsf{K}^{\mathsf{ser}}, \mathsf{K}^{\mathsf{r}}, \mathsf{K}^{\mathsf{rs}}, \mathsf{K}^{\mathsf{rt}}, \mathsf{K}^{\mathsf{rst}}$ each language $\mathcal{L}_{\mathsf{j}}$ is such that

---

[2] We have not illustrated how some of the "strange" connectives in many-valued languages can be recovered from possible world models; however, our treatment below of intuitionistic logic and the logic of conditionals will, in effect, provide examples of this. In the case of relevance logic, such recovery was made in part by introducing ternary rather than binary acccess relations and impossible as well as possible worlds. In a more general mathematical context, we would speak here of set-theoretic representations of the associated algebras.

» MODELS: An $\mathcal{L}_j$-*model* is a triple $\mathcal{M} = \langle \mathcal{W}, \mathcal{R}, v \rangle$ wherein $\mathcal{W}$ is non-empty, $\mathcal{R}$ is part of $\mathcal{W} \times \mathcal{W}$ and such that

$\mathcal{R}$ is serial, if $j = K^{ser}$

$\mathcal{R}$ is reflexive, if $j = K^{r}$

$\mathcal{R}$ is reflexive and symmetric, if $j = K^{rs}$

$\mathcal{R}$ is reflexive and transitive, if $j = K^{rt}$

$\mathcal{R}$ is an equivalence relation, if $j = K^{rst}$

and v is a map from $\mathcal{W} \times S_m$ to $\{1, 0\}$ such that

$v(w, {\sim}A) = 1$ iff $v(w, A) = 0$

$v(w, A \wedge B) = 1$ iff $v(w, A) = v(B, w) = 1$

$v(w, \Box A) = 1$ iff $v(w', A) = 1$, for all w' st $\langle w, w' \rangle \in \mathcal{R}$

» ADMISSIBLE VALUATIONS: Admissible valuations of $\mathcal{L}_j$ are the functions $v(w, \ldots)$ such that there is an $\mathcal{L}_j$-model $\mathcal{M}$ with w in $\mathcal{W}$. Such a valuation satisfies sentence A iff $v(w, A) = 1$.

TOWARDS NATURAL DEDUCTION

We would like to provide soundness and completeness proofs for the logics standardly associated with each $\mathcal{L}_j$. We already have, in §5, tableaux systems presented as formulations of these logics. Those tableaux systems are unlike those for CPL in that, in addition to the sentences of the modal syntax, we also see expressions such as 'w' occurring in their lines. What this reflects is that, while such systems are logical systems, they are really formulated for a richer language. The reason such systems are formulated for a richer language is that they are designed to mechanize the production of counterexamples, in the sense of models with valuations that refute invalid arguments. To be sure, the systems of §5 capture precisely the theorems and derivations of the standard normal modal logics, but that is because each—the tableaux system and the standard logic—is sound and complete for the language in question.

What is missing from our story, then, is the standard normal modal logics themselves, formulated precisely in the modal syntax itself (which is historically how they were introduced) and the soundness and completeness proofs for those logics. What will come as no surprise is that, for the most part, so formulating the standard logics will consist in simply adding the "characteristic formulas" that were displayed in §5, plus a rule such as what was there called 'Necessitation', to CPL(NAT). We turn now to the task. (To save space we will in places uses 'SNML' to abbreviate 'Standard Normal Modal Logics', which denotes the set of languages $\mathcal{L}_j$, with index j as above.)

THE SYSTEMS

As above, each of the logics is constructed by augmenting CPL(NAT). Before specifying the relevant additions we first give the "characteristic formulas" in the requisite form and we specify a new Connective Rule:

- CHARACTERISTIC FORMULAS:
  - (Ser □): $\Box A \vdash {\sim}\Box{\sim}A$
  - (Refl □): $\Box A \vdash A$
  - (Sym □): $A \vdash \Box{\sim}\Box{\sim}A$
  - (Tran □): $\Box A \vdash \Box\Box A$
- CONNECTIVE RULE:
  - (□ Intro): If $A_1, \ldots, A_n \vdash B$ then $\Box A_1, \ldots, \Box A_n \vdash \Box B$.

Note that (□ Intro) includes the theorem-creating rule as a special case: if A is a theorem so is $\Box A$.[3]

Constructing the six systems is now straightforward:[4]

- System K: Add (□ Intro) to CPL(NAT).
- System D: Add (Ser □) to K.
- System T: Add (Refl □) to D.
- System B: Add (Sym □) to T.
- System S4: Add (Tran □) to T.
- System S5: Add (Sym □) to S4.

As an exercise we leave the proof that T is also just K plus (Refl □), with (Ser □) provable from that much. Note also that S5 is K plus all five new rules added.

ADEQUACY OF THE SYSTEMS

While we plan to adapt the Completeness Template Theorem here, we will begin by constructing a special model for each language (sometimes called its *canonical structure*, in view of the role we will see it playing). The "worlds" in this model will simply be the maxi-sets of the pertinent logic.

- The *canonical structure* for language $\mathcal{L}_j$ is $\langle \mathcal{W}(j), \mathcal{R}(j), v \rangle$ where
  - in each case $\mathcal{R}(j)$ is defined for elements w, w' of $\mathcal{W}(j)$ by:

[3] This is what we previously called 'Necessitation'.

[4] Of course, by 'add to CPL(NAT)' we mean *add to the rules*, as the respective syntaxes are not the same (though the modal syntax is gained by merely augmenting the classical one).

$\langle w, w' \rangle \in \mathcal{R}$ iff for all $A \in \mathcal{S}$, if $\Box A \in w$ then $A \in w'$.

» $\mathcal{W}(j)$ is the set of all maxi-sets of:

K if $j = K$

D if $j = K^{ser}$

T if $j = K^{r}$

B if $j = K^{rs}$

S4 if $j = K^{rt}$

S5 if $j = K^{rst}$

» the valuation v is defined by the conditions

$v(w, A) = 1$ if A is in w

$v(w, A) = 0$ if A is not in w

Most of the work, to which we now turn, will go into proving that the canonical structure for language $\mathcal{L}_j$ is in fact an $\mathcal{L}_j$-model. After that, it should be clear sailing, for things are now set up so as to provide easy proofs for the lemmas needed for an application of the Completeness Template Theorem.

To begin we can prove for all cases that if the structure fulfils the other conditions for being a model, then v is an admissible valuation.

LEMMA 12.1 *For all sentences* A, B *of the modal sentential syntax, and all maxi-sets* w *of any of the given logics:*

$\sim$A *is in* w	*iff*	A *is not in* w
$(A \wedge B)$ *is in* w	*iff*	A *and* B *are in* w
$\Box$A *is in* w	*iff*	A *is in all* w' *st* $\langle w, w' \rangle \in \mathcal{R}(j)$

PROOF LEM 12.1 The proof for the first two is just as for CPL(NAT). To prove the third we draw on the definition of $\mathcal{R}(j)$ from which it follows that if $w\mathcal{R}(j)w'$ then A is in w' if $\Box$A is in w.

Suppose now that $\Box$A is not in w. Then $\sim\Box$A is in w. Consider the set $\mathcal{N}(w) = \{B : \Box B \text{ is in } w\}$. We claim that this set plus $\sim$A is consistent. Suppose not. Then $\mathcal{N}(w) \vdash A$, a fact we know already from CPL(NAT). But, then, $\mathcal{N}(w)$ must have a finite subset $\{A_1, \ldots, A_n\}$ which logically implies A, in which case, by ($\Box$ Intro), it follows that $\Box A_1, \ldots, \Box A_n \vdash \Box A$ and, by Weak, that $w \vdash \Box A$, for maxi-set w. But, now, $\Box$A is in w, contrary to supposition.

Hence, by the Extension Theorem, the set $\mathcal{N}(w) \cup \{\sim A\}$ is part of a maxi-set w' which does not contain A but is clearly such that $w\mathcal{R}(j)w'$. QED

Before turning to the next lemma we note that the foregoing proof does not rule out that, for a given world w, there is no world w' such that $w\mathcal{R}(\mathsf{j})w'$, in which case w will contain $\Box\mathsf{A}$ for every sentence A. In logic K, such a case is consistent, and so it should indeed not have been ruled out; however, in the other logics, to which we now turn, it is not consistent.

LEMMA 12.2 *If* $\mathsf{j} = \mathsf{K}^{ser}$ *then* $\mathcal{R}(\mathsf{j})$ *is serial; and if* $\mathsf{j} = \mathsf{K}^{r}$ *then* $\mathcal{R}(\mathsf{j})$ *is reflexive; and if* $\mathsf{j} = \mathsf{K}^{rs}$ *then* $\mathcal{R}(\mathsf{j})$ *is reflexive and symmetric; and if* $\mathsf{j} = \mathsf{K}^{rt}$ *then* $\mathcal{R}(\mathsf{j})$ *is reflexive and transitive; and if* $\mathsf{j} = \mathsf{K}^{ser}$ *then* $\mathcal{R}(\mathsf{j})$ *is reflexive, symmetric, and transitive.*

PROOF LEM 12.2 This must be proved from the specific rules added to K to construct the other logics. For the first we look at D and note that we must prove that if w is any maxi-set then there is another maxi-set w' such that $w\mathcal{R}(\mathsf{K}^{ser})w'$. Recalling the notation $\mathcal{N}(w)$ from the preceding lemma, it will suffice to show that $\mathcal{N}(w)$ is consistent in this case, for any maxi-set w of D.

Let w be such a maxi-set and suppose that $\mathcal{N}(w)$ is not consistent, so that $\mathcal{N}(w) \vdash \bot$. As before we note that $\mathcal{N}(w)$ must then have members $\mathsf{A}_1, \ldots, \mathsf{A}_n$ such that $\mathsf{A}_1, \ldots, \mathsf{A}_n \vdash \bot$, and by ($\Box$ Intro) it follows then that $\Box\mathsf{A}_1, \ldots, \Box\mathsf{A}_n \vdash \Box\bot$. By Weak this implies that $w \vdash \Box\bot$. But in D that has the consequence that also $w \vdash {\sim}\Box{\sim}\bot$, which, in turn, implies that w is inconsistent, given that $\vdash \Box{\sim}\bot$ in each of the given logics (Exercise).

We will leave some parts of the proof of Lemma 12.2 as exercises, but we note that the relevant condition for T is met: if any maxi-set of T contains $\Box\mathsf{A}$ for any sentence A then it also contains A itself, due to (Refl $\Box$). In other words, w will contain the whole of $\mathcal{N}(w)$, and so $w\mathcal{R}(\mathsf{K}^{r})w$. QED

LEMMA 12.3 *The canonical structure for language* $\mathcal{L}_\mathsf{j}$ *is an* $\mathcal{L}_\mathsf{j}$*-model, for each index* $\mathsf{j} = \mathsf{K}^{ser}, \mathsf{K}^{r}, \mathsf{K}^{rs}, \mathsf{K}^{rt}, \mathsf{K}^{rst}$.

PROOF LEM 12.3 This follows at once from the preceding two lemmas. QED

THEOREM 12.1 (COMPLETENESS OF SNML) *The logics* K, D, T, B, S4, *and* S5 *are strongly complete for the languages* $\mathcal{L}_\mathsf{K}$, $\mathcal{L}_{\mathsf{K}^{ser}}$, $\mathcal{L}_{\mathsf{K}^{r}}$, $\mathcal{L}_{\mathsf{K}^{rs}}$, $\mathcal{L}_{\mathsf{K}^{rt}}$, *and* $\mathcal{L}_{\mathsf{K}^{rst}}$, *respectively.*

PROOF THM 12.1 This follows from the preceding lemmas using the Completeness Template Theorem. Note that the Separation Lemma for this case has essentially the same proof as for CPL in §11. QED

SOUNDNESS OF THE SYSTEMS

We will prove the soundness of D in its current formulation; adapting this proof to the other systems is something we leave to the exercises. To formulate a natural deduction system for D we begin with CPL(NAT); we add

» CONNECTIVE RULES:
  » □ Intro: If $A_1, \ldots, A_n \vdash B$ then $\Box A_1, \ldots, \Box A_n \vdash \Box B$.
  » Ser □: $\Box A \vdash \sim\Box\sim A$

We will divide the rules into two classes—those that simply give us a statement of logical consequence, and those that go beyond that:

» CLASS 1
  » Prime: If A is in $\mathcal{X}$, then $\mathcal{X} \vdash A$.
  » ⊥ Intro: $A, \sim A \vdash \bot$
  » ⊥ Elim: $\bot \vdash A$
  » DNeg: $A \vdash \sim\sim A$
  » ∧ Intro: $A, B \vdash (A \wedge B)$
  » ∧ Neg: $A, \sim B \vdash \sim(A \wedge B)$
    $\sim A, B \vdash \sim(A \wedge B)$
    $\sim A, \sim B \vdash \sim(A \wedge B)$
  » Ser □: $\Box A \vdash \sim\Box\sim A$

» CLASS 2
  » Weak: If $\mathcal{X} \vdash A$ then $\mathcal{X}, \mathcal{Y} \vdash A$.
  » Trans: If $\mathcal{X} \vdash A_1$, and $\mathcal{X} \vdash A_2, \ldots$, and $\mathcal{X} \vdash A_n$ and also $A_1, A_2, \ldots, A_n \vdash B$, then $\mathcal{X} \vdash B$.
  » Excl: If $\mathcal{X}, B \vdash A$ and $\mathcal{X}, \sim B \vdash A$, then $\mathcal{X} \vdash A$.
  » □ Intro: If $A_1, \ldots, A_n \vdash B$ then $\Box A_1, \ldots, \Box A_n \vdash \Box B$.

DEFINITION: A sentence A is a logical consequence of set $\mathcal{X}$ of sentences in logic D iff there is a finite sequence $\mathcal{X}_1 \vdash A_1, \mathcal{X}_2 \vdash A_2, \ldots, \mathcal{X}_2 \vdash A_n$ such that the last one is $\mathcal{X} \vdash A$ and each of them is *either*

» an instance of a CLASS 1 rule of CPL(NAT), *or*

» an instance of Ser □, *or*

» follows from preceding members by a CLASS 2 rule of CPL(NAT), *or*

» follows from preceding members by □ Intro.

TO PROVE: If k is a number between 1 and n (inclusive), then $\mathcal{X}_k \Vdash A_k$ in $\mathcal{L}_{K^{ser}}$.

HYPOTHESIS (of Induction): This is so for all numbers i from 1 to k − 1.

CASES:

» CPL: $\mathcal{X}_k \vdash A_k$ is an instance of a CLASS I rule of CPL(NAT) or follows from preceding members by a rule of CPL(NAT). Then [by Hypothesis, those preceding members correspond to valid implications in our language, and so] $\mathcal{X}_k \Vdash A_k$ because our language is an extension of the language of CPL.

» Ser□: $\mathcal{X}_k \vdash A_k$ is an instance of Ser□. Then $\mathcal{X}_k \vdash A_k$ (proved in §5).

» Intro: $\mathcal{X}_k \vdash A_k$ follows from a preceding member $\mathcal{X} \vdash A$ by □ Intro. Then, by Hypothesis, that preceding member was such that $\mathcal{X} \Vdash A$; and so $\mathcal{X}_k \Vdash A_k$ (proved in §5).

This ends the proof.

EXERCISES 12.2.1

1 With the usual definitions of the remaining CPL connectives prove $\Box(A \supset B) \vdash \Box A \supset \Box B$. You may use any previous results concerning what is provable in CPL(NAT).

2 Prove that the logical systems K, B, S4, and S5 are sound for their respective languages.

3 Prove the unproved parts of Lemma 12.2.

4 Revisit Exercises 5.6.1 using the natural deduction formulation of the normal modal logics to prove your results.

5 Spell out the proof of the Completeness Theorem.

12.3 LOGICS OF CONDITIONALS

We shall focus on the "ceteris paribus" ("everything being equal") conditionals mentioned in §6.3. The syntax S_{ck} is that of $\mathcal{L}_{CPL}$ (but with our restriction to just two primitive connectives) augmented with the binary connective $\Rightarrow$. The set of S_{ck}-sentences is $\mathcal{S}_{ck}$. We read $\Rightarrow$ as 'If... then..., ceteris paribus'. The assumption in constructing a semantics for this sort of discourse is that the content of the 'everything being equal' depends solely on the antecedent and not on the consequent.[5]

[5]This assumption may in general have to be relaxed to allow for other contextual factors; but we shall not do so here.

We shall begin minimally by generalizing the structures introduced for the basic normal modal logic K. Accordingly, we will call the target language: $\mathcal{L}_{\mathsf{CK}}$.

THE LANGUAGE

For each world w and each sentence A there is to be a class $\mathcal{R}^w_{\mathsf{A}}$ of worlds which are intuitively just like w, except that A may be true in them—that is, "everything else is equal". There is a small technical point here: we do not want $\mathcal{R}^w_{\mathsf{A}}$ to depend on insignificant syntactic features of A, we want it to be the same (for example) for A and $\sim\sim$A, and so forth. By keying the selection of $\mathcal{R}^w_{\mathsf{A}}$ to the set of worlds in which A is true, rather than to A's syntactic features, we can achieve the goal.

» MODELS: An $\mathcal{L}_{\mathsf{CK}}$-*model* is a triple $\mathcal{M} = \langle \mathcal{W}, \mathcal{R}, v \rangle$ wherein $\mathcal{W}$ is non-empty, $\mathcal{R}$ is a relation from $\mathcal{W} \times \wp(\mathcal{W})$ to $\mathcal{W}$, and v is a map from $\mathcal{W} \times \mathcal{S}_{\mathbf{ck}}$ to $\{1, 0\}$ such that

  $v(w, \sim\mathsf{A}) = 1$ iff $v(w, \mathsf{A}) = 0$

  $v(w, \mathsf{A} \wedge \mathsf{B}) = 1$ iff $v(w, \mathsf{A}) = v(\mathsf{B}, w) = 1$

  $v(w, \mathsf{A} \Rightarrow \mathsf{B}) = 1$ iff $v(w', \mathsf{A}) = 1$, for all w' such that $v(w', \mathsf{A}) = 1$ and $\mathcal{R}(w, v(\mathsf{A}), w')$

  where, *nota bene*, $v(\mathsf{A}) = \{w' : v(w', \mathsf{A}) = 1\}$.

» ADMISSIBLE VALUATIONS: An admissible valuation of $\mathcal{L}_{\mathsf{CK}}$ is any function $v(w, \ldots)$ such that there is an $\mathcal{L}_{\mathsf{CK}}$-model $\mathcal{M} = \langle \mathcal{W}, \mathcal{R}, v \rangle$ with w in $\mathcal{W}$. Such a valuation satisfies sentence A iff $v(w, \mathsf{A}) = 1$.

This formulation should raise a question: Is there problem in appealing to the proposition which v assigns to A in the middle of a specification of how v is to assign propositions to sentences? The reason it *is* all right is that A is shorter than A $\Rightarrow$ B. That said, a more perspicuous formulation will be useful:

» MODELS: An $\mathcal{L}_{\mathsf{CK}}$-*model* is a triple $\mathcal{M} = \langle \mathcal{W}, \mathcal{R}, v \rangle$ wherein $\mathcal{W}$ is non-empty, $\mathcal{R}$ is a relation from $\mathcal{W} \times \wp(\mathcal{W})$ to $\mathcal{W}$, and v is a map from S_{m} into $\wp(\mathcal{W})$ ("propositions") such that

  $v(\sim\mathsf{A}) = \mathcal{W} - v(\mathsf{A})$

  $v(\mathsf{A} \wedge \mathsf{B}) = v(\mathsf{A}) \cap v(\mathsf{B})$

  $v(\mathsf{A} \Rightarrow \mathsf{B}) = \{w : v(\mathsf{A}) \cap \mathcal{R}^w_{v(\mathsf{A})} \subseteq v(\mathsf{B})\}$

  where $\mathcal{R}^w_{\mathcal{U}} = \{w' : \mathcal{R}(w, \mathcal{U}, w')\}$, with $\mathcal{U} \in \wp(\mathcal{W})$.

» ADMISSIBLE VALUATIONS: An *admissible valuation* of $\mathcal{L}_{\mathsf{CK}}$ is any function $v_w(\ldots)$ defined from an $\mathcal{L}_{\mathsf{CK}}$-model $\mathcal{M} = \langle \mathcal{W}, \mathcal{R}, v \rangle$ and element w of $\mathcal{W}$ via the condition

$v_w(A) = 1$ if $w \in v(A)$, and otherwise $v_w(A) = 0$.

Such a valuation *satisfies* A iff it assigns 1 to A.

In either case we have a formulation of the idea that the conditional is true in a world just in case the consequent is true in exactly those "antecedent-relevant" worlds in which the antecedent is true.

CHOICES MADE EXPLICIT

Although $\mathcal{L}_{CK}$ is a very minimal construction we did make one significant choice. What difference would it make if we omitted '$v(A)\cap$' from the clause for $v(A \Rightarrow B)$? In that case the conditional could be true even though its antecedent would be false in any antecedent-relevant world at all, in which case one could truly assert such sentences as

> If I were a merchant then I would be rich, but it is not the case that if I were a merchant then I would be a rich merchant.

Our given choice guarantees the "characteristic principle"

($\Rightarrow$ Consequent) $\quad A \Rightarrow B \Vdash A \Rightarrow (A \wedge B)$.

Logics of conditionals, as mentioned in §6.3, were originally formulated rigorously by Robert Stalnaker and David Lewis; they agreed on some conditions to impose on $\mathcal{R}$ but differed on others:

» SPECIAL CONDITIONS:

Weak Factuality: If $w \in \mathcal{U}$ then $w \in \mathcal{R}^w_{\mathcal{U}}$.

Strong Factuality: If $w \in \mathcal{U}$ then $\mathcal{R}^w_{\mathcal{U}} = \{w\}$.

Uniqueness: $\mathcal{U} \cap \mathcal{R}^w_{\mathcal{U}}$ has at most one member.

Union: $\mathcal{R}^w_{\mathcal{U}\cup\mathcal{Y}}$ is either $\mathcal{R}^w_{\mathcal{U}}$, $\mathcal{R}^w_{\mathcal{Y}}$, or $\mathcal{R}^w_{\mathcal{U}} \cup \mathcal{R}^w_{\mathcal{Y}}$.

Order: If $\mathcal{R}^w_{\mathcal{U}} \subseteq \mathcal{Y}$ and $\mathcal{R}^w_{\mathcal{Y}} \subseteq \mathcal{U}$ then $\mathcal{R}^w_{\mathcal{U}} = \mathcal{R}^w_{\mathcal{Y}}$.

The motivations for Weak and Strong Factuality are pretty clear: If A is true then our world is certainly like itself in all respects aside from whether A is true. Likewise (strong form), if A is true, why look any further than this world to see whether 'if A then B' is true? Weak Factuality guarantees (and has as "characteristic principle")

(Modus Ponens) $\quad A, A \Rightarrow B \Vdash B$

while Strong Factuality guarantees the stronger "this-worldly" characteristic principle

(Centering) $\quad A, B \Vdash A \Rightarrow B$.

Uniqueness, on the other hand, was more debatable; it was part of Stalnaker's logic and not Lewis'. Uniqueness guarantees

(Conditional Excluded Middle) $\Vdash (A \Rightarrow B) \vee (A \Rightarrow {\sim}B)$.

Finally, while the Union and Order conditions may appear recondite they were implicitly prevalent in logics of this sort. Where (to save space) $\mathbb{A}$ abbreviates $(A \vee B) \Rightarrow A$ and $\mathbb{B}$ abbreviates $(A \vee B) \Rightarrow B$, the Union condition guarantees

$$\Vdash \mathbb{A} \vee \mathbb{B} \vee [[(A \vee B) \Rightarrow C] \Leftrightarrow (A \Rightarrow C) \wedge (B \Rightarrow C)]$$

The Order condition, in turn, guarantees

$$A \Rightarrow B, B \Rightarrow A, A \Rightarrow C \Vdash B \Rightarrow C$$

This last principle really establishes in the context of at least the stronger such logics that if A and B imply each other *ceteris paribus* then they can be substituted for each other everywhere—they are equivalent in all the ways that could possibly show up in this logical context.

THE LOGIC CK

Just as for the normal modal languages and logics, we can use the above Special Conditions and their corresponding "characteristic" sentences to define a series of logics of conditionals. But since it is quite obvious how to do that we shall be content here to focus just on the language $\mathcal{L}_{CK}$. We provide a logic similar to K but with a *conditionalized necessity* as follows:

» The logic CK is CPL(NAT) plus the rule we call '(⇒ Intro)', namely:

If $A_1, \ldots, A_n \vdash B$ then $C \Rightarrow A_1, \ldots, C \Rightarrow A_n \vdash C \Rightarrow B$.

COMPLETENESS

We proceed to the completeness proof, in what should by now be a familiar format.

» The *canonical structure* for $\mathcal{L}_{CK}$ is the triple $\langle \mathcal{W}, \mathcal{R}, v \rangle$ where $\mathcal{W}$ is the set of maxi-sets of CK, v is a function that assigns to each sentence A the set $v(A) = \{w \in \mathcal{W} : A \in w\}$, and $\mathcal{R}$ is the relation defined by:

» $\mathcal{R}^w_{\mathcal{U}} = \{w' \in \mathcal{W} : B \in w'$ for all B st $A \Rightarrow B$ is in $w\}$, if $\mathcal{U} = v(A)$

» if $\mathcal{U} \neq v(A)$ for any sentence A, then $\mathcal{R}^w_{\mathcal{U}} = \mathcal{W}$.[6]

LEMMA 12.4 *For all* A, B *of* $\mathcal{L}_{CK}$, *and all maxi-sets* w *of* CK

[6]This last choice is arbitrary; it plays no role in what follows but only serves to complete the definition of $\mathcal{R}$.

$\sim$A *is in* w *iff* A *is not in* w

(A $\wedge$ B) *is in* w *iff* A *and* B *are in* w

A $\Rightarrow$ B *is in* w *iff* B *is in all* w′, *such that* $w' \in \mathcal{R}^{w}_{\nu(A)}$

PROOF LEM 12.4 The proof for the first two is just as for CPL(NAT). To prove the third we draw on the definition of $\mathcal{R}$, from which it follows that if A $\Rightarrow$ B is in w and w' is in $\mathcal{R}^{w}_{\nu(A)}$, then B is in w.

Suppose now that A $\Rightarrow$ B is not in w. Then $\sim$(A $\Rightarrow$ B) is in w. Consider the set $\mathcal{N}(A, w) = \{B : A \Rightarrow B \text{ is in } w\}$. In this canonical structure $\mathcal{R}^{w}_{\nu(A)}$ is the set of worlds w' such that $\mathcal{N}(A, w) \subseteq w'$.

We claim that $\mathcal{N}(A, w) \cup \{\sim B\}$ is consistent. Suppose otherwise. Then $\mathcal{N}(A, w) \vdash B$, a fact from CPL(NAT). But, then, $\mathcal{N}(A, w)$ must have a finite subset $\{A_1, \ldots, A_n\}$ that implies B. By the ($\Rightarrow$ Intro) it follows that $A \Rightarrow A_1, \ldots, A \Rightarrow A_n \vdash A \Rightarrow B$, in which case, by Weak, $w \vdash A \Rightarrow B$, for maxi-set w, and hence A $\Rightarrow$ B is in w after all, contrary to supposition.

By the Extension Theorem $\mathcal{N}(A, w) \cup \{\sim B\}$ is part of a maxi-set w' which does not contain B but is clearly in $\mathcal{R}^{w}_{\nu(A)}$. QED

LEMMA 12.5 *The canonical structure for language* $\mathcal{L}_{CK}$ *is an* $\mathcal{L}_{CK}$*-model.*

PROOF LEM 12.5 This follows from the preceding two lemmas and definitions. QED

THEOREM 12.2 (COMPLETENESS) *The logic* CK *is strongly complete for the language* $\mathcal{L}_{CK}$.

PROOF THM 12.2 This follows now from the preceding lemmas using the Completeness Template Theorem. QED

EXERCISES 12.3.1

1 Prove that ($\Rightarrow$ Consequent) holds in CK.

2 Prove the soundness of logic CK with respect to language $\mathcal{L}_{CK}$.

3 Prove that the Special Conditions do indeed guarantee their corresponding characteristic principles.

4 If, with $\vdash$ replacing $\Vdash$, we add the given characteristic principles to CK, do we obtain complete logical systems for the corresponding languages?

12.4 INTUITIONISTIC LOGIC

To facilitate our proofs we take the liberty of slightly modifying both the syntax and semantics of the language $\mathcal{L}_I$, which was presented in §6.4. We shall take the set of (primitive) connectives to be $\mathcal{C} = \{\wedge, \vee, \rightarrow, \bot\}$, where $\bot$ is a 0-place connective that plays the grammatical role of a (primitive) sentence. Negation, in turn, is *defined* in terms of $\bot$ and $\rightarrow$. Specifically, the negation of A is $(A \rightarrow \bot)$. (It will be provable in the target logic that $\bot$ and $p \wedge {\sim}p$ are equivalent.)

THE LANGUAGE

As in §6.4 the language $\mathcal{L}_I$ is simply adapted from normal modal logic, with the access relation reflexive and transitive:

» An $\mathcal{L}_I$-*model* is a triple $\langle \mathcal{W}, \mathcal{R}, \nu \rangle$ with $\mathcal{W}$ a non-empty set (the "stages"), $\mathcal{R}$ a reflexive, transitive binary relation on $\mathcal{W}$ ("access") and ν a function which assigns to each world and sentence the value 1 or 0 subject to the following conditions, for all $w \in \mathcal{W}$ and all sentences A and B:

  » $\nu(w, \bot) = 0$

  » $\nu(w, A \vee B) = 1$ iff $\nu(w, A) = 1$ or $\nu(w, B) = 1$ or both

  » $\nu(w, A \wedge B) = 1$ iff $\nu(w, A) = 1$ and $\nu(w, B) = 1$

  » $\nu(w, A \rightarrow B) = 1$ iff $\nu(w', B) = 1$ for all w' such that $w\mathcal{R}w'$ and $\nu(w, 1) = 1$

  » If $\nu(w, A) = 1$ and $w\mathcal{R}w'$ then $\nu(w', A) = 1$

Note that the last condition on ν is what in §6.4 we called *heredity*, but here it applies to all sentences (not just atomics).

THE LOGIC

For our logic, which we will call 'I-NAT', we will start as for CPL(NAT) but add the rules for the new connectives while omitting those for ~. We will also add some rules that were not needed as long as we had classical negation.

» STRUCTURAL RULES

  Prime: If A is in $\mathcal{X}$ then $\mathcal{X} \vdash A$.

  Weak: If $\mathcal{X} \vdash A$ then $\mathcal{X}, \mathcal{Y} \vdash A$.

  Trans: If $\mathcal{X} \vdash A_1, \ldots, \mathcal{X} \vdash A_n$ and $A_1, \ldots, A_n \vdash B$, then $\mathcal{X} \vdash B$.

» CONNECTIVE RULES

  $\bot$ Elim: $\bot \vdash A$

$\wedge$ Intro: $A, B \vdash (A \wedge B)$

$\wedge$ Elim: $(A \wedge B) \vdash A$
$(A \wedge B) \vdash B$

$\vee$ Intro: $A \vdash (A \vee B)$
$B \vdash (A \vee B)$

$\vee$ Elim: If $\mathcal{X}, A \vdash C$ and $\mathcal{X}, B \vdash C$ then $\mathcal{X}, (A \vee B) \vdash C$

$\rightarrow$ Intro: If $\mathcal{X}, A \vdash B$ then $\mathcal{X} \vdash (A \rightarrow B)$

$\rightarrow$ Elim: $A, (A \rightarrow B) \vdash B$

PROOFS WITHOUT CLASSICAL NEGATION

The absence of classical negation requires some unaccustomed ingenuity when constructing proofs in I-Nat. We will illustrate this by proving two important distribution principles.[7]

» Distribution:

$$A \wedge (B \vee C) \vdash (A \wedge B) \vee (A \wedge C)$$

$$(A \vee B) \wedge (A \vee C) \vdash A \vee (B \wedge C)$$

To prepare for their proofs we list some theorems as exercises:

T1. If $A, B \vdash C$ then $A \wedge B \vdash C$
T2. If $\mathcal{X}, A \vdash B$ and $\mathcal{X}, A \vdash C$ then $\mathcal{X}, A \vdash B \wedge C$
T3. $A \vee (B \vee A) \vdash A \vee B$
T4. If $E, A \vdash C$ and $E, B \vdash C$ and $E, G \vdash (A \vee B)$ then $E, G \vdash C$

We shall appeal to (T1)–(T4) in what follows.[8] We shall also feel free to replace formulas by the results of *commuting* conjunctions and disjunctions in them; that is, we shall freely replace $A \wedge B$ by $B \wedge A$, and similarly for disjunction. When we do this we shall write 'Comm' to the side. That commuting is all right in this context can be shown in each case by means of simple derivations; we leave those as exercises. The proofs for Distribution (both principles) run as follows.

[7]Students familiar with abstract algebra may be somewhat surprised to see that these are provable here. The rules that appear in I-NAT look very much like the general laws for lattices, and there are certainly lattices in which the distributive laws do not hold. Contrary to appearances, therefore, I-NAT does more than just echo the lattice laws. Intuitionistic logic can be regarded as the theory of a special sort of distributive algebras or lattices—*Brouwer algebras*, *Heyting lattices*. See Exercises 12.4.1.

[8]Note that in (T4) E may be absent or be replaced by any set of premises; the theorem still holds with those variations.

T5. $A \wedge (B \vee C) \vdash (A \wedge B) \vee C$.

PROOF:

1. $A, B \vdash (A \wedge B)$	$\wedge$ Intro
2. $A \wedge B \vdash (A \wedge B) \vee C$	$\vee$ Intro
3. $A, B \vdash (A \wedge B) \vee C$	(1),(2), Trans
4. $C \vdash (A \wedge B) \vee C$	$\vee$ Intro, Comm
5. $A, C \vdash (A \wedge B) \vee C$	(4), Weak
6. $A, (B \vee C) \vdash (A \wedge B) \vee C$	(3),(5), $\vee$ Elim
7. $A \wedge (B \vee C) \vdash (A \wedge B) \vee C$	*Invoke T1*

T6. $A \wedge (B \vee C) \vdash (A \wedge B) \vee (A \wedge C)$.[9]

PROOF:

1. $A \wedge (B \vee C) \vdash A$	$\wedge$ Elim
2. $A \wedge (B \vee C) \vdash (A \wedge B) \vee C$	*Invoke T5*
3. $A \wedge (B \vee C) \vdash A \wedge [(A \wedge B) \vee C)]$	(1),(2), $\wedge$ Intro,Trans
4. $A \wedge (B \vee C) \vdash A \wedge [C \vee (A \wedge B)]$	Comm
5. $A \wedge (B \vee C) \vdash (A \wedge C) \vee [A \wedge (A \wedge B)]$	(4), *Invoke T5*
6. $(A \wedge C) \vdash (A \wedge B) \vee (A \wedge C)$	$\vee$ Intro, Comm
7. $A \wedge (A \wedge B) \vdash (A \wedge B) \vee (A \wedge C)$	$\wedge$ Elim,$\vee$ Intro,Trans
8. $A \wedge (B \vee C) \vdash (A \wedge B) \vee (A \wedge C)$	(5)–(7), *Invoke T4*

T7. $(A \vee B) \wedge C \vdash A \vee (B \wedge C)$.

PROOF:

1. $C \wedge (B \vee A) \vdash (C \wedge B) \vee A$	*Invoke T5*
2. $(A \vee B) \wedge C \vdash A \vee (B \wedge C)$	(1), Comm (several times)

T8. $(A \vee B) \wedge (A \vee C) \vdash A \vee (B \wedge C)$.

PROOF:

1. $(A \vee B) \wedge (A \vee C) \vdash (A \vee C) \wedge (A \vee B)$	Comm
2. $(A \vee C) \wedge (A \vee B) \vdash A \vee [C \wedge (A \vee B)]$	*Invoke T7*
3. $(A \vee B) \wedge (A \vee C) \vdash A \vee [C \wedge (B \vee A)]$	(1),(2), Trans, Comm
4. $A \vdash A \vee (B \wedge C)$	$\vee$ Intro
5. $C \wedge (B \vee A) \vdash (C \wedge B) \vee A$	*Invoke T5*
6. $C \wedge (B \vee A) \vdash A \vee (B \wedge C)$	(5), Comm
7. $(A \vee B) \wedge (A \vee C) \vdash A \vee (B \wedge C)$	(3),(4),(6), *Invoke T4*

Various theorems involving $\rightarrow$ and the defined negation may perhaps give more of the flavor of intuitionistic logic than the foregoing theorems; however, we shall leave those to exercises and briefly turn to some preliminaries for the target completeness proof.

[9]Note that (3) and (7) of this proof involve multiple steps.

TOWARDS COMPLETENESS

To prepare ourselves for the completeness proof, which will proceed somewhat differently from the preceding ones, we need to discuss a few points about theories in intuitionistic logic.

A set of sentences is inconsistent if all sentences are derivable from it, and consistent otherwise. So, $\mathcal{X}$ is inconsistent iff $\mathcal{X} \vdash \bot$. As before, a theory is a set of sentences closed under deduction. What we need to introduce is the notion of *prime theories*.

DEFINITION 12.1 A *prime theory* is a theory such that for any sentences A and B, if $A \vee B$ is in the theory, so is A or B (or both).

In our earlier explanation of the semantics (see §6.4) we imagined the access relation in terms of *knowledge growth*, stages of knowledge growth, with knowledge only increasing—never suffering loss of memory. The content of such a stage of knowledge can be represented by a theory: the set of sentences known, or better, the ones that have already been established or proved by that time. Since intuitionists insist that a disjunction can be asserted as known only if at least one of the disjuncts is already known, these theories must be prime theories.

Are there prime theories? Certainly. At the very least maxi-sets are prime theories: if $\mathcal{X}$ contains $A \vee B$ but $\mathcal{X}, A \vdash \bot$ and $\mathcal{X}, B \vdash \bot$, then by our rules $\mathcal{X} \vdash \bot$. So, if nothing can be added to $\mathcal{X}$ without creating an inconsistent set, then if $\mathcal{X}$ contains a disjunction it must be consistent with one of the disjuncts. If, in addition, $\mathcal{X}$ is maximal, then it must have one such disjunct in it, lest there exist a larger consistent set, which is impossible, given that $\mathcal{X}$ is maximal. That said, we shall have to prove something stronger for purposes of the completeness proof, to which we now turn.

COMPLETENESS

We begin, as usual, with the relevant canonical structure:

» The canonical structure for language $\mathcal{L}_I$ is $\langle \mathcal{W}, \mathcal{R}, v \rangle$ wherein $\mathcal{W}$ is the set of *prime theories* of I-NAT, and $\mathcal{R}$ is defined by:

  $w\mathcal{R}w'$ iff $w \subseteq w'$

  and the valuation v is defined by the conditions

  » $v(w, A) = 1$ iff A is in w

  » $v(w, A) = 0$ if A is not in w

We note that $\mathcal{R}$ is reflexive and transitive, and that the heredity condition is clearly satisfied. What we need to prove is that v meets the other conditions to make this a model of the language; we prove that by proving

LEMMA 12.6 *For all* w *in* $\mathcal{W}$ *and all sentences* A, B

i) $A \wedge B$ *is in* w *iff both* A *and* B *are in* w

ii) $A \vee B$ *is in* w *iff* A *or* B *is in* w *(or both are)*

iii) $A \rightarrow B$ *is in* w *iff* B *is in all* w' *such that* $w \subseteq w'$ *and* A *is in* w'

PROOF LEM 12.6 That (i) holds is proved exactly as for theories in CPL. That (ii) holds follows at once from our choice of prime theories as "worlds". Moreover, the rld of (iii) holds because $\rightarrow$ obeys *modus ponens* (see ($\rightarrow$ Elim)).

What is left to prove is the lrd of (iii): Suppose $A \rightarrow B$ is not in w. Then there must be a prime theory w' such that $w \subseteq w'$ and A is in w' but B is not. By our $\rightarrow$ rules and the fact that any theory w contains all its own consequences, $A \rightarrow B$ is in w iff $w, A \vdash B$. Hence, Lemma 12.6 is proved by proving

LEMMA 12.7 *If* $\mathcal{X}$ *is a prime theory such that it is not the case that* $\mathcal{X}, A \vdash B$ *then* $\mathcal{X}, A$ *can be extended into a prime theory that does not contain* B.

PROOF LEM 12.7 In proving Lemma 12.7 we assume that the sentences of the language are ordered in some fashion (say, alphabetically); reference to the *first* sentence and so on is to be understood relative to the ordering. We now define a series of sets starting with $\mathcal{X}$ and A.

$$\begin{aligned} \mathcal{X}^{\star}(1) &= \mathcal{X} \cup \{A\} \\ \mathcal{X}^{\star}(k+1) &= \text{B-}\textit{fillet}(\{C : \mathcal{X}^{\star}(k) \vdash C\}) \end{aligned}$$

where B-*fillet* is the following operation on sets of sentences:[10]

» For any set of sentences $\mathcal{Z}$ the series $\mathcal{Z}^{\text{ф}}_{m}$ is defined:

$$\begin{aligned} \mathcal{Z}^{\text{ф}}_{1} &= \mathcal{Z} \\ \mathcal{Z}^{\text{ф}}_{m+1} &= \mathcal{Z}^{\text{ф}}_{m} \cup \{D\} \end{aligned}$$

where D is the first disjunct of the mth disjunction in $\mathcal{Z}^{\text{ф}}_{m}$ neither of whose disjuncts is in $\mathcal{Z}^{\text{ф}}_{m}$ such that it is not the case that $\mathcal{Z}^{\text{ф}}_{m} \cup \{D\} \vdash B$. (We shall call this adding of a disjunct the *filleting* of the disjunction in question.)

» B-*fillet*$(\mathcal{Z})$ is the union of all the sets $\mathcal{Z}^{\text{ф}}_{m}$, with $m = 1, 2, \ldots$

---

[10] We choose this term to echo a famous remark in the first review of the work that introduced Intuitionism: "A fish can be filleted but not the Universe!"

Finally, we define $\mathcal{X}^\star$ thus

» $\mathcal{X}^\star$ is the union of all the sets $\mathcal{X}^\star(k)$, with $k = 1, 2, \ldots$

With these definitions in hand we claim now that $\mathcal{X}^\star$ is a prime theory which contains $\mathcal{X}$ and A but not B. First of all, $\mathcal{X}$ is a theory; for if C is derivable from $\mathcal{X}^\star$ in I-NAT then it is derivable from some finite subset $\mathcal{Y}$, which must therefore belong to $\mathcal{X}^\star(k)$ for some k, but all consequences of $\mathcal{Y}$ will belong to $\mathcal{X}^\star(k+1)$ and hence to $\mathcal{X}^\star$. Secondly, unless the filleting is blocked at some point (which, course, would block the entire construction) then $\mathcal{X}^\star$ is prime; for if any disjunction occurs in $\mathcal{X}^\star$ it must occur in some $\mathcal{X}^\star(k)$, in which case one of its disjuncts will occur in $\mathcal{X}^\star(k+1)$. Finally, again with the same proviso, it cannot be the case that $\mathcal{X}^\star$ contains B. Suppose $B \in \mathcal{X}^\star$. Then B must have been added in one of the construction stages. Suppose that B was added in the formation of $\mathcal{X}^\star(k+1)$, in which case it was not in $\mathcal{X}^\star(k)$, not derivable from $\mathcal{X}^\star(k)$, and closing $\mathcal{X}^\star(k)$ under deduction will not add B. But neither can it be added by the filleting process; hence, $B \notin \mathcal{X}^\star$.

What remains, then, is to establish the proviso that the construction process is never blocked. There is only one way in which it could be blocked, which is that, for some number m, in the construction of $\mathcal{Z}^{\pitchfork}_{m+1}$ we find for the first time that the disjunction to be filleted is recalcitrant; that is, that $\mathcal{Z}^{\pitchfork}_{m}$ contains a disjunction $D \vee E$, and while B is not derivable from $\mathcal{Z}^{\pitchfork}_{m}$, it is derivable both from $\mathcal{Z}^{\pitchfork}m \cup \{D\}$ and from $\mathcal{Z}^{\pitchfork}_{m} \cup \{E\}$. But that is impossible, by (T4).

QED

EXERCISES 12.4.1

1 DISTRIBUTION:

1. Show that the converses of the two distribution principles can be derived.
2. Show $A \wedge B \vdash C$ and $A \vdash B \vee C$ then $A \vdash C$.[11]

2 Show that I-NAT is sound for language $\mathcal{L}_{\mathsf{I}}$.

3 Prove (T1)–(T4).

4 Prove at least several cases in which formulas can be derived from the result of commuting conjunctions and/or disjunctions in them.

[11] This second part of the first exercise corresponds to a condition on lattices that is equivalent to distributivity. See Chapter 4 (section B3) of Curry's [25].

5 Prove

1. $\vdash A \to (B \to A)$
2. $A \to (B \to C), A \to B \vdash A \to C$
3. $A \to (B \to C) \vdash (A \to B) \to (A \to C)$

6 With the negation symbol ~ defined by $\sim A = (A \to \bot)$, prove the following:

1. If $A \vdash B$ then $\sim B \vdash \sim A$
2. $A \vdash \sim\sim A$
3. $\sim\sim\sim A \vdash \sim A$
4. $\vdash \sim(A \wedge \sim A)$
5. $\sim A \vee B, A \vdash B$

7 The completeness proof is really implicitly by mathematical induction. Make this form explicit.

12.5 A Simple Relevance Logic

In §7.3 we discussed the logic FDE, known as the logic of first degree entailment or of *tautological entailment*. This logic was first formulated by Anderson and Belnap [1] to capture the intuition that a conclusion should be derivable from premises only if those premises are non-redundantly and directly *relevant* to the conclusion. FDE was the first and simplest of their family of relevance logics.

From a contradiction such as $A \wedge \sim A$ Anderson and Belnap maintained that both A and ~A are derivable, but not just any old sentence. This required certain deletions from classical logic, such as the principle that B is derivable in general from $\sim A \vee B$ and A (the principle of *material modus ponens* or, perhaps better, *disjunctive syllogism*). Given that principle one could argue as C. I. Lewis [64] argued, for any (irrelevant) sentence B:

1. $A \wedge \sim A$	
2. A	$\wedge$ Elim
3. $\sim A$	$\wedge$ Elim
4. $\sim A \vee B$	(3), $\vee$ Intro
5. B	(2), (4), *Disjunctive Syllogism*

Primitive Tautological Entailments

As a paradigm of genuine derivability Anderson and Belnap took cases like this: From

$$A_1 \wedge A_2 \wedge \ldots \wedge A_n$$

the sentence

$$B_1 \vee B_2 \vee \ldots \vee B_k$$

is derivable precisely if one of the disjuncts B_j is the same as one of the conjuncts A_i. The most pristine examples of this sort are the ones in which all those conjuncts and disjuncts are either atomic sentences or negations of atomic sentences. In that case let us call the premise and conclusion respectively a *basic conjunction* and a *basic disjunction*, and both of them *basic expressions*. Those pristine paradigm examples are called *primitive tautological entailments*. Clearly it is possible to tell directly, by inspection, whether we have a primitive tautological entailment before us or not.

ARGUMENT NORMAL FORM

Next, Anderson and Belnap considered a similar sort of case. An *argument* is said to be in *normal form* if its premise is a disjunction of basic expressions and its conclusion a conjunction of basic expressions. Then for this argument to be a genuine derivation, each of those conjuncts in the conclusion must be genuinely derivable (by a primitive tautological entailment) from every disjunct in the premise. That is, $B \wedge C$ is derivable from $A \vee D$ only if B and C are each derivable from A and also each derivable from D—a glaringly strict requirement! But, again, one can see that it is possible to decide simply by inspection whether we have such a case before us.

Finally Anderson and Belnap accepted a family of principles to turn all arguments into ones in normal form, principles that were already used in classical logic. The given principles are traditionally known as Commutation, Association, Distribution, Double Negation, and De Morgan. We won't go into the details here (see exercises) but such principles suffice to reduce every question about whether a given argument (in the target syntax) has its conclusion genuinely derivable from its premises to the previous case.

TABLEAUX AND NATURAL DEDUCTION

Reducing all such questions to ones about arguments in normal form is just the sort of procedure that tableaux methods are typically meant to mechanize. This method we will now examine, and relate to the natural deduction format. Our syntax will be much the same as in §7.3 but we will now take $\sim$, $\vee$, and $\wedge$ as our three primitive connectives, leaving all others as defined in the standard way.

We will liberalize the natural deduction format somewhat. Let us allow lists on both sides of the turnstile $\vdash$ so we get formulas of form:

$$A_1, A_2, \ldots, A_m \vdash B_1, B_2, \ldots, B_n$$

We will think of the premises as parts of a long conjunction and the list of conclusions as a long disjunction (but in any order); so understood, the displayed sentence (above) is the (syntactic) claim meant to correspond to the (semantic) validity claim:

» If all of $A_1, \ldots, A_m$ are true (designated) then *at least one* of $B_1, \ldots, B_n$ is true (designated) as well.

FDE Tableaux Recast

We use the format above to rewrite the tableau rules. When setting up a tableau we begin by displaying a claim of form

$$\mathcal{X} \vdash A$$

and then use the tableau rules (to be given below) to simplify or "resolve" the given claim in an effort towards showing that it is *incorrect*.[12]

In the FDE tableaux of §7.3 we marked each of the premises in $\mathcal{X}$ with $\oplus$ (designated) and the conclusion A with $\ominus$ (undesignated). To write the same rules in a way more reminiscent of natural deduction symbols, let us just keep $\mathcal{X} \vdash A$ in that form and indicate that anything on the left of the turnstile is to be thought of as marked with $\oplus$ and anything to the right of it as marked with $\ominus$, without writing down those markers. With this convention the FDE *resolution rules* may be formulated thus:

$$\frac{\mathcal{X}, A \wedge B, \mathcal{Y} \vdash \mathcal{Z}}{\mathcal{X}, A, B, \mathcal{Y} \vdash \mathcal{Z}} \qquad \frac{\mathcal{X} \vdash \mathcal{Y}, A \wedge B, \mathcal{Z}}{\mathcal{X} \vdash \mathcal{Y}, A, \mathcal{Z} \text{ or } \mathcal{X} \vdash \mathcal{Y}, B, \mathcal{Z}}$$

$$\frac{\mathcal{X}, {\sim}(A \wedge B), \mathcal{Y} \vdash \mathcal{Z}}{\mathcal{X}, {\sim}A, \mathcal{Y} \vdash \mathcal{Z} \text{ or } \mathcal{X}, {\sim}B, \mathcal{Y} \vdash \mathcal{Z}} \qquad \frac{\mathcal{X} \vdash \mathcal{Y}, {\sim}(A \wedge B), \mathcal{Z}}{\mathcal{X} \vdash \mathcal{Y}, {\sim}A, {\sim}B, \mathcal{Z}}$$

$$\frac{\mathcal{X}, A \vee B, \mathcal{Y} \vdash \mathcal{Z}}{\mathcal{X}, A, \mathcal{Y} \vdash \mathcal{Z} \text{ or } \mathcal{X}, B, \mathcal{Y} \vdash \mathcal{Z}} \qquad \frac{\mathcal{X} \vdash \mathcal{Y}, A \vee B, \mathcal{Z}}{\mathcal{X} \vdash \mathcal{Y}, A, B, \mathcal{Z}}$$

$$\frac{\mathcal{X}, {\sim}(A \vee B), \mathcal{Y} \vdash \mathcal{Z}}{\mathcal{X}, {\sim}A, {\sim}B, \mathcal{Y} \vdash \mathcal{Z}} \qquad \frac{\mathcal{X} \vdash \mathcal{Y}, {\sim}(A \vee B), \mathcal{Z}}{\mathcal{X} \vdash \mathcal{Y}, {\sim}A, \mathcal{Z} \text{ or } \mathcal{X} \vdash \mathcal{Y}, {\sim}B, \mathcal{Z}}$$

$$\frac{\mathcal{X}, {\sim\sim}A, \mathcal{Y} \vdash \mathcal{Z}}{\mathcal{X}, A, \mathcal{Y}, \mathcal{Z}} \qquad \frac{\mathcal{X} \vdash \mathcal{Y}, {\sim\sim}A, \mathcal{Z}}{\mathcal{X} \vdash \mathcal{Y}, A, \mathcal{Z}}$$

[12] Note well: we continue to regard expressions like '$\mathcal{X}$', '$\mathcal{X}$, A' to stand for sets of sentences, just as for previous natural deduction systems, but they can be written out in practice; so our capital scripted letters $\mathcal{X}$, $\mathcal{Y}$, $\mathcal{Z}$ will stand for *finite* sets of sentences. (Although it is useful to think of them as conjunctions of premises and disjunctions of conclusions, that is just a mnemonic.)

In thinking about these rules it is useful to recall that a tableau construction is an attempt to produce a counterexample, that is, to refute the claim of derivability that was to be examined. So, for example, the second resolution rule (top right column) is to be read as:

» If $\mathcal{X} \vdash \mathcal{Y}, A \wedge B, \mathcal{Z}$ is *incorrect* then *either* $\mathcal{X} \vdash \mathcal{Y}, A, \mathcal{Z}$ *or* $\mathcal{X} \vdash \mathcal{Y}, B, \mathcal{Z}$ is *incorrect*.

Natural Deduction

To be sure, the foregoing system still does not look like a natural deduction system, but that is no surprise. After all, a natural deduction is meant to *prove* such claims, while tableaux are designed to *refute* them. So the two sorts of construction move in opposite directions. We would "contrapose" to formulate the corresponding natural deduction system. To the second tableau rule, for example, would correspond

» If $\mathcal{X} \vdash \mathcal{Y}, A, \mathcal{Z}$ and $\mathcal{X} \vdash \mathcal{Y}, B, \mathcal{Z}$ then $\mathcal{X} \vdash \mathcal{Y}, A \wedge B, \mathcal{Z}$.

and this rule would be the FDE-NAT version of ($\wedge$ Intro Right). We will leave it as an exercise to formulate the entire corresponding natural deduction system. For now, we return to the tableaux rules in their new formulation, with an eye on establishing completeness.

Completeness

We want to prove the completeness of the foregoing system with respect to $\mathcal{L}_{\mathsf{FDE}}$ (understood here with the minimal syntax). Notice that, unlike the tableaux of §7.3, there is now no sign of blocking; the "blocked" or resolved formulas simply disappear as we go down the tree. The tree does not end till not a single rule is applicable to the last nodes. But it will end. After all, every application of a rule reduces the complexity of the sentences present[13] and so the process has to end, since none of the lists involved have infinite complexity.

The question is: What will the end nodes look like? Every sentence of the language has one of the following forms:

p (atomic)	~p (negated atomic)
~~A	
$A \wedge B$	$\sim(A \wedge B)$
$A \vee B$	$\sim(A \vee B)$

That is all. If any such sentence occurs in our tree it will be eliminated in favor of less complex sentences unless they are of the first two forms (top row). Hence, the end nodes are all of the form:

[13] unlike in some other systems, nothing new is ever introduced in the current system

» END NODE FORM: $A_1, \ldots, A_m \vdash B_1, \ldots, B_n$ (with each A_i and B_j either an atomic or negated atomic sentence, for $i = 1, \ldots, m$ and $j = 1, \ldots, n$).

Accordingly, each end node is in effect a derivability claim for basic expressions (as understood above, page 208). Hence, by Anderson and Belnap's criteria, such a claim is correct if and only if it is a *primitive tautological entailment*, that is, if and only if at least one of the sentences on the right *is identical with* one of the sentences on the left. That corresponds in the original tableaux precisely to having one sentence occur with both markers $\oplus$ and $\ominus$ in the same branch.

With the foregoing in mind we can now move towards the completeness result. Suppose that a given endnode

$$A_1, A_2, \ldots, A_m \vdash B_1, B_2, \ldots, B_n$$

is *not* a primitive tautological entailment. Then we can make the following four-valued assignment to atomic sentences:

$v(p) = 1$ if p but not $\sim p$ is one of the A_i

$v(p) = 0$ if $\sim p$ but not p is one of the A_i

$v(p) = \mathsf{b}$ if each of p and $\sim p$ is one of the A_i

$v(p) = 0$ if p but not $\sim p$ is one of the B_j

$v(p) = 1$ if $\sim p$ but not p is one of the B_j

$v(p) = \mathsf{n}$ if each of p and $\sim p$ is one of the B_j

That this is a consistent assignment to all the atomic sentences occurring in the given endnode (call it 'e') is plain: By supposition, e is not a primitive tautological entailment, in which case no sentence in e occurs on both the left and right of the turnstile. Note, too, that we can extend v to all other atomic sentences in the language, in any way we like; that will play no role in the completeness proof. (Of course, v is extended to all the complex sentences in the language by means of the four-valued matrix for FDE.)

LEMMA 12.8 *Endnode* $A_1, \ldots, A_n \vdash B_1, \ldots, B_n$ *is such that it is not the case that* $A_1, \ldots, A_n \Vdash B_1, \ldots, B_n$.

PROOF LEM 12.8 The assignment v satisfies all the premises of the argument depicted in the given endnode because it gives each of them one of the designated values (1 or b); however, v does not satisfy any member of the conclusion given that it assigns each B_j one of the undesignated values (n or 0). Therefore, the argument depicted in such an endnode is not valid in the four-valued semantics for this language. QED

To finish the completeness proof for this system we need now establish:[14]

LEMMA 12.9 *If the argument depicted in any node in the tree after the origin is not valid then neither is the immediately preceding node in the same branch.*

PROOF LEM 12.9 This is proved by showing that it holds for each of the rules used to produce the tree. Suppose, for example, that the node in question was produced by the last rule, which eliminates double negation on the right. Then we have to prove:

» If it is not the case that $\mathcal{X} \Vdash \mathcal{Y}, A, \mathcal{Z}$ then it is not the case that $\mathcal{X} \Vdash \mathcal{Y}, {\sim}{\sim}A, \mathcal{Z}$

That means: if any valuation assigns designated values to all of $\mathcal{X}$ but undesignated values to all of $\mathcal{Y}, A, \mathcal{Z}$ then it assigns designated values to all of $\mathcal{X}$ but undesignated values to all of $\mathcal{Y}, {\sim}{\sim}A, \mathcal{Z}$. This is easy enough to prove from the matrix since ${\sim}{\sim}A$ and A always receive the same value. Similarly, suppose the node in question was created through the resolution rule for $\wedge$ on the right. Without loss of generality suppose it was the one written to the left of the two new nodes that were created by application of the rule. We have to prove:

» If it is not the case that $\mathcal{X} \Vdash \mathcal{Y}, A, \mathcal{Z}$ then it is not the case that $\mathcal{X} \Vdash \mathcal{Y}, A \wedge B, \mathcal{Z}$

Suppose that a given valuation v assigns all designated values to members of $\mathcal{X}$ but all undesignated values to all members of $\mathcal{Y}, A, \mathcal{Z}$. Then $v(A)$ is either n or 0. A look at the matrix shows that this implies that $v(A \wedge B)$ is also either n or 0.

We leave the other cases in the proof of Lemma 12.9 as exercise (but we will none the less mark the end of proof here). QED

EXERCISES 12.5.1

1 In the indicated way, formulate the natural deduction system FDE-NAT. The structural rules are the usual ones, but formulated for multiple entries on the right of the turnstile as well. (What must Prime be for this case? Should Weak be allowed on the right side as well?) The Connective Rules are produced from the above version of the tableau rules, in the way we illustrated for ($\wedge$ Intro Right).

2 Note that each case involved in the proof of Lemma 12.9 is in effect equally part of the soundness proof of the corresponding natural deduction rule. With that in mind, prove the soundess of FDE-NAT with respect to the four-valued semantics for $\mathcal{L}_{FDE}$.

[14]For convenience we call the first node of any tree (within the current system) the *origin*.

3 How does our completeness proof for the tableaux system translate into a completeness proof for FDE-NAT? Answer informally.

4 In order to equate sentences with their standard normal form, Anderson and Belnap utilized the following principles in their original formulation of FDE.

Commutation: $A \wedge B = B \wedge A$

$$A \vee B = B \vee A$$

Association: $A \wedge (B \wedge C) = (A \wedge B) \wedge C$

$$A \vee (B \vee C) = (A \vee B) \vee C$$

Distribution: $A \wedge (B \vee C) = (A \wedge B) \vee (A \wedge C)$

$$A \vee (B \wedge C) = (A \vee B) \wedge (A \vee C)$$

Double Negation: $\sim\sim A = A$

De Morgan: $\sim(A \wedge B) = (\sim A \vee \sim B)$

$$\sim(A \vee B) = (\sim A \wedge \sim B)$$

Show that in each case the equated formulas are deducible from each other, using either the tableaux rules in their new formulation or your system FDE-NAT.

12.6 ISSUES OF (IN-) FINITUDE

At numerous points along the way we have mentioned infinity and emphasized differences between the infinite and the finite. In a tableau construction it could sometimes happen that a branch would continue forever, so that the tableau would not be closed at any step, nor would any step show definitively that the tableau would remain open. By human ingenuity one might detect that it was so, but a machine or computer set to carry out the construction would simply continue forever. That is just one example where infinity enters very naturally; there were others. In this section we will begin with some negative points, which may suggest that the tasks of logic can be seriously hampered once we stray outside the realms of the finite. But then we shall show that for various logics, and indeed in the most familiar ones, problems can be reduced to their finite case.

FUNCTIONAL COMPLETENESS

We begin with functional completeness of many-valued languages, where we restricted ourselves to those which have a finite adequate matrix. In fact, if a language has only an infinite adequate matrix (such as Łukasiewicz's infinite-valued language) it cannot possibly be functionally complete. Let $A_1, A_2, \ldots, A_k, \ldots$ be all the sentences in the language which contain only one atomic sentence (call it p) and suppose the matrix has distinct values $u_1, u_2, \ldots, u_n, \ldots$. We now think of the "truth table" made up with the corresponding values for these sentences when p takes those different values:

p	A_1	A_2	$\cdots$	A_k	$\cdots$
u_1	$u(1,1)$	$u(2,1)$	$\vdots$	$u(k,1)$	$\vdots$
u_2	$u(1,2)$	$u(2,2)$	$\vdots$	$u(k,2)$	$\vdots$
u_3	$u(1,3)$	$u(2,3)$	$\vdots$	$u(k,3)$	$\vdots$
$\vdots$	$\vdots$	$\vdots$	$\vdots$	$\vdots$	$\vdots$

and so forth. Thus the language is such that A_1 has value $u(1,3)$ when p has value 3 and, more generally, A_k has value $u(k,j)$ when p has value j. Understand this well: $u(k,j)$ is in fact one of the values u_m, since those are all the values there are; hence, the expression '(k,j)' denotes one of the numbers $1, 2, 3, \ldots$. Each of the sentences A_i expresses a unary operator.

Now define the operator δ as follows, for every number j,

$$\delta(u_j) = u(j,j) + 1$$

What this means is that operator sends (for example) the value u_2 into the value that comes right after $u(2,2)$. When p has value u_2 then A_2 has value $u(2,2)$, but a sentence that expressed δ would have value $u(2,2)+1$. Hence, the sentence A_2 does not express δ. But this goes not only for 2; it goes similarly for every number $1, 2, 3, \ldots$ We conclude that none of the A_i expresses δ. Hence, the language is not functionally complete.

The foregoing method of proof is called *Cantor's diagonal method*.[15] The method is often useful for showing that something cannot be done when we are dealing with an infinite case and have relatively limited means of description.

CONSEQUENCE RELATIONS AND DEDUCTIVE VALIDITY

Much of our work has consisted in relating two sorts of consequence relations to each other: the semantic consequence (valid argument) relation $\Vdash$

[15] Do you see the pertinent diagonal in the "truth table"?

in a language and the logical consequence (derivability) relation $\vdash$ in a logical system. The latter, in each kind of logical systems we have introduced, is *finitary* in the following sense:

DEFINITION 12.2

» A *property* F of sets is *finitary* just in case any set $\mathcal{X}$ has property F iff some finite subset of $\mathcal{X}$ has F.

» Let $\mathcal{R}$ be a relation the domain of which includes sets. Then $\mathcal{R}$ is *finitary* just in case any set $\mathcal{X}$ bears $\mathcal{R}$ to something iff some finite subset of $\mathcal{X}$ bears $\mathcal{R}$ to it.

Suppose $\mathcal{X}$ contains infinitely many sentences. While the statement that $\mathcal{X} \vdash A$ makes perfect sense and may be true, our derivation rules act only on *finite* subsets of $\mathcal{X}$. Hence, if $A \vdash B$ then it is also the case that $\mathcal{X}, A \vdash B$, no matter how large $\mathcal{X}$ may be (Weak). But, then, $\mathcal{X}$ is only along for the ride; it is not affected in any way, nor plays any part, in that ride. Each step in a derivation—as indeed in a tableau construction—alters or replaces only finitely many sentences.

The semantic consequence relation $\Vdash$ is different; there is no guarantee that it is finitary. Early on, when these notions were introduced, we mentioned a language designed by Rudolf Carnap which illustrates the situation. The syntax is just that of our familiar quantificational logic, but the admissible valuations of the language are such that

$$\{Fa_1, Fa_2, \ldots, Fa_n, \ldots\} \Vdash (\forall x)Fx$$

where $a_1, a_2, \ldots, a_n, \ldots$ are all the names in the language, as many as there are natural numbers. In this language the semantic consequence relation is not finitary.

This language would not lend itself to our general method for proving completeness. The maxi-sets would have a familiar look, but a maxi-set could contain all those premises and also the negation of the conclusion; it would be deductively consistent, but there would be no admissible valuation that satisfied it.

DECISION PROCEDURES

The *decision problem* as first formulated by David Hilbert early in the 20th century consisted in finding a procedure that would allow us to determine in a finite number of steps whether any given sentence in first-order quantificational logic is provable or not provable. Such a procedure would be a *decision procedure* for that logic, and if such a procedure existed the logic would be *decidable*. But as it turns out there is not and cannot be any such procedure: that logic is *undecidable*.[16]

[16]This was proved by Alonzo Church [21].

Of course the problem was generalized, and we can pose it for any given logic. For CPL all logic students learn the solution early on. Truth tables provide a straightforward decision procedure for CPL, as does, in a different way, the tableaux method. For any sentence of CPL a tableau construction must certainly end in finitely many steps since each step reduces the complexity of what is given, and no sentence is infinitely complex. The case of any finite matrix language is similar. But we have encountered cases in which tableaux can have branches that never stop growing, because the rules introduce new symbols in certain kinds of steps.[17]

ON THE POSITIVE SIDE: FINITARY CONSEQUENCE RESULTS

Having canvassed some rather negative news about our encounters with infinity, we will now go on to find that there is a good deal of positive news as well.

To begin, the fact that we cannot have a complete logic (of the sorts we have discussed here, at least) for a language whose semantic consequence relation is infinitary does have a contrapositive after all! We have in fact found completeness proofs for logics pertaining to a number of languages that include modal and other non-standard connectives. It follows then that their semantic consequence relations are finitary.

Are there also more direct ways of proving such results, without detouring through a completeness proof for a logical system? Certainly.[18] But we will content ourselves here with the less direct way, and note that we have actually proved that the semantic consequence relation is finitary for a number of cases here, as implicit corollaries to our completeness proofs. So we know at this point that the following eleven languages:

» The language of classical propositional logic $\mathcal{L}_{\mathsf{CPL}}$

» Łukasiewicz's three-valued language with Słupecki's connective added $\mathcal{L}_{Ł}^{\pi}$

» The six languages $\mathcal{L}_{\mathsf{K}}$, $\mathcal{L}_{\mathsf{K}}^{\mathsf{ser}}$, $\mathcal{L}_{\mathsf{K}}^{\mathsf{r}}$, $\mathcal{L}_{\mathsf{K}}^{\mathsf{rs}}$, $\mathcal{L}_{\mathsf{K}}^{\mathsf{rt}}$, $\mathcal{L}_{\mathsf{K}}^{\mathsf{rst}}$, which correspond to the six familiar normal modal (propositional) logics

» The language $\mathcal{L}_{\mathsf{CK}}$

» The language $\mathcal{L}_{\mathsf{I}}$ of intuitionistic (propositional) logic

» The language $\mathcal{L}_{\mathsf{FDE}}$ of tautological entailment (first-degree entailment)

all have finitary semantic consequence relations.

[17]That is also the case when the tableaux method is adapted for first-order quantificational logic. Monadic quantificational logic (the logic restricted to one-place predicates) is decidable; as soon as even a binary relation is introduced, decidability is lost. Boolos, Burgess and Jeffrey [14] provide full discussion.

[18]van Fraassen [101] provides an extensive treatment on this topic.

MATTERS OF SIZE IN NORMAL MODAL LOGIC

We will present one related topic with positive results here, for modal logic. Before doing so, we should introduce some terminology and distinctions that make a difference in our study of languages, so that our results here will not keep a deceptively general look.

First of all, when a logic is an extension of CPL there are certain nice features which other logics may not share and which make a difference here. Let us distinguish:

- Language $\mathcal{L}$ has a finitary consequence relation.
- Language $\mathcal{L}$ has the *compactness property*: any set of sentences is satisfiable if and only if all its finite subsets are satisfiable.

In classical logic and its extensions it is not necessary to distinguish the two (why not?), and the word 'compactness' tends to be used interchangeably for either feature. But even in many-valued languages the two may not be equivalent at all.

In CPL we can afford to think solely in terms of single sentences when addressing logical questions. After all, A is derivable from $\mathcal{X}$ if and only if B $\supset$ A is a logical truth, for some finite conjunction B of members of $\mathcal{X}$. But, in general, we always face in principle three distinct questions:

- What are the logical truths?
- What are the satisfiable sets?
- What are the valid arguments?

That said, we shall content ourselves here with looking at SNML where various pertinent nice features of CPL are inherited.

Finite Model Property

A tableaux construction for a modal logic may not end. When it does, it is finite, and the counterexample it allows us to construct is a finite set of worlds with a relation on it—a finite model. Imagine, for a moment, that the following is true for one of the languages—call it $\mathcal{L}$—of normal modal logic:

- $\mathcal{L}$ has the *finite model property*: any sentence of $\mathcal{L}$ is satisfiable only if it is satisfiable in a finite model.[19]

If $\mathcal{L}$ has this interesting property $\mathcal{L}$ is a close neighbor of the family of finite matrix languages. As we have seen, the propositions in a model form a

[19] In view of the nice features inherited from CPL, this has immediate corollaries for the universally valid sentences and for arguments with finitely many premises: Exercise.

base for its valuations. In a finite model there are only finitely many propositions (say, n); so, we have there a base which, together with any one of the finitely many worlds, forms an n-valued matrix. Of course, n can still be any natural number, so we can then think of the modal language $\mathcal{L}$ as having not a single adequate finite matrix but a family of finite matrices that "together" (so to speak) are adequate. And to determine whether a sentence is satisfiable we would in principle have to construct and, in turn, inspect all the 1-valued, 2-valued, 3-valued, ... matrices in that family.[20] Still, the infinite models are one and all irrelevant to logical truth in this language. Size matters, but only up to a point: *infinite* sizes do not matter!

The question is: Do the languages of normal modal logic have the finite model property? We will study this question for the language $\mathcal{L}_K^T$, corresponding to the basic normal modal (alethic) logic T, in which the access relation is reflexive. (Hence, in this language necessity implies truth: what is necessary is actual.)

Filtration

We shall show that $\mathcal{L}_K^T$ has the finite model property. The method we will use does not detour through the logical system but, rather, pertains directly to the models; it is called the *method of filtration*. Intuitively, given a model which may be infinite we "filter" it through a finite set of sentences that are our topic of concern; in doing so, we thereby construct a finite model that plays the same role as the original for those particular sentences.

THEOREM 12.3 *$\mathcal{L}_K^T$ has the finite model property:*

» *A sentence of $\mathcal{L}_K^T$ is logically true iff it is valid in every finite $\mathcal{L}_K^T$-model.*

» *A sentence of $\mathcal{L}_K^T$ is satisfiable iff it is satisfied in some finite $\mathcal{L}_K^T$-model.*

PROOF THM 12.4 The two parts of the theorem are equivalent to each other; so we need only prove one. As a preliminary we introduce a *syntactic* notion—the set $\nabla(A)$ of *subformulas* of A:

DEFINITION 12.3 (THE SET $\nabla(A)$) For any sentence A in $\mathcal{L}_K^T$

1. A is in $\nabla(A)$.
2. If $\sim$B or $\Box$B is in $\nabla(A)$ then B is in $\nabla(A)$.
3. If $(B \wedge C)$ is in $\nabla(A)$ then B and C are in $\nabla(A)$.
4. Nothing is in $\nabla(A)$ except by virtue of (1)–(3).

[20] When the matrix elements are all the propositions (sets of worlds) in a possible world model, their number must of course be a power of 2.

We take it here that all other connectives are defined in terms of the three listed (above). Note that each clause after the first introduces shorter sentences as subformulas; therefore, the set $\nabla(A)$ is finite.

Now suppose that A is a sentence in $\mathcal{L}_K^\tau$ and that $\mathcal{M} = \langle \mathcal{W}, \mathcal{R}, v \rangle$ is an $\mathcal{L}_K^\tau$-model such that, where $w \in \mathcal{W}$, $v(w, A) = 1$, in which case A is satisfied in model $\mathcal{M}$. We shall show that there is a finite $\mathcal{L}_K^\tau$-model

$$\mathcal{M}^{\nabla(A)} = \langle \mathcal{W}^\nabla, \mathcal{R}^\nabla, v^\nabla \rangle$$

such that $v^\nabla(w^\nabla, A) = 1$ as well, where $w^\nabla \in \mathcal{W}^\nabla$.

The worlds in $\mathcal{W}^\nabla$ will themselves be sets, namely, sets of worlds in $\mathcal{W}$. For each world u in $\mathcal{W}$ we define:[21]

- $u^\nabla = \{w \in \mathcal{W} : v(w, B) = v(u, B),$ for all B in $\nabla(A)\}$
- $\mathcal{W}^\nabla = \{u^\nabla : u \in \mathcal{W}\}$
- $\mathcal{R}^\nabla$ is the set of all pairs $\langle u^\nabla, w^\nabla \rangle$ such that for all B, if $\Box B$ is in $\nabla(A)$ and $v(u, \Box B) = 1$, then $v(w, B) = 1$.

The first question is whether $\mathcal{W}^\nabla$ is finite. It is. After all, there are only finitely many formulas in $\nabla(A)$. If u^∇ is not the same as w^∇ then $v(u, B)$ and $v(w, B)$ must differ for some sentence B in $\nabla(A)$. But there are only finitely many different ways to assign 1s and 0s to a finite set of sentences; hence, there can't be more than finitely many sets that are in $\mathcal{W}^\nabla$.

The next question is whether $\mathcal{R}^\nabla$ is well-defined. Our definition of $\mathcal{R}$ is in trouble unless the following is the case:

LEMMA 12.10 *Suppose that* $u^\nabla = u'^\nabla$ *and* $w^\nabla = w'^\nabla$, *and that* $\Box B$ *in in* $\nabla(A)$. *Then the following are equivalent:*

a) if $v(u, \Box B) = 1$ *then* $v(w, B) = 1$

b) if $v(u', \Box B) = 1$ *then* $v(w', B) = 1$

PROOF LEM 12.10 We know that if $\Box B$ is in $\nabla(A)$ then so is B, in which case, by our definition of the sets u^∇ and so on, B has the same truthvalue in u' as in u, and similarly for w' and w. QED

LEMMA 12.11 $\mathcal{R}^\nabla$ *is reflexive.*

PROOF LEM 12.11 This follows at once from the reflexivity of $\mathcal{R}$. Specifically, u^∇ must bear $\mathcal{R}^\nabla$ to itself because $u\mathcal{R}u$ and, hence, if $v(u, \Box B) = 1$ then $v(u, B) = 1$. QED

[21] We will get to v^∇ in due course.

Beyond its being well-defined and reflexive, we can say something more, and more important, about $\mathcal{R}^\nabla$, namely, that it mimics $\mathcal{R}$ to just the extent that we need:

LEMMA 12.12 *If* $u\mathcal{R}w$ *then* u^∇ *bears* $\mathcal{R}^\nabla$ *to* w^∇.

PROOF LEM 12.12 Suppose that $u\mathcal{R}w$ and that $\Box B$ is in $\nabla(A)$. Suppose, further, that $v(u, \Box B) = 1$. In that case, $v(w, B) = 1$ by the conditions on v. But, then, by definition u^∇ bears $\mathcal{R}^\nabla$ to w^∇. QED

We are now (finally) ready to introduce the valuation v^∇ in an obvious way. We define it inductively, trying to go for an assignment of truthvalues that will mimic v for the subformulas of A, while not really caring about what it does to any other sentence.

DEFINITION 12.4 (THE FUNCTION v^∇) Let p be any atomic sentence and B any sentence.

a) If p is in $\nabla(A)$ then $v^\nabla(p) = \{u^\nabla : u \in v(p)\}$.

b) If p is not in $\nabla(A)$ then $v^\nabla(p) = \emptyset$.

c) $v^\nabla({\sim}B) = \mathcal{W}^\nabla - v^\nabla(B)$.

d) $v^\nabla(B \wedge C) = v^\nabla(B) \cap v^\nabla(C)$.

e) $v^\nabla(\Box B) = \{u^\nabla : \text{ for all } w \in \mathcal{W}, w^\nabla \in v^\nabla(B) \text{ if } u^\nabla \mathcal{R} w^\nabla\}$.

We further define

$$v^\nabla(u^\nabla, B) = \begin{cases} 1 & \text{if } u^\nabla \in v^\nabla(B) \\ 0 & \text{otherwise.} \end{cases}$$

LEMMA 12.13 $\mathcal{M}^{\nabla(A)} = \langle \mathcal{W}^\nabla, \mathcal{R}^\nabla, v^\nabla \rangle$ *is a finite* $\mathcal{L}_{K^\tau}$*-model.*

PROOF LEM 12.13 This is proved by the preceding lemmas and remarks, plus the definition of v^∇ which carefully obeys the constraints on valuations in such models.

LEMMA 12.14 $v^\nabla(B) = \{u^\nabla : u \in v(B)\}$, *for all sentences* B *in* $\nabla(A)$.

PROOF LEM 12.14 We note that Lemma 12.14 marks the most important stage of our reasoning; once it is proved the proof of Theorem 12.3 is thereby complete.

The proof is via (strong) induction on the length of sentences in $\mathcal{L}_K^\tau$. Accordingly, let B be any given sentence in $\nabla(A)$.

» HYPOTHESIS OF INDUCTION. If sentence C is of length less than B and C is in $\nabla(A)$ then $v^{\nabla}(u^{\nabla}, C) = v(u, C)$, for all worlds u in $\mathcal{W}$.

» CASES. Let u be any world in $\mathcal{W}$.

1. B is atomic. Then, by clause (a) of Def 12.4,

$$v^{\nabla}(u^{\nabla}, B) = v(u, B).$$

2. B has form ~C. Then, by the Induction Hypothesis,

$$v^{\nabla}(u^{\nabla}, B) = 1 - v^{\nabla}(u^{\nabla}, C) = 1 - v(u, C) = v(u, B).$$

3. B has form $(C \wedge D)$. Then, by the Induction Hypothesis,

$$\begin{aligned} v^{\nabla}(u^{\nabla}, B) &= v^{\nabla}(u^{\nabla}, C) \cdot v^{\nabla}(u^{\nabla}, D) \\ &= v(u, C) \cdot v(u, D) \\ &= v(u, B). \end{aligned}$$

4. B has form $\Box$C. In this case there are two subcases which jointly prove that $v^{\nabla}(u^{\nabla}, B) = 1$ iff $v(u, B) = 1$. Since $\mathcal{L}_{K}^{r}$ is only two-valued, this suffices.

a. $v(u, B) = 1$. We must prove that $v^{\nabla}(u^{\nabla}, B) = 1$, which requires that if $\langle u^{\nabla}, w^{\nabla}\rangle \in \mathcal{R}^{\nabla}$ then $v^{\nabla}(w^{\nabla}, C) = 1$, for all w^{∇}. So, suppose that $\langle u^{\nabla}, w^{\nabla}\rangle \in \mathcal{R}^{\nabla}$. Then, by definition, if $v(u, B) = 1$ then $v(w, C) = 1$. The Induction Hypothesis applies to C and w, and hence $v^{\nabla}(w^{\nabla}, C) = 1$, as was required.

b. $v^{\nabla}(u^{\nabla}, B) = 1$. We must prove that $v(u, B) = 1$, which requires that if $u\mathcal{R}w$ then $v(w, C) = 1$, for all w. By Def 12.4 it follows that $v^{\nabla}(w^{\nabla}, C) = 1$ for all w^{∇} such that $\langle u^{\nabla}, w^{\nabla}\rangle \in \mathcal{R}^{\nabla}$. The Induction Hypothesis applies to C and all such worlds w^{∇}, and so

If $\langle u^{\nabla}, w^{\nabla}\rangle \in \mathcal{R}^{\nabla}$ then $v(w, C) = 1$.

But Lemma 12.12 implies that $\langle u^{\nabla}, w^{\nabla}\rangle \in \mathcal{R}^{\nabla}$ if $u\mathcal{R}w$. So we conclude:

If $u\mathcal{R}w$ then $v(w, C) = 1$,

which is what was required.

QED

Decidability of Certain Modal Logics

Knowing that a language has the finite model property does not by itself give us a decision procedure. If a sentence is satisfiable it is satisfiable in some finite model, but there are infinitely many finite sizes so the search for a counterexample to a given sentence might still go on forever.

That said, Proof 12.4 actually established something more than we explicitly mentioned in the theorem. When we pointed out that $\mathcal{W}^{\nabla}$ is finite, that was based on the fact that there are only finitely many ways for worlds to disagree on the truthvalues of subformulas of A. That would be so even if we allowed random assignments of 1s and 0s to the given subformulas—if there are n subformulas then there are 2^n such assignments. But, then, clearly we know much more about the filtration-produced model than that it is finite! No matter what the size of $\mathcal{M}$, the model $\mathcal{M}^{\nabla(A)}$ will have at most 2^n worlds in it. So, there will be no need to inspect models of larger size. Accordingly, in proving Theorem 12.3 we have (in effect) proved:

Theorem 12.5 *Validity and satisfiability in $\mathcal{L}_K^{\tau}$ are decidable.*

Finishing the proof requires removing one last doubt. In particular, suppose we want to check whether sentence A is valid in all $\mathcal{L}_K^{\tau}$-models. What we do is check whether ~A is satisfied by any valuation in any model that has at most 2^n worlds in it. The question is: Do we need to check only finitely many valuations on finitely many models?

The answer is: Yes. Let the cardinality of $\mathcal{W}$ in a given model be m. Then the size k of the set of couples of worlds equals m^2 and the possible binary access relations are sets of such couples and, so, there are just 2^k of them. Given $\mathcal{W}$ and $\mathcal{R}$, could there now be *infinitely* many different valuations that we need to check? There certainly are infinitely many valuations, given that there are infinitely many atomic sentences. But by inspection of Proof 12.4 we once again see that we need look only at one valuation for each possible truthvalue-assignment to atomic subformulas of ~A (for each world). Both these numbers (possible such assignments and worlds) are finite; hence, we are still in the realm of the finite. And that is all.

Exercises 12.6.1

1 Can Proof 12.4 be adapted to the other languages of normal modal logic? What of intuitionistic logic? What of FDE?

Further Reading

For natural deduction, algebras, and lattices, consult Curry's [25].

Sometimes, quotations just don't fit.
– Authors

Bibliography

[1] Alan Ross Anderson and Nuel D. Belnap. *Entailment: The Logic of Relevance and Necessity*, Volume 1. Princeton University Press, Princeton, 1975. ‹see vii, 91, 92, 208›

[2] Alan Ross Anderson, Nuel D. Belnap, and J. Michael Dunn. *Entailment: The Logic of Relevance and Necessity*, Volume 2. Princeton University Press, Princeton, 1992.

[3] Aristotle. "On Interpretation". In J. Barnes, editor, *The Complete Works of Aristotle: The Revised Oxford Translation*, Volume 1. Princeton University Press, Princeton, NJ, 1984. ‹see 4›

[4] Emmon Bach. *Informal Lectures on Formal Semantics*. SUNY Press, Albany, 1989. ‹see 34›

[5] Jon Barwise and John Etchemendy. *The Liar*. Oxford University Press, Oxford, 1987. ‹see 129›

[6] JC Beall. "Is Yablo's paradox non-circular?". *Analysis*, 61(3):176–187, 2001. ‹see 129›

[7] JC Beall, editor. *Liars and Heaps: New Essays on Paradox*. Oxford University Press, Oxford, 2003. Forthcoming. ‹see 145›

[8] JC Beall and Greg Restall. "Logical Pluralism". *Australasian Journal of Philosophy*, 78:475–493, 2000. ‹see 9›

[9] JC Beall and Greg Restall. *Logical Pluralism*. Oxford University Press, Oxford, 2003. Forthcoming.

[10] John L. Bell, David DeVidi, and Graham Solomon. *Logical Options: An Introduction to Classical and Alternative Logics*. Broadview Press, 2001. ‹see 47›

[11] Ethan D. Bloch. *Proofs and Fundamentals: A First Course in Abstract Mathematics*. Birkhäuser, Boston, 2000. ‹see 158›

[12] I. M. Bocheński. *A History of Formal Logic*. Chelsea, New York, 1961. ‹see 9›

[13] D. Bochvar. "On a Three-Valued Calculus and Its Application to the Analysis of Contradictories". *Matématčéskij Sbornik*, 4:287–308, 1939. Reviewed by A. Church in *Journal of Symbolic Logic* 4:98–99, 1939. ‹see 126›

[14] George S. Boolos, John P. Burgess, and Richard C. Jeffrey. *Computability and Logic*. Cambridge University Press, Cambridge, Fourth edition, 2002. ‹see 158, 217›

[15] David Bostock. *Intermediate Logic*. Oxford University Press, Oxford, 1997. ‹see 47›

[16] L. E. J. BROUWER. *Over de Grondslagen der Wiskunde*. Maas & van Suchtelen, Amsterdam, 1907. English title, *Foundations of Mathematics*, English translation in [47]. ‹see 95›

[17] ROBERT A. BULL AND KRISTER SEGERBERG. "Basic Modal Logic". In DOV M. GABBAY AND FRANZ GÜNTHNER, editors, *Handbook of Philosophical Logic, Vol. II*, Volume 3, pages 1–83. Reidel, Dordrecht, 2001. ‹see 84›

[18] RUDOLPH CARNAP. *Meaning and Necessity*. University of Chicago Press, Chicago, 1947. ‹see 52›

[19] RUDOLPH CARNAP. *Logical Syntax of Language*. Routledge and Kegan Paul, London, 1949. ‹see 34›

[20] BRIAN F. CHELLAS. *Modal Logic: An Introduction*. Cambridge University Press, Cambridge, 1980. ‹see 84, 102›

[21] ALONZO CHURCH. "A note on the *Entscheidungsproblem*". *Journal of Symbolic Logic*, 1:40–41, 1936. ‹see 216›

[22] B. J. COPELAND. "The Genesis of Possible World Semantics". *Journal of Philosophical Logic*, 31:99–137, 2002. ‹see 9›

[23] M. J. CRESSWELL. *Logics and Languages*. Methuen and Co., London, 1973. ‹see 34›

[24] HASKELL B. CURRY. "The Inconsistency of Certain Formal Logics". *Journal of Symbolic Logic*, 7:115–17, 1942. ‹see 128›

[25] HASKELL B. CURRY. *Foundations of Mathematical Logic*. Dover, New York, 1977. ‹see 185, 207, 223›

[26] DIRK VAN DALEN. "Intuitionistic Logic". In LOU GOBLE, editor, *The Blackwell Guide to Philosophical Logic*. Blackwell, Oxford, 2001. ‹see 102›

[27] MICHAEL DUMMETT. *Elements of Intuitionism*. Oxford University Press, Oxford, 2000. 2nd Edition. ‹see 102›

[28] J. M. DUNN AND GARY HARDEGREE. *Algebraic Methods in Philosophical Logic*. Oxford University Press, Oxford, 2001. ‹see 118›

[29] J. MICHAEL DUNN. *The Algebra of Intensional Logics*. PhD thesis, University of Pittsburgh, 1966. ‹see 106, 108›

[30] J. MICHAEL DUNN. "Natural Language versus Formal Language". Presented at the joint APA-ASL symposium, New York, Dec.27, 1969. ‹see 106›

[31] J. MICHAEL DUNN. "Partiality and Its Dual". *Studia Logica*, 65:5–40, 2000. ‹see 106›

[32] H. B. ENDERTON. *Elements of Set Theory*. Academic Press, 1977. ‹see 21›

[33] KIT FINE. "Models for Entailment". *Journal of Philosophical Logic*, 3:347–372, 1974. ‹see 120›

[34] KIT FINE. "Vagueness, Truth and Logic". *Synthese*, 30:265–300, 1975. ‹see 145›

[35] GRAEME FORBES. *Modern Logic*. Oxford University Press, Oxford, 1994. ‹see 34›

[36] DOV M. GABBAY AND HEINRICH WANSING, editors. *What is Negation?* Kluwer Academic Publishers, 1999. ‹see 119›

[37] ROD GIRLE. *Modal Logics and Philosophy*. McGill-Queen's University Press, London, 2000. ‹see 84›

[38] LOU GOBLE, editor. *The Blackwell Guide to Philosophical Logic*. Blackwell, Oxford, 2001. ‹see 102›

[39] NELSON GOODMAN. *Fact, Fiction, and Forecast*. Harvard University Press, Cambridge, MA, 1955. ‹see 93›

[40] DELIA GRAFF AND TIMOTHY WILLIAMSON, editors. *Vagueness*. International Research Library of Philosophy, Ashgate Aldershot, 2002. ‹see 144›

[41] ANIL GUPTA AND NUEL BELNAP. *The Revision Theory of Truth*. MIT Press, 1993. ‹see 129›

[42] S. HAACK. *Deviant Logic: Some Philosophical Issues*. Cambridge University Press, 1974. Reissued as *Deviant Logic, Fuzzy Logic: Beyond the Formalism* [43]. ‹see 9›

[43] SUSAN HAACK. *Deviant Logic, Fuzzy Logic: Beyond the Formalism*. Cambridge University Press, Cambridge, 1996. ‹see 227›

[44] PAUL R. HALMOS. *Naive Set Theory*. Springer-Verlag, New York, 1960. ‹see 21›

[45] W.L. HARPER, R. STALNAKER, AND G. PEARCE, editors. *Ifs*. Reidel, Dordrecht, 1981. ‹see 229›

[46] AREND HEYTING. *Intuitionism: An Introduction*. North Holland, Amsterdam, 1956. ‹see 95›

[47] AREND HEYTING. *Brouwer Collected Works I*. North Holland, Amsterdam, 1975. ‹see 226›

[48] JAAKKO HINTIKKA. *Time and Necessity: Studies in Aristotle's Theory of Modality*. Oxford University Press, Oxford, 1987. ‹see 9›

[49] L. HORN. *A Natural History of Negation*. University of Chicago Press, Chicago, 1989. ‹see 118›

[50] COLIN HOWSON. *Logic with Trees: An introduction to symbolic logic*. Routledge, 1996. ‹see 47›

[51] G. HUGHES AND M. CRESSWELL. *A New Introduction to Modal Logic*. Routledge, London, 1996. ‹see 67, 84, 91, 102›

[52] DOMINIC HYDE. "From Heaps and Gaps to Heaps of Gluts". *Mind*, 106:641–660, 1997. ‹see 145›

[53] DALE JACQUETTE, editor. *A Companion to Philosophical Logic*. Blackwell, Oxford, 2002. ‹see 102›

[54] RICHARD C. JEFFREY. *Formal Logic: its scope and its limits*. McGraw Hill, Third edition, 1991. ‹see 47›

[55] ROSANNA KEEFE AND PETER SMITH, editors. *Vagueness: A Reader*. MIT Press, Cambridge, MA, 1997. ‹see 144›

[56] S. C. KLEENE. *Introduction to Metamathematics*. North-Holland, 1952. ‹see 120, 126›

[57] WILLIAM KNEALE AND MARTHA KNEALE. *The Development of Logic*. Oxford University Press, 1962. ‹see 9›

[58] SAUL A. KRIPKE. "Semantical Analysis of Modal Logic I: Normal Modal Propositional Calculi". *Zeitschrift für Mathematische Logik und Grundlagen der Mathematik*, 9:67–96, 1963. ‹see 8, 53›

[59] Saul A. Kripke. "Semantical Considerations on Modal Logic". *Acta Philosophica Fennica*, 16:83–94, 1963. ‹see 8, 53›

[60] Saul A. Kripke. "Semantical Analysis of Intuitionistic Logic I". In M. A. E. Dummett and J. N. Crossley, editors, *Formal Systems and Recursive Functions*, pages 92–130. North-Holland Publishing Co, Amsterdam, 1965. ‹see 96›

[61] Saul A. Kripke. "Semantical Analysis of Modal Logic II: Non-Normal Modal Propositional Calculi". In Addison et al., editor, *The Theory of Models*, pages 206–220. North-Holland Publishing Co, 1965. ‹see 86, 91›

[62] C. I. Lewis. "Implication and the Algebra of Logic". *Mind*, 21:522–531, 1912. ‹see 6, 90›

[63] C. I. Lewis. "The Issues Concerning Material Implication". *Journal of Philosophy, Psychology, and Scientific Methods*, 14:350–6, 1917. ‹see 90›

[64] C. I. Lewis and C. H. Langford. *Symbolic Logic*. The Century Co, New York and London, 1932. ‹see 6, 90, 208›

[65] David K. Lewis. *Counterfactuals*. Blackwell, 1973. ‹see 94›

[66] David K. Lewis. *On the Plurality of Worlds*. Basil Blackwell, Ltd., Oxford, 1986. ‹see 7, 53›

[67] Jan Łukasiewicz. "On Determinism". In L. Borkowski, editor, *Selected works*. North Holland, Amsterdam, 1970. ‹see 9›

[68] Jan Łukasiewicz. *Selected Works*. North-Holland, Amsterdam, 1970. Edited by L. Borkowski. ‹see 122, 140›

[69] Robert L. Martin, editor. *The Liar Paradox*. Yale University Press, New Haven, 1970. ‹see 129›

[70] Robert L. Martin, editor. *Recent Essays on Truth and the Liar Paradox*. Oxford University Press, New York, 1984. ‹see 129›

[71] Vann McGee. *Truth, Vagueness, and Paradox*. Hackett, Indianapolis, 1991. ‹see 129›

[72] Robert K. Meyer. *Topics in Modal and Many-Valued Logic*. PhD thesis, University of Pittsburgh, 1966. ‹see vii›

[73] John Pollock. "Henkin style completeness proofs in theories lacking negation". *Notre Dame Journal of Formal Logic*, 12:509–511, 1971. ‹see 182›

[74] Emil Post. "Introduction to a General Theory of Elementary Propositions". *American Journal of Mathematics*, 43:163–185, 1921. ‹see 119›

[75] Michael D. Potter. *Sets: An Introduction*. Oxford University Press, Oxford, 1990. ‹see 21›

[76] Graham Priest. "The Logic of Paradox". *Journal of Philosophical Logic*, 8:219–241, 1979. ‹see 123›

[77] Graham Priest. *In Contradiction: A Study of the Transconsistent*. Martinus Nijhoff, The Hague, 1987. ‹see 129›

[78] Graham Priest. "What is a Non-Normal World?". *Logique et Analyse*, 35:291–302, 1992. ‹see 102›

[79] Graham Priest. *An Introduction to Non-Classical Logic*. Cambridge University Press, Cambridge, 2001. ‹see 47, 84, 102›

[80] WILLARD VAN ORMAN QUINE. *Set Theory and its Logic*. Harvard University Press, 1963. ‹see 21›

[81] WILLARD VAN ORMAN QUINE. *The Ways of Paradox and Other Essays*. Random House, New York, 1966. ‹see 119›

[82] P. T. RAJU. "The Principle of Four-Cornered Negation in Indian Philosophy". *Review of Metaphysics*, 7:694–713, 1954. ‹see 105, 118›

[83] STEPHEN READ. *Thinking about Logic*. Oxford University Press, 1995. ‹see 9›

[84] GREG RESTALL. "Ways Things Can't Be". *Notre Dame Journal of Formal Logic*, 39:583–596, 1997. ‹see 102›

[85] GREG RESTALL. *An Introduction to Substructural Logics*. New York: Routledge, 2000. ‹see 118›

[86] GREG RESTALL. *Logic: The Fundamentals of Philosophy*. University College London Publications, London, 2001. ‹see 47›

[87] BERTRAND RUSSELL. "On Denoting". *Mind*, 14, 1905. ‹see 9›

[88] HEINRICH SCHOLZ. *Concise History of Logic*. Philosophical Library, New York, 1961. ‹see 9›

[89] KEITH SIMMONS. *Universality and The Liar*. Cambridge University Press, 1993. ‹see 129›

[90] R. M. SMULLYAN. *First-Order Logic*. Springer-Verlag, Berlin, 1968. Reprinted by Dover Press, 1995. ‹see 47›

[91] RAYMOND M. SMULLYAN. *Gödel's Incompleteness Theorems*, Volume 19 of *Oxford Logic Guides*. Oxford University Press, New York, 1992. ‹see 173›

[92] ROY SORENSEN. *Vagueness and Contradiction*. Clarendon, Oxford, 2001. ‹see 133›

[93] ROBERT STALNAKER. "A Theory of Conditionals". *Studies in Logical Theory, American Philosophical Quarterly*, Monograph Series 2 (Oxford: Basil Blackwell), 1968. Reprinted in [45]. ‹see 94›

[94] ROBERT R. STOLL. *Set Theory and Logic*. W. H. Freeman Press, San Francisco, 1963. ‹see 21›

[95] ALFRED TARSKI. *Logic, Semantics, Metamathematics: papers from 1923 to 1938*. Clarendon Press, Oxford, 1956. Translated by J. H. Woodger. ‹see 172›

[96] ALFRED TARSKI. "On the Concept of Logical Consequence". In *Logic, Semantics, Metamathematics: papers from 1923 to 1938*, chapter 16. Clarendon Press, Oxford, 1956. Translated by J. H. Woodger. ‹see 32›

[97] PETER UNGER. "There are No Ordinary Things". *Synthese*, 4:117–54, 1979. ‹see 133›

[98] ALASDAIR URQUHART. "Many-Valued Logics". In DOV M. GABBAY AND FRANZ GÜNTHNER, editors, *Handbook of Philosophical Logic, Vol. II*, Volume 2, pages 249–296. D. Reidel, Dordrecht, 2001. ‹see 129, 145›

[99] BAS C. VAN FRAASSEN. "Presupposition, Implication and Self-Reference". *Journal of Philosophy*, 65:136–52, 1968. ‹see 145›

[100] BAS C. VAN FRAASSEN. "Truth and Paradoxical Consequences". In R. MARTIN, editor, *The Paradox of the Liar*, pages 13–23. Yale University Press, 1970. ‹see 145›

[101] Bas C. van Fraassen. *Formal Semantics and Logic*. The Macmillan Company, New York, 1971. ‹see 158, 217›

[102] Achille Varzi. *An Essay in Universal Semantics*, Volume 1 of *Topoi Library*. Kluwer Academic Publishers, Boston, 1999. ‹see 145›

[103] Heinrich Wansing, editor. *Negation: A Notion in Focus*. de Gruyter, Berlin, 1996. ‹see 119›

[104] Samuel C. Wheeler. "Reference and Vagueness". *Synthese*, 30:367–79, 1967.

[105] Alfred North Whitehead and Bertrand Russell. *Principia Mathematica*. Cambridge University Press, 1925–1927. ‹see 91›

[106] Timothy Williamson. *Vagueness*. Routledge, 1994. ‹see 133, 144›

[107] John Woods. *Paradox and Paraconsistency*. Cambridge University Press, Cambridge, 2003. ‹see 129›

[108] Stephen Yablo. "Truth and Reflection". *Journal of Philosophical Logic*, 14:297–349, 1985. ‹see 128›

[109] Stephen Yablo. "Paradox Without Self-Reference". *Analysis*, 53:251–252, 1993. ‹see 128›

Index